Grand Urban Rules

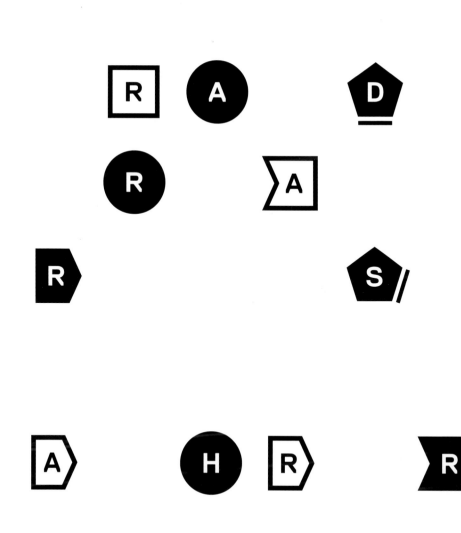

GRAND URB

010 Publishers, Rotterdam 2009

The content of this book is based on research conducted at the ETH Zürich: at the Chair of Prof. Kees Christiaanse and the Chair of Prof. Dr. Ludger Hovestadt.

N RULES

Alex Lehnerer

0

The City of Averuni and its Code

This is an imaginary city, whose physical appearance is the result of the effect of a specific set of urban rules, selected by its residents from the best rules in the world, at the moment when unwritten conventions were no longer able to control private interests. The city's building code therefore is an ideal code, its rules working both individually and as an integrated body.

The city of Averuni lies somewhat more than two flight hours northeast of New York on an island of the same name in the middle of the Atlantic Ocean. Travel time by air to this small island from London is approximately 5 1/2 hours. The land on the island consists more or less exclusively of Averuni's metropolitan region and a mountain chain to the north. Alongside a narrow strip of coastline, this protected natural park serves as the principal local recreational area for residents of the city. With 1480 km², the city and its metropolitan region take up 80% of the island's total surface area. With its 3665 inhabitants per square kilometer, population density is comparable to Paris' unité urbaine—in surface area, however, the city is only slightly more than half its size. As a consequence of its Atlantic location, Averuni is markedly western and North American in character—but elements of European or even Asian influence are not altogether absent. This is observable in the city's layout as well as in its population, formed by heavy immigration from all parts of the world over the past two centuries. The island's constitution and its democratically legitimated institutions strongly resemble those of the United States of America. The city's history can be documented back to 1348. This is, then, a relatively old city, if one that experienced explosive growth, covering the entire island, only in the early 20th century. This growth is the cause of one of the city's hitherto unrecognized characteristics: it became crowded. Increasingly, close proximity between neighbors became a source of conflict; in order to augment living area, the city was prepared to permanently eradicate the last remaining natural area, the Averuni Foothills. In short, the city began at some point to suffer from problems very similar to those afflicting many other urban settlements elsewhere. This situation was recognized by the city's mayor. If, until recently, Averuni regarded building and zoning ordinances as superfluous (on the assumption that residents somehow automatically preserved the general welfare precisely by pursuing their particular and private interests), then the municipal administration has recently arrived at the conclusion that the city's public interests absolutely require formal protection.

At this point, things had to proceed quickly. And yet it takes time to develop specifically-tailored building and zoning ordinances. But the mayor had an idea: he formed the so-called Grand Urban Rules Group (GURG), composed of recognized architects from the city, and commissioned the group to search out cities worldwide closely resembling Averuni in character, or those whose urban problems were in some way exemplary in relation to those facing Averuni. Beyond this, they were to investigate the rules by which such cities had sought to mediate between private and public interests, and the consequences of these efforts for the form of the city. The result was a selection of 19 cities which comprised Berlin, Chicago, Hong Kong, Houston, Las Vegas, London, Los Angeles, New York, Paris, Philadelphia, Buffalo, Portland, San Francisco, San Gimignano, Santa Barbara, Seattle, Stuttgart, Vancouver, and Zürich.

And as luck would have it (and the circumstance is perhaps of no more than anecdotal interest), it is a curious fact that the averages of the longitudes and latitudes of these 19 cities give us a location of 41° northern latitude and 54° western longitude—precisely the location of Averuni's central business district, with its imposing high-rises.

After inspecting all of the relevant building ordinances and their contexts, the GURG began by identifying the rules of special interest to Averuni, to sort them according to scale, and to coordinate them with one another. This was followed by an attempt to derive an all-encompassing set of ordinances for Averuni. The resultant code is not only an administrative steering instrument, but at the same time a telling description of the city, and of the future that was sketched out for it years ago—a future that has increasingly become a reality. The current state of the *Code* is the result of a series of changes introduced over the past 10 years—in part because certain rules initially failed to deliver the desired results in practice, but also because the city has learned from the histories of other cities that such rules possess only a relative permanence, and that the calibrated revision of such regulations is thoroughly necessary and contributes to the city's liveliness and diversity.

§x

Motivation

- **A** Aesthetic Regimes: public beauty, visual appearance
- **H** Hygiene: separation of incompatible uses, programme, land use
- **C** Contextual Regimes: issues depending on the immediate context and its preservation, economic and social regimes, traditions, etc.
- **R** Rights of Light: enough light and air for everybody
- **V** View Management: preservation of important views of the city
- **M** Managing Bulk: basic stipulations regarding the object's form and bulk

Rule Category

The Kind of Rule

Absolute: fixed limit   A   R   Relative: reference, ratio, dependency

Zone related   □   ■   Not zone related

Min   ◧ ◨   Max

Domain

- **D** Density and Distribution Regulator
- **P** Programmatic Regulation
- **F** Form Regulator
- **H** Height
- **S** Style

Provenience

The individual rules are supplemented by a set of plans which, if need be, specify the areas of effectiveness of individual rules geographically within the territory of the city.

Abbreviation
§ Paragraph

C A D P F H S   Provenience

Title Rule

Descriptive explanation. [reference(s)]

⬡C ⬡R ⬡D ⬡P ⬡F ⬡H ⬡S General

Common Law of Nuisance

CLN
§1.01

The individual shall comport himself in such a way that his actions do not represent a nuisance to others. [p.78]

[no nuisance]

⬡C ⬡R ⬡D ⬡P ⬡F ⬡H ⬡S Adam Smith

Invisible Hand

IH
§1.02

In pursuing his own objectives, each individual shall in some way contribute automatically to the common welfare. [p.78]

⬡C ⬡A ⬡D ⬡F ⬡H ⬡S Supreme Court Decision, USA

Rights to Beauty

RTB
§1.03

In cases wherein §1.01 and §1.02 do not apply, the city (administration) has the right to define the public interest and subject it to police powers. This interest includes aesthetic desiderata. [p.112]

PPI
§1.04

🅒 🅡 🄓 🄟 🄕 🄗 🅢   General

Public & Private Interests

Public interests are always derived from private ones. This does not mean, however, that the public interest cannot be opposed to private ones and cannot constrain them. [p.81]

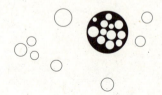

RC
§1.05

🅒 🅡 🄓 🄟 🄕 🄗 🅢   Chicago / New York / General

Revision Cycles

These officially proclaimed rules are complemented by a series of unwritten social and economic norms. These are also binding for the city. The degree of force of such unwritten norms changes with time. For this reason, the rules adopted herein must also be subject to modification. Furthermore, such changes in regulation contribute to a desired morphological diversity. [p.90, 222, fig.105]

FAC
§1.06

🅒 🅡 🄓 🄟 🄕 🄗 🅢   Friedrich A. Hayek

Freedom & Coercion

Freedom is the absence of coercion. [p.64]

x - coercion = freedom

C R D P F H S Hugh Ferriss

Proximity Coercion

Proximity elevates coercion. [p.146, 246, 249, 251]

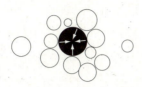

C R D P H The commons, Garret Hardin

Tendency towards Overexploitation

There is a tendency for publicly usable space to be overexploited by individuals. For public areas where privatization is out of the question, rules must be established designed to moderate private interests on the one hand, and to mediate effectively between private and public interests on the other. [p.78, 118, 177, 251, fig.9]

$$+1 - 1/x = >0$$

C R D P F H S General

Rules and Freedoms

Rules adjust the general degree of determination (coercion). Found within these rules, therefore, are certain freedoms. Pure freedom does not exist: at most, we enjoy restricted freedoms. When rules are in force, certain freedoms are automatically valid as well. [p.65]

PSA
§1.10

Ⓒ Ⓐ Ⓓ Ⓟ   Ⓢ   William H. Whyte / New York

Public Space Acceptance

It is difficult to design a place that will not attract people. What is remarkable is how often it's been accomplished. People like to sit, where there are places to sit. [p.179]

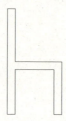

§2 Superordinate Land Use Rules

ROT
§2.01

Ⓒ Ⓐ Ⓓ   Ⓕ Ⓗ Ⓢ   New York

Rule of Three

During the past century, a number of inner-city parcels have been rebuilt up to three times. The city has the discretion to grant certain buildings historic land-mark status and place them under permanent protection. [p.141]

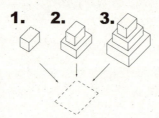

GT
§2.02

Ⓒ Ⓡ   Ⓟ   New York

Glut Tendency

Diverse or mixed use tends to self-destruct to the extent that especially successful uses tend to glut a given area. In order to diminish the tendency and danger that certain successful utilizations will tend toward glut, land use regulations possess the force of law for a maximum of 10 years (i.e., if not additionally constrained by other provisions). Ensuing thereafter will be a fundamental revision of the regulations proclaimed herein. [p.220]

Ⓐ▣ 🏠 Ⓢ New York

Style Rules

Also necessary is the revision of the rules in force in accordance with §1.05, because the city holds the view that urban regulations cannot be effective independently of societal transformations. Among these are evolving perceptions with regard to urban and architectural form. [p.182, 183, fig.79]

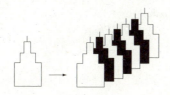

Ⓒ▣ William H.Whyte

Land Preservation

The best way to save land is to buy it. [p.99]

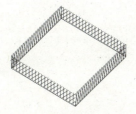

Ⓒ▣🏛 Houston compared to Chicago

Population to Overall Street Length

The relationship between population size and the total length of the infrastructure serving them varies from city to city, and there exists no direct proportionality between the two magnitudes. [p.196, 246]

RLP
§ 2.06

◉ ⊠ 🏠   🏠 Ⓗ   Hong Kong

Ridge Line Protection

In order to allow the city to remain visibly a settlement at the edge of mountainous terrain, the ridgeline of the mountain range is protected. The city has the discretion to determine the number of meters of ridgeline that must be visible from the harborside lying opposite. [p.134, fig.48]

SDP
§ 2.07

◉ ⊠ 🏠 🏚 🏠 Ⓗ   Mulholland Drive, Los Angeles

Scenic Drive Protection

The view from the cliffside mountain road down onto the city shall not be blocked by buildings, nor shall buildings be visible from this road at all (as measured from a height of 4 ft (1.2 m)). [p.206, fig.100c]

BP
§ 2.08

◉ Ⓡ 🏠   🏠 Ⓗ   Vancouver

Backdrop Preservation

Three-dimensional view corridors ensure (in conjunction with § 7.06) views between high-rises and onto the distant mountain panorama. [p.132, 202, 249, 251, 254, fig.46]

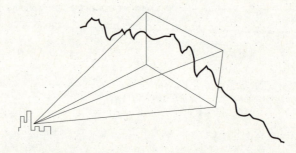

V R D F H Philadelphia

Where is William ?

William P. Averuni stands on his pedestal looking out over the entire city from the heights. No building may be taller than this landmark. [p.228, fig.111]

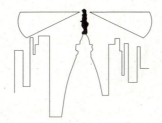

V R D F H London

London View Management

Through the heights of the adjacent buildings, the upper space around the cathedral shall remain unencumbered by visual interference. Tall structures will be permitted to stand in the cathedral's view shadow. [p.136, 249, 251, 254, fig.49–52]

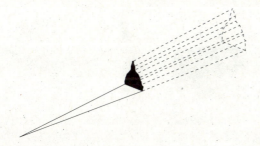

C R D F H Vancouver / Zürich

Towers at Primary Streets

Large buildings shall stand on broad avenues. [p.251, 254]

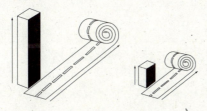

UE
§ 2.12

Ⓜ Ⓐ ⬠   Ⓕ Ⓗ   Seattle

Urban Envelope

The three-dimensional urban envelope fixes the maximum developable volume within a given district. The sole criterion is the fixed height of development throughout the district. All subsequent form-determining regulations work within this envelope. [p.201, 249, 252, 254, 258, fig.94]

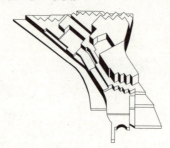

SUL
§ 2.13

Ⓜ Ⓐ ⬠ ⬠   Ⓗ   Houston

Sub Urban Loop

The highway loop 610 subdivides the city into an urban and a suburban zone. All regulations concerning minimums (minimum distances § 6.11, minimum plot size § 6.02) are augmented outside of this ring. [p.197, fig.91]

NSG
§ 2.14

Ⓒ Ⓐ   Mulholland Drive, Los Angeles

No Site Grading

The natural topography should be preserved. [p.206]

C A D P F H   New York

Special Districts

§ 3.01
SD

Within geographically defined areas, the city has the discretion to give special consideration to local particularities through special regulations, and otherwise to suspend or modify citywide regulations. This rule will be supplemented and supported by the corresponding planning materials. [p.97, 160, 199, 210, 216, 252, fig.93]

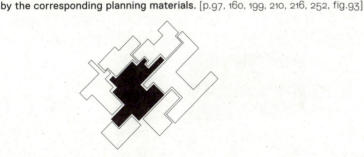

C R D   H   Vancouver

Taper Down to Shoreline

§ 3.02
TDS

The maximum permissible building height is reduced progressively as the water's edge is approached. [p.132, 134]

C R D   F H   New York

Gentlemen's Agreement

§ 3.03
GA

An agreement exists according to which taller structures will maintain an appropriate distance from the UN Secretariat Building. This is true at least for all buildings taller than the 38 stories of the UN tower. [p.223]

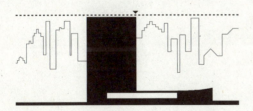

SWS
§ 3.04

A R ⬠ F H   San Francisco

Skyline Wall Syndrome

High-rises built around the same time and motivated by speculation tend to be similar in appearance and size. When they stand alongside one another, the effect is of a homogenous wall of buildings. It is a task of the planning authorities to adopt appropriate measures designed to counteract this tendency. [p.131, 251, 252, fig.45]

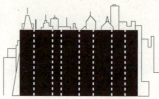

BOB
§ 3.05

C R ⬠ H   New York

Boom Behavior

The tallest buildings are erected toward the end of an economic boom. In many cases, the result is a superfluity of office space in subsequent years. The city has the authority to adopt prompt countermeasures. [p.90]

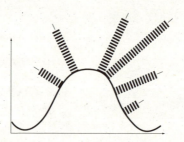

DQ
§ 3.06

M A ⬠ H   Proposition M in San Francisco

Development Quota

In the central business district, a maximum of 475,000 square (44,000 sqm) feet of office space can be built annually. [p.128]

475,000 SQFT/YEAR

Ⓜ Ⓐ Ⓓ   Ⓗ   Seattle

Height Range

HR
§ 3.07

Altogether 55 high-rise projects are approved for the next 8 years, and these have to be graduated in height. A building is a high-rise if it is at least 25 m in height (§ 7.02–1). [p.202, 252, fig.95]

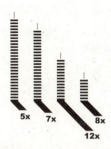

Ⓗ Ⓐ   Ⓟ   New York

Use Groups

UG
§ 3.08

Uses are categorized, defined geographically, and subdivided into zones. These then form districts. The basic subdivisions consist of residential, commercial, and industrial uses. There are 18 use groups in all. [p.85, 246, 249, 252, fig.13]

Ⓒ Ⓐ Ⓓ Ⓟ Ⓕ Ⓗ   Wilshire Boulevard, Los Angeles

Transition Zoning

TS
§ 3.09

Special regulations apply to the boundaries of these zones (§ 3.08). [p.213]

AC
§ 3.10

Ⓗ Ⓐ   Ⓟ   SoHo, New York

Artists Certification

Only certified artists may own a home in the Art District. [p.220]

CAN
§ 3.11

Ⓒ Ⓡ Ⓓ   Ⓗ   New York

Canyoning Land Value Peaks

Building lot prices are highly differentiated by location. The highest prices often lie just a few meters from average prices. The city has the authority to employ regulatory measures in order to counteract this development. [p.96, fig.20]

DCM
§ 3.12

Ⓐ Ⓡ Ⓓ   Ⓕ Ⓗ   San Francisco

Downtown's Castle Moat

Found in the immediate vicinity of the financial district are neighborhoods having the city's lowest densities. [—]

C R P   Jane Jacobs   **MFS**
Multi Function Streets   **§ 4.01**

A street or district serves a variety of primary functions. [p.67]

C A F   Jane Jacobs   **SHB**
Short Blocks   **§ 4.02**

Block lengths shall be short. [p.196, fig.90]

C R P F H S   Jane Jacobs   **DIM**
Difference Max   **§ 4.03**

In each street, the buildings shall form contrasts by virtue of their respective age, condition, and use. [p.67, 254]

AAH
§4.04

Ⓐ ▣ ⬠   Along US Highways

Adopt a Highway

Private·citizens, small shops, and institutions may display advertising signage at the street's edge as long as they attend to the maintenance and cleaning of these sections of the street and remove trash from them. [p.118, fig.38]

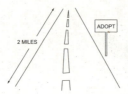

QSV
§4.05

Ⓐ ▣ ⬠   Ⓕ Ⓗ Ⓢ   San Francisco

Quality of Street Views

By virtue of their locations, topographies, or buildings, certain streets possess special visual qualities. These stand under special protection. A *quality of street view* map specifies the view relationships and visual peculiarities that are to be protected. [p.128, 252, 254, fig.43]

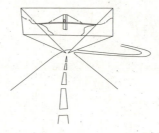

DM
§4.06

Ⓐ ▣   Ⓕ   Ⓢ   Mulholland Drive, Los Angeles

Dirt Mulholland

A street's potholes provide some of the most pervasive experiences of users. [p.206]

Ⓒ Ⓐ 🄳 🅟 🅕 🄷   Seattle

Pedestrian Streets

Streets used principally by pedestrians are classified as Class I, Class II, and Green Streets. Adjacent buildings that contribute to enhancing the quality of such streets may thereby earn utilization bonuses. Requirements vary according to the street's classification. [p.202, 220, 254, fig.96–97]

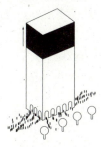

Ⓐ Ⓡ   🅟 🅕   🅢   Seattle

Façade Transparency

In Class I pedestrian streets, at least 60% of ground-level façades must be transparent. Nontransparent surfaces may be no more than 15 ft (4.6 m). For Class II pedestrian streets, transparency must be at least 30%, with utmost 30 ft (9.1 m) of blank façade. [p.204]

Ⓒ 🄰   🅟   Midtown Manhattan, New York / San Francisco

Retail Frontage Continuity

Ground-floor zones shall form strips of retail uses that go beyond the dimensions of the single block. [p.220, fig.104a]

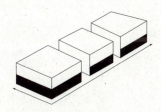

SFD
§ 4.10

Ⓒ Ⓡ   Ⓟ Ⓕ   Seattle

Shop Front Diversity

A shopping street with small retail businesses cannot have a larger shop whose frontage is longer than 1 ½ times the average length of the neighboring shops. [fig.104b]

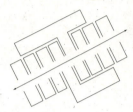

SWC
§ 4.11

Ⓒ Ⓐ Ⓓ   Ⓕ   New York

Street Wall Continuity

Toward the street, buildings shall stand directly on the edges of their parcels. This endows the street with a continuous streetscape. [p.186, 220, fig.84]

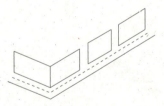

SWL
§ 4.12

Ⓜ Ⓐ Ⓓ   Ⓕ   R4 Residence Districts, New York

Street Wall Length

The maximum length of a building façade shall be 185 ft (56 m). [p.67, fig.3]

Ⓡ Ⓡ Ⓓ Ⓕ Ⓗ   New York   **SSR**
    § 4.13

Setback Street Ratio

Above a certain height, each building shall spring back at distances having (depending upon the district or zone: § 3.01, § 3.08) either twice, 1 ½ times, or the same width as the adjacent street. This creates a feeling of enclosure without a canyon-like impression. [p.82, 107, 158, 175, 218, 254, fig.63]

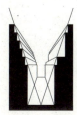

Ⓜ Ⓐ Ⓓ Ⓕ   Houston   **SW**
    § 4.14

Street Width

Streets shall have ideal widths of at least 100 ft (30 m). [p.196]

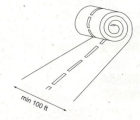

min 100 ft

Ⓒ Ⓡ   General   **ROB**
    § 4.15

Robustness

Streets are more robust, that is to say permanent, than building lots, and building lots are more robust than buildings. This robustness determines the hierarchy of the individual elements. [p.196, 246]

NH
§ 5.01

C A General

Neighbor

Designated as a neighbor is whoever or whatever lies directly along the edge of the building lot. This definition remains in force until it is supplanted by a·new one. [p.145]

VSR
§ 5.02

C R D P F H S New York

Virgin Site Rule

The street grid cuts relationships between neighboring blocks. This independence persists until new regulations concerning neighbors generate new interdependencies. [p.100]

106
§ 5.03

H R P F London

Section 106 Agreements

A new housing development over a given threshold size, commonly 15 dwellings (the figure varies between local authorities), is required to provide a predetermined proportion as affordable housing. [p.163]

C R ⌂ **F ⌂ S**   Kevin Lynch

LMI
§ 5.04

Landmarks and Icons

A building's significance is determined by its contrast with the immediate vicinity (i.e. with neighbors: § 5.01) and its lucidity of form. It lies within the powers of the city administration to encourage these distinctions to emerge more strongly in a given project, or instead to attenuate them. Such decisions are contingent upon the corresponding strategies of differentiation. [p.228, 254]

M A ⌂   **⌂**   London

MS
§ 5.05

Metropolitan Sanction

Public buildings are permitted to surpass the otherwise generally valid height limits up to a maximum height of 30 m. [p.105]

M A ⌂   **⌂**   Chicago

FC
§ 5.06

Flat Cap

The maximum permissible building height is 35 ft (11 m). This threshold may be surpassed only under certain conditions (e.g. § 4.07, § 5.14, § 7.01–4). [p.90, fig.18]

HDM
§ 5.07

C R D ⬠   H   Mulholland Drive, Los Angeles

Height Difference Max

Height differences between individual buildings are highly desirable, but at the same time an excessively strong contrast between neighboring structures detracts from a district's physical coherence. For this reason, neighboring buildings shall not differ in height by more than 50% of their total heights. [p.209, 254, fig.100f]

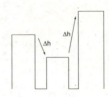

2H
§ 5.08

R R D P F H   Zürich

2h Shadow

A high-rise may not place a neighboring residential building in shadow for more than two hours per day. (See high-rise definition § 7.01–2). [p.149, 191, 251, 252, 254, 258, 260, fig.58]

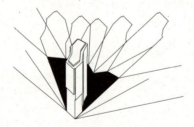

NC
§ 5.09

A R D P F H S   Mulholland Drive, Los Angeles

Neighborhood Compatibility

New construction projects must be adapted in form, function, and landscaping to neighboring buildings within a circumference of 100 feet (30 m). Neighboring buildings are defined by § 5.01, or by further stipulations within special districts § 3.01. [p.209, 220, 252, 254, fig.100g]

🏠 🏠 🏠 🏠 🏠 🏠   New Mexico

Solar Access

Those operating solar facilities shall enjoy unimpeded rights to the sunshine to which the premises are exposed. [p.152]

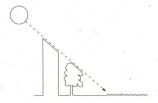

🏠 🏠 🏠 🏠 🏠 🏠   London

Ancient Lights Doctrine

If sunlight has entered a certain window for 20 years or more, then the owner has a right to expect that this shall be the case in the future as well. [p.151, 254]

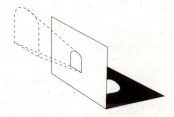

🏠 🏠 🏠   Kenmore, Buffalo

Yard Maintenance

Plants present in private gardens may not interfere with or disturb neighbors. The general appearance of the garden must be consistent with that of adjacent gardens.[p.114]

HH
§ 5.13

C R F H   Santa Monica

Hedge Height

A simple parcel hedge has up to four ideal heights. First, that of the owner, second, that of the immediate neighbor, third, that prescribed by the municipality, and fourth, that of the hedge's own intrinsic or ideal growth height. [p.146, fig.57]

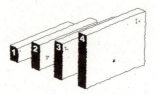

TDR
§ 5.14

C R D H   New York

Transfer of Development Rights

If a parcel is not developed to the maximum allowable height, then the owner can permanently sell this potential to a neighboring site. If all of these sites have already been built to their height capacity, then the city administration has the authority to extend the vicinity surrounding the building in question in order to ensure the continued transfer of development rights. This happens within the area of a specially devised district (§ 3.01). [p.143, 160, 225, fig.65]

VIS
§ 5.15

A R F H S   Mulholland Drive, Los Angeles

Visibility Study

The views of a new building project are critical and need to be assessed within a radius of ¾ of a mile (1,200 m) around it. [p.206, fig.100b]

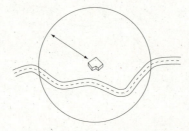

🅐 🆁　　🅕 🅗 🆂⃝　　San Francisco

Opposition Drawing

Opponents of a new building project need to produce opposition drawings, which explain the deficiencies of the critical project within its context. Otherwise they will not get heard. [p.124, 252]

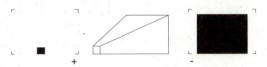

§ 6 Plot/Block Rules

🅜 🅐 🅓⃝　🅕⃝　　New York

Block Width

A block is delimited on all sides by streets, public spaces, parks etc. [—]

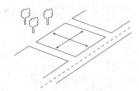

🅜 🅐⃝ 🅓⃝ 🅟⃝　　Houston / Los Angeles

Lot Size Requirements

A building site where a single-family house is to stand must have a minimum size of 5000 sqft (465 sqm). [p.191, 196, 210, 246]

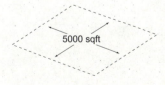

5000 sqft

COS
§6.03

Ⓜ ⊠ Ⓓ   🅕   Houston

Compensating Open Space

A site can be less than the officially valid minimum size provided that a certain quantity of open space on the site remains undeveloped by way of compensation. [p.197]

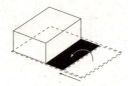

FYD
§6.04

Ⓜ ⊠ Ⓓ   🅕   R1–1 Residence Districts, New York

Front Yard Depth

Front yards shall have minimum depths of 20 ft (6 m). [p.67, fig.3]

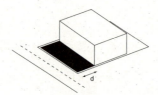

RYD
§6.05

Ⓜ ⊠ Ⓓ   🅕   R2 Residence Districts, New York

Rear Yard Depth

Back yards shall have minimum depths of 20 ft (6 m). [p.67, fig.3]

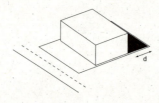

M R D P — Ebenezer Howard, Garden City

Fodder Ratio

Gardens must be of sufficient size to allow proprietors to provide themselves with foodstuffs through their own agricultural labor. [p.191]

C A P — New York

Lot Assembly

A building lot that has been assembled from a number of individual lots is more valuable than the sum of its individual parts. [p.143, fig.55]

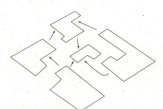

M A D F — R2 Residence Districts, New York

Lot Width

In order to preserve the character of a low-density neighborhood, the minimum width of a building lot is 40 ft (12 m). This can vary according to zone. [p.67, fig.3]

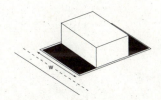

OSR
§ 6.09

Ⓜ 🄡 Ⓓ   Ⓕ   R6 Residence Districts, New York

Open Space Ratio

The quantum of undeveloped, open space on a given zoning lot is given as a percentage of the total FAR on the lot. This Open Space Ratio must amount to at least 20% per zone. [—]

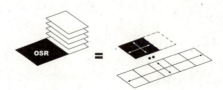

LC
§ 6.10

Ⓜ 🄐 Ⓓ   Ⓕ   R3–1 Residence Districts, New York

Lot Coverage

A building may occupy a maximum of 35% of the surface of a building lot. This value can vary according to zone. [p.67, fig.3]

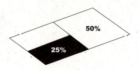

BD
§ 6.11

Ⓜ 🄑 Ⓓ   Ⓕ   R3X Residence Districts, New York

Building Distance

The minimum distance between buildings is 8 ft (2.4 m). [p.67, fig.3]

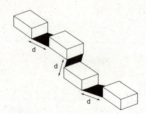

Ⓜ ⊠ Ⓓ Ⓕ   R3–1 Residence Districts, New York

SYW
§ 6.12

Side Yard Width

The width of the surrounding gardens strips is altogether 13 ft (4 m), with each side having a width of at least 5 ft (1.5 m). [p.67, fig.3]

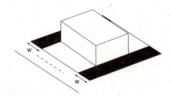

Ⓐ ⊠ Ⓕ Ⓢ   R6 Residence Districts, New York

POA
§ 6.13

Planted Open Areas

All open surfaces between the street wall and the front lot line are to be landscaped with plants. [—]

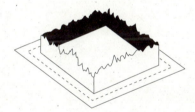

Ⓐ Ⓡ Ⓓ Ⓕ Ⓗ Ⓢ   Mulholland Drive, Los Angeles

LSS
§ 6.14

Landscape Screening

In protected natural areas, visible portions of buildings are to be masked by plants and vegetation. [p.209, fig.100e]

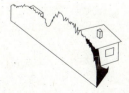

JFO
§ 6.15

Ⓐ🅰   Ⓕ Ⓢ/   Town of Mentz, Port Byron

Junkyard Fence Order

Junkyards are to be surrounded by fences which block views to their interiors.
[p.113, fig.31]

§ 7 Building Rules

FAR
§ 7.01–1

Ⓜ Ⓡ Ⓓ Ⓟ Ⓕ Ⓗ   New York

Floor Area Ratio

The maximum ratio between the total usable surface area of the building's full stories and the surface of the building lot is dependent upon the utilization zone where the lot is located. The zones are more precisely specified through plans. Maximum space usage may also be conditioned by other regulations (for ex. § 7.01–4).
[p.67, 68, 175, 183, 218, fig.3, 74]

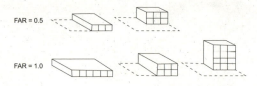

FAR = 0.5

FAR = 1.0

LH
§ 7.01–2

Ⓜ🅰Ⓓ   Ⓗ   Switzerland / Germany

Lowest Highrise

A high-rise is defined as being at least 25 m tall. [p.149]

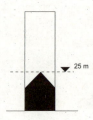

25 m

M **R** **D**   **H**   Paris

5-Story Rule of Paris

Buildings cannot be taller than the height residents and users are prepared to climb using stairs. For buildings without elevators, this threshold has been reached at a height of five stories. [p.106]

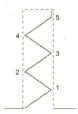

M **R** **D** **P** **F** **H**   New York / Seattle

Plaza Bonus

In exchange for providing certain public amenities, buildings may in some cases surpass the maximal values that normally apply (max. building height, utilization, etc.). A catalog specifies the levels of such bonuses for specific public features. [p.98, 176, 183, 190, 203, 225, 230, fig.75]

C **R** **D**   **F** **H**   San Gimignano / New York

Engineering Height

Current knowledge of building construction allows the erection of structures only up to a certain height (no longer valid: a reworking of this rule is proposed). [p.88, fig.14]

EH
§ 7.01–6

C R D P F H New York / Chicago

Economic Height

Beginning at a certain building height, one encounters the law of diminishing returns, i.e., the sales of additional stories no longer cover the costs of their construction and maintenance. This Economic Height will be taken into consideration when determining a generally valid height limit. [p.89, 131, 184, 237, fig.81–83]

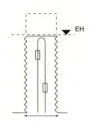

SB
§ 7.02–1

M A D F H R2 Residence Districts, New York / Paris

Set Back

Beginning at a certain height, the building's volume shall spring back, forming an eaves height. [p.82, 106, 111, 252, 254, fig.12]

PWH
§ 7.02–2

M A D F H R2A Residence Districts, New York

Perimeter Wall Height

The height of a terminal, vertical outer wall before a potential setback can be up to 21 ft (6.4 m). [p.67, fig.3]

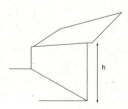

Ⓜ Ⓐ Ⓓ Ⓕ Ⓗ   R6 Residence District, New York

BAH
§ 7.02–3

Base Height

The maximum height of a front façade behind which the upper volume of the building is stepped back is 35 ft (11 m). [fig.12]

Ⓒ Ⓡ Ⓓ Ⓕ Ⓗ   New York

CB
§ 7.02–4

Contextual Base

All buildings have uniform eaves heights. New buildings must be oriented in this regard to neighboring buildings. [p.220, fig.12]

Ⓡ Ⓡ Ⓓ Ⓕ Ⓗ   New York

DEC
§ 7.02–5

Daylight Evaluation Chart

The Daylight Evaluation Chart measures and regulates the shadows cast on the street by the building. [p.155, 251, 252, fig.62]

SEP
§ 7.02–6

R A D F H   New York

Sky Exposure Plane

The Sky Exposure Plane is a virtual surface that is inclined toward the inside from the boundaries of the zoning lot and beginning at a certain height. The gradient varies by district, and such surface can be interrupted only under certain conditions. This allows light and air into the street. [p.149, 183, 233, 252, fig.12]

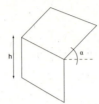

BB
§ 7.02–7

M A D F H   Berlin

22m Berlin Block

A citywide ordinance states that unless exceptions apply, the eaves height within a block and adjacent to its courtyards is **22 m**. [p.106, fig.28]

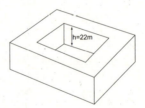

DTE
§ 7.02–8

M R D F H   R10 Residence Districts, New York

Down to Earth

At least **55%** of a building's volume is found below a height of 150 ft (46 m). [p.252, fig.12]

A R D F H   Mulholland Drive, Los Angeles

NSL
§ 7.02–9

No Skylighting

A building silhouette as visible from the street against the sky should be inconspicuous. [p.206]

A A D P F H S   New York

SH
§ 7.02–10

Shoehorning

As long as the maximum allowable site utilization has not been attained, and no landmark protection provisions apply, an existing building may be extended in height by putting another one on top of it. [p.141]

M A D F S   Weissenhofsiedlung, Stuttgart

FR
§ 7.02–11

Flat Roof

All roofs are flat. [p.106]

SP
§ 7.02–12

ⓐ ⓡ ⬠   ⬠ ⓗ   Mulholland Drive, Los Angeles

Stepped Profile

Sloping sites: all buildings follow the slope of the site in their volumetry and roof termini. [p.206, fig.100a]

BBK
§ 7.02–13

ⓜ ⓐ ⬠   ⬠   San Francisco

Building Bulk

The maximum length of a diagonal line drawn through the building's ground plan of 1.45 x the sideline lenght restricts its horizontal extension. This avoids a slab effect in the case of high-rises. [p.128, 251, 252, 258, fig.42]

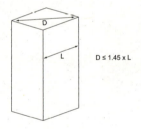

NLD
§ 7.02–14

ⓡ ⓓ ⬠ ⬠ ⬠   New York

Naturally Lit Office Depth

Offices shall never be too deep to be illuminated by natural light. [p.169, fig.69]

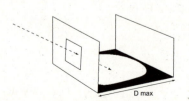

London

Sky Factor

Provided that 0.2% of the total visual field is visible through the window as sky from a certain position within a room, then the room is adequately lit from this position by natural light. [p.153, fig.60]

 New York

Bulky Block Type

Economic pressures compel the utilization of a given building lot all the way to applicable legal limits. These limits then determine the building's form. If a building is constructed which, despite all restrictions, fails to have the desired appearance, then the city has the authority to determine the proportions / shape of its volumetry by means of additional regulations. The utilization coefficient, however, remains constant. [p.170, 222, 240, fig.70]

R2 Residence Districts, New York

Driveway Width

The width of driveways in front of garages is at least 18 ft (5.5 m). [p.67, fig.3]

CCS
§ 7.03–2

R4 Residence Districts, New York

Curb Cut Spacing

Curb cuts must be spaced at least 16 ft (4.9 m) apart. This measurement has an influence on the location of the site's driveway. [p.67, fig.3]

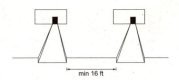

min 16 ft

VA
§ 7.03–3

New York

Vertical Assembly

A pair of buildings each of which is explicitly functionally distinct may not only stand alongside one another, but may also be stacked one above the other. [p.232, fig. 114]

OZ
§ 7.03–4

C1 Overlay Districts, New York

Overlay Zones

In a mixed-use development, residential use shall always be positioned above commercial use. [p.213, fig.102]

SHOP

C ⊠ D P   Los Angeles / Houston   **PR**
§ 7.03–5

Parking Requirements

There must be 1.33 parking spaces for each bedroom. [p.193, 196, fig.89]

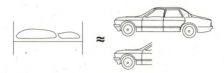

H A   P   San Francisco   **LL**
§ 7.03–6

Laundry Law

For reasons of fire protection, laundries are to be constructed of stone, never of wood. [p.68, 190]

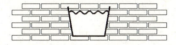

A A D   F H S   Santa Barbara   **CMO**
§ 7.04–1

City Make Over

All buildings erected after 1929 must conform to a Spanish–colonial ideal of beauty. [p.103, 112]

ARL
§ 7.04–2

A R   F H S   San Francisco

Anti Refrigerator Look

Special roof termini on high-rises generate a more visually attractive and varied skyline. [p.128, fig.44]

VL
§ 7.04–3

A R   P F   S   Las Vegas

Vegas' Lighting

At least 75% of the façades of casinos must be covered with advertising in fluorescent lighting. [p.118, fig.33–37]

CW
§ 7.04–4

A R   S   Mulholland Drive, Los Angeles

Color Wheel

For buildings in special nature protection zones, the colors of the building and its outer parts must be compatible with the seasonal coloration of the surrounding natural environment. [p.106, 209, fig.100d]

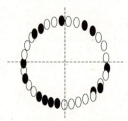

A A   S   Weissenhofsiedlung, Stuttgart

Color Stipulation

The color of all outside façades is as a rule white. [p.106]

CLN

no nuisance

IH

RTB

PPI

RC

FAC

x - coercion = freedom

PC

TOE

+1 - 1/x = >0

RF

PSA

ROT

1. 2. 3.

GT

SR

LP

PSL

RLP

SDP

BP

WIW

LVM

TPS

UE

SUL

NSG

SD

TDS

GA

SWS

BOB

DQ

475.000 SQFT/YEAR

HR

5x 7x 8x 12x

UG

TS

AC

CAN

DCM

MFS

SHB

DIM

AAH

QSV

DM

PS

FT

30%

RFC

SFD

SWC

SWL

SSR

SW

ROB

NH

1a 1 1b

VSR

106

LMI

MS

FC

HDM

2H

NC

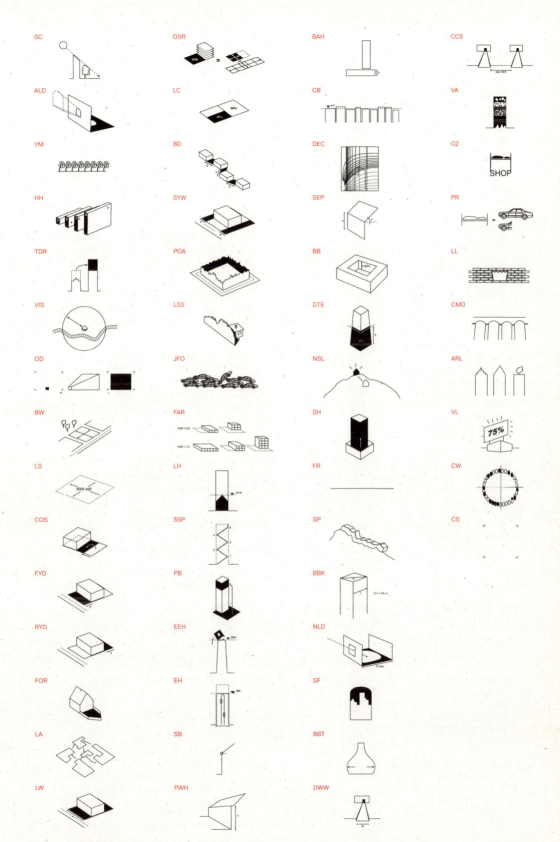

SC

ALD

YM

HH

TDR

VIS

OD

BW

LS

COS

FYD

RYD

FOR

LA

LW

OSR

LC

BD

SYW

POA

LSS

JFO

FAR

LH

5SP

PB

EEH

EH

SB

PWH

BAH

CB

DEC

SEP

BB

DTE

NSL

SH

FR

SP

BBK

NLD

SF

BBT

DWW

CCS

VA

OZ

PR

LL

CMO

ARL

VL

CW

CS

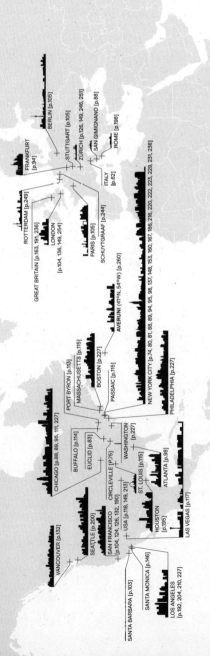

HONG KONG [p.132]

BERLIN [p.105]

STUTTGART [p.105]

ZÜRICH [p.126, 149, 246, 251]

SAN GIMIGNANO [p.88]

ROME [p.198]

FRANKFURT [p.94]

ITALY [p.62]

ROTTERDAM [p.249]

LONDON [p.104, 136, 149, 254]

GREAT BRITAIN [p.163, 191, 236]

PARIS [p.105]

SCHUYTGRAAF [p.244]

AVERUNI (41°N, 54°W) [p.260]

NEW YORK CITY [p.74, 80, 81, 88, 89, 94, 95, 98, 137, 148, 153, 160, 167, 186, 216, 220, 222, 223, 229, 231, 236]

PORT BYRON [p.113]

MASSACHUSETTS [p.115]

BOSTON [p.227]

PASSAIC [p.115]

PHILADELPHIA [p.227]

CHICAGO [p.88, 90, 95, 111, 227]

BUFFALO [p.114]

EUCLID [p.83]

CIRCLEVILLE [P.76]

WASHINGTON [p.227]

ST. LOUIS [p.115]

ATLANTA [p.98]

USA [p.104, 124, 126, 132, 190]

HOUSTON [p.195]

LAS VEGAS [p.177]

VANCOUVER [p.132]

SEATTLE [p.200]

SAN FRANCISCO [p.104, 124, 126, 132, 190]

SANTA MONICA [p.146]

SANTA BARBARA [p.103]

LOS ANGELES [p.192, 204, 210, 227]

1

Rules as Tools—A Token of Affection

There are books about great cities, books about spectacular streets... and there are books about great architects. You have in your hands a book about *great rules*.

This volume deals with 115 different rules. All of the authors, designers, and inventors of these rules are celebrated personalities. Their names are known throughout the world: Hong Kong, Chicago, Berlin, New York, London ...

Each merits an individual monograph—and in fact, there exist numerous studies devoted to each. All of them share a drive to develop mechanisms in the form of rules—rules designed to influence, to safeguard, even to ward off their own destinies. In this regard, they are united by a certain collegiality: sets of rules are regularly exchanged between them in order to address similar problematics and to learn from one another. But our various cities can also be distinguished from one another by their varying degrees of delight in experimentation. Some are bold inventors that never shy away from self-exploration—even to the point of causing considerable damage to themselves, only to be called upon by the authorities to moderate themselves through the establishment of rules that are only dissipated, finally, in hundreds of revisions. Others will adopt a rule only once it has brought about the desired results elsewhere. Also shared among our cities is a certain optimism, one that regards it as necessary and positive to subject private desires to a certain degree of steering and canalization in order to formulate and to propagate overarching public interests.

This optimism also characterizes the architect and urban designer for whom this book is written. The enterprise of urban design—that is to say, the linking together of various design visions via the negotiation of a diversity of private and public interests—consists more of the conscious positing of rules than the drawing up of plans.

To express a vision in the form of precise plans has always been the core occupation of the designer. And that is what architects are trained to do. The plan is among our most powerful tools. We are less trained to cope with urban rules. We adhere to them more-or-less consciously, and in the rarest of instances, we draft them ourselves. As a rule, we leave this work to municipal building authorities, to their administrators, to lawyers, and to economists.

Still, as professional amateurs with regard to the city, its evolution, and its form, we can hardly avoid acknowledging the significant role played by rules and regulations in shaping our built environment. At the same time, our dealings with rules represents a decisive expansion of our design methods. As integrated, operational tools in planning and design, rules possess special qualities. Their implementation enables the precise formulation of degrees of freedom for specified areas and for the protagonists of the planning process. These freedoms are decisive for the generation of ephemeral qualities such as urban diversity, difference and vitality. Consciously deployed freedoms, moreover, endow planning with a certain sustainability and permanence in confronting an unpredictable future. And finally, rules are helpful instruments in structuring the work of design itself. They simultaneously constitute guidelines for producing a design as well as criteria for evaluating it.

Rules are precise and unambiguous formulations, yet they produce a multiplicity of alternative realities. There exists no special discipline or special location for them, only a context, which takes the form of—once again—still more rules. In this case, it is the city—the city as a totality of rules which circumscribe it and the building code constitutes an abstract chronicle, or notes for one, one that knows no past tense, and one that can be periodically updated almost unproblematically.

The story they narrate constitutes an authentic portrait of a given city. At the same time, they furnish the impulses that culminate in its monumental action. The universality of such portraits is astonishing. It is a question of negative episodes, of controversies, of private interests masked as public ones and vice versa.

The impact of rules always occurs in the present tense, its effects are always temporary, yet they rework and transform continuing events whose origins lie in the past into guidelines for future action. This reprocessing is determinative (as is always the case with the writing of history), and its inertia provides the city with continuity and reliability. Regulations construct permanent realities within rapid processes of change.

Rules are everywhere—they are infrastructural. They hang like a fog above our built and non-built environments. They remain in force in locations that no street will ever reach. They dominate the air, just as they do the ground and that which lies beneath it. As an abstract and immaterial urban infrastructure, they constitute a connection between built structures, land, and its use. They link the physical with the social city, connecting quality with quantity and latent characteristics to manifest ones. Rules are universal and discrete guiding instruments, and they create an almost poetic, standardized irrationality.

Rules do not act, but they do remain in force. It is not rules themselves that are productive, but instead those who adhere to them. Because of this inherent passivity, regulations initially lead a shadow existence within discussions of the urban will-to-form and the will-to-change.

Still: cities are neurotic. Their self-imposed constraints, whether factual or normative (whether alterable or not), are pervasive, and are at least as responsible for determining the form of our built environment as its individual and primary elements: streets, buildings, and architects.

Legal fiction: the specialized discussion taking place between lawyers, politicians, administrators, sociologists, etc., about regulative administrative mechanisms is not in itself the goal.

This work is instead written for architects who, as urbanists, voluntarily assume the status of subversive civil servants.

It is a question of research into the behavior of buildings and of our built environment: how do buildings react to external and internal pressures, how do they interact with one another to form (compulsory) communities?

Here too, it is a question of a rehabilitation: of the detachment of rules from their bureaucratic torpor and from the deterministic context of building ordinances and laws, of the possibility of converting them into the active and powerful design and steering instruments of an operational, project-based urban design.

Rules supply design principles that represent alternatives and expansions of the conventional plan. They render design control adjustable—ranging from a determinism that resembles automatism to an existential aura of personal responsibility.

This adjustability is one of the most important preconditions for urban diversity, participation, vitality, and not least of all for urban design that is successful in the long-term. Here, conventional design techniques are fused with political instruments.

Welcome aboard! We are embarking on a journey to the showplaces of a rule-based steering of the built environment! To places where rules are the protagonists, where they are thoroughly capable in their totality of generating an encyclopedic context.

The result is a list of 115 regulations (synthesized within the Code of Averuni) in which each of our found rules receives a new and artificial context formed by, again, still other rules and regulations. The inventorying of selected rules by degrees of scale is only one of many possibilities of classification. A different one might read as follows: a) regulations that only remain in force for a year, b) which allow multiple possibilities, c) regularities, and d) those unfair to minorities, e) those which pass judgment on questions of beauty and aesthetics, f) those that fix maximum thresholds, g) imported regulations, h) those which are frequently broken, i) regulations still to be drawn up, k) those which appear in every North American city with the exception of Houston, l) but have never been written down, m) those adopted in 1961, n) those concerned with the provision of light and air, o) those concerned with commercial law, p) those which are negotiable, q) those limited to certain territories, r) those whose motives are no longer evident, and s) those still valid today. [1]

At least to begin with, an inventory of the rules found at various locations and an attempt to classify them can only be conceived as a collection, and not as a set of instructions for use. Rather, these rules are representative of attempts at guiding urban destinies. They mirror the wealth of inventiveness of cities which strive actively to influence their own forms and characters.

The 115 rules assembled here are not intended as a set of instructions for high-quality urban design. They are methodological tools, and not universally deployable monkey wrenches. The method of a rule-based steering can be generalized, but not the rules arising from it. These are highly specialized, and are tailored to address equally specific contexts. They represent creative acts that solve definite urban problems—and sometimes even create them.

This collection of rules demonstrates the variety of the areas they seek to guide, the spectrum of criteria which they cover, and the multifarious types of rules that exist. Following a discussion of the individual regulations within the specific situations they address, it serves as an inspiration to emulate these cities in their attempts to develop rule-based instruments designed to guide urban design.

Still, the proviso that rules and regulations which function well at one location will not automatically have the same beneficial impact on another has been ignored by many municipal administrations in the past. Many American cities went further than simply drawing inspiration from regulations adopted by other cities—in particular by New York City and its comprehensive rule-based guidance system, introduced in 1916. In many

---

[1]   In imitation of a certain Chinese encyclopedia mentioned in Jorge Luis Borges (1966), 'Die Analytische Sprache John Wilkins', cited from Michel Foucault (1971), *Die Ordnung der Dinge— Eine Archäologie der Humanwissenschaften*, 17.

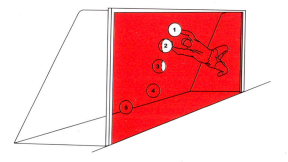

1 The method of scoring according to the FiFA rules: 1–3 No Goal, 4–5 Goal.

places, the New York approach was regarded as a universal panacea for urban problems in general: large portions of New York's zoning ordinances—the first adopted nationally—were simply copied in the years after 1916 by a series of North American cities. New York had attempted to derive an algorithm for the solution of its metropolitan problems. In many cities, the problems of the time were similarly apparent. Different forms of use collided with one another, generating individual conflicts which soon became public problems. These general problems were answered in an equally universal form: even the printing errors contained in New York's zoning ordinances proliferated rapidly within those of a number of other North American cities. This enforced mobility of certain regulations led to the widespread fallacy that specific regulations could function as a universal panacea.

An Ostensibly Bad Reputation

Rules have a bad reputation. Architects in particular are not terribly fond of them. In the form of building laws, they count as primary determinants, and are often conceived as nothing but constraints on artistic creativity. Louis Sullivan, for example, once warned: "Formulas are dangerous things. They are apt to prove the end of a genuine art, however hopeful they may be in the beginning to the individual. The formula of an art remains and becomes more and more dry, rigid, and vanishes forever."[2] And in 1937, Le Corbusier remarked, also as a sideswipe at an—in his opinion—over-regulated New York: "The spirit of France is not rule-bound except in periods of lethargy and ossification. Today, when a new world is surging up under the impulse of technical miracles, the officials of the City of Lights apply regulations. And soon there will be no lights in the City."[3] Kevin Lynch makes a distinction concerning the general, societal perspective of urban planning, regulation, and design: "Controls are widely accepted if they are limitations on use, density, and the layout of circulation—even if they should not be. They are viewed with greater suspicion when applied to visual form. Controls are negative and passive measures, as opposed to the positive technique of design. They stifle innov-

[2] Louis H. Sullivan and Claude Fayette Bragdon (1934), *Kindergarten Chats on Architecture, Education and Democracy*, 139.
[3] Le Corbusier (1964), *When the Cathedrals Were White*, 20. Quoted by John J. Costonis (1989), *Icons and Aliens: Law, Aesthetics, and Environmental Change*, 114.

ation and restrict individual freedom."[4]

In the realm of games and sports, on the other hand, rules are accepted without much distrust at all. They are even regarded as necessary preconditions designed to ensure an exciting game or play. Even when the FIFA required more than 130 pages of explanations in order to provide a comprehensive explanation of the 17 official regulations of football.[5] For one of the most popular sports of our time, the objection to over-regulation would have some force. But urban design is no game.

Still (and without attempting to elaborate on the distinctions between building regulations and game rules), it can be said that there are good and bad regulations, those that restrict freedom of movement, and those that actually generate it in the first place.

An Attempt at Abstraction

[Actor]
Palladio and Rules

[Location]
Italy

Rules belong to no specific discipline. In an abstract sense, a rule to begin with simply characterizes a relationship. It can be derived from a certain orderliness, or won from experience and knowledge, and is then fixed in the form of an accord.

In this context, an interesting contribution was made by two American architectural historians, George Hersey and Richard Freedman, in their book *Possible Palladian Villa—Plus a Few Instructively Impossible Ones*. In 1992, they attempted to disclose the code underlying the works of Palladio, which is to say, to describe the organization, proportions, and morphology of his villas by means of explicit rules. They did so with such precision that a computer programme was developed that was capable of re-synthesizing new (in fact, an infinite number of) possible Palladian villas on the basis of their rules. The question poses itself: how can one do such a thing to Palladio? To define the work of a man regarded as one of the most influential architects of all time on the basis of a pair of unspectacular rules? Would it not cast doubt on his originality and genius, virtually reducing his achievements to a kind of game? Or could this exercise further elevate our regard for his achievements precisely because he apparently worked with a system, with an underlying, rule-based continuity, rather than proceeding impulsively in each separate instance with a new inspiration?

With good reason, Hersey and Freedman avoid offering any conclusive or explicit reply to this question. Important for them was the experiment itself, and not an evaluation of a medium of description. And by decomposing and representing the works of a generally recognized artist into formulae, they indirectly deprive Sullivan's critique regarding the relationship between rules and artistic creativity of its force.

But rules are more than simply abstract forms of description. They possess an inherited character: if something obeys a specific rule, then it is likely that such compliance will persist as well. This inertia, designated as orderliness, thereby produces reliability and calculability for an otherwise unpredictable future. Danish director Thomas Vinterberg replied to the question why he was so fond of rules: "I love them, without them I am

4   Kevin Lynch (1971), *Site Planning*, 238.
5   See FIFA (2008), *Laws of the Game*.

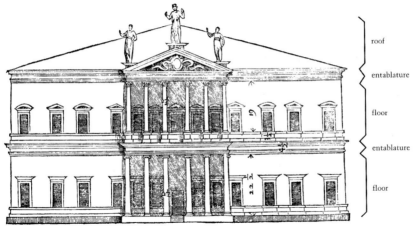

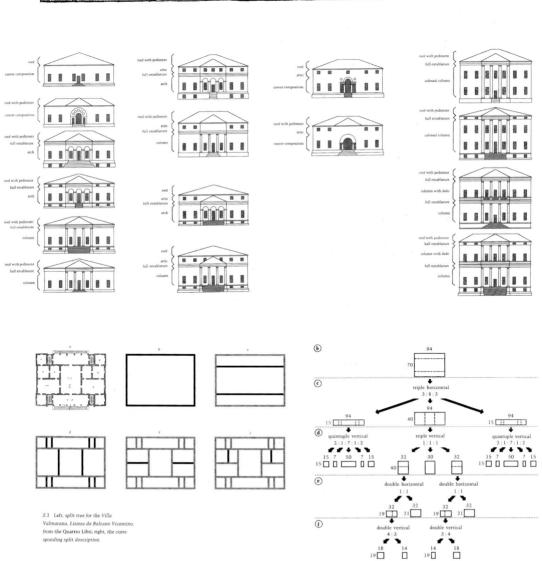

2.3 Left, split tree for the Villa Valmarana, Lisiera da Balzano Vicentino, from the Quattro Libri; right, the corresponding split description.

2 Analyzing Palladio and the subsequent resynthesis.

disoriented. Many people don't understand that, it's like with a calendar: once you have decided how your day looks, you can relax about it. Through rules, life becomes free."[6]

Rules are Ubiquitous

No social fabric, not even the most individualistic society, can manage without general rules. But only a few of them are instituted in the form of laws or formally codified. By far the greater proportion of regulations rein in the form of unwritten conventions, customs, norms, maxims, and traditions. They change over time, some disappear and are replaced by new ones. According to political economist Friedrich von Hayek, such implicit rules play a very special role in our society. Hayek claims that "the readiness to submit to such rules constitutes... an essential precondition for the general development and perfection of the rules of collective social life; ... self-evidently, shared conventions and traditions make it possible for a group of people to work together easily and effectively with far less formal organization and compulsion compared with a group of people lacking such a common background."[7] Hayek thereby underlines not only the existence of informal determinants, but also the way in which these cooperate with formal regulations. Formal and informal forms of organization reinforce one another as context. We need not determine whether it is theoretically possible for an informal order to render a formal, administrative order superfluous. Extremely dubious, in any event, is the assertion that the degree of determination would be less for the individual. In all likelihood, the constraints or obligations that would remain in force would simply no longer be perceived as such.

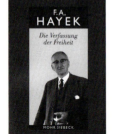

Freedom & Coercion
[FAC] §1.06

Making Control Adjustable

Emerging already in the course of this initial discussion of regulations have been a pair of interdependent terms, neither one of which is entirely simple to define: constraint on the one hand, and freedom on the other. It would be naïve to speak of universal freedom, and discussions of compulsion usually tend in the direction of legal-philosophical issues of little interest to architects. Going beyond hippie fantasies, we take up now a preliminary definition of freedom. Friedrich von Hayek supplies us with the following one: "Freedom is the absence of coercion [FAC]." The justification for this negative definition is the fact that freedom is "essential in order to allow space for the unanticipated and the unpredictable; we desire [freedom] because we have learned to expect from it opportunities to realize many of our objectives."[8] Any other direct relationship to a specific purpose, that is to say, any positive characterization of freedom as a precondition for attaining a specific goal would immediately destroy this quality, thereby contradicting the fundamental character of the idea of freedom—the freedom from something, not the freedom toward something!

This optimism, this opportunity to attain something that is both desirable and unpredictable, is also our motivation for anchoring the idea of freedom

6   Interview Thomas Vinterberg in *Die Zeit*, Aug 2004.
7   Friedrich August von Hayek (1952), *Individualismus und Wirtschaftliche Ordnung*, 37.
8   Friedrich August von Hayek (1972), *The Constitution of Liberty*, 38.

as a fixed component of an urban development and planning discourse. To the extent that this discussion of freedom is relevant to the area of operational urban design, it quickly becomes clear that freedom as such does not exist as a totality; at most, we have specific freedoms, those grounded in specific definitions [RF]. In the hands of the city planner, these freedoms range from the conscious but passive granting of a certain leeway all the way to the active generation of specific choices and options. Work with rules as methodical planning tools permits the adjustment of this degree of freedom—or better: degree of compulsion—within precisely delimited areas. The planning imperative "it must be" is expanded to include the "potentially allowable," the "conceivably permissible," and the "desirable under certain circumstances." The examples contained in this book attempt to clarify the ways in which spaces of conscious freedom can be allowed on the basis of the formulation of regulations, even in cases where full awareness of the ultimate consequences of such indeterminacies is lacking; departing from an approach that wants to control everything, and moving toward a non-fatalistic form of "adjustable control." The freedom contained in a rule consists precisely in that which it does not specify. A conscious lack of specificity becomes a design necessity.

Stay Operational!

The idea of urban complexity serves on the one hand as an excuse for the necessary paucity of explanations when faced with urban phenomena, while directly perceptible in it, on the other hand, for many is a characteristic urban quality. Finally, from Christopher Alexander we know that the city is no simple tree[9] with hierarchical dependencies, but instead an intricate network. Robert Venturi even loves complex and contradictory things. And Benoît Mandelbrot is probably not entirely wrong when he makes the general assertion that "the goal of science has always been to reduce the complexity of the world to simple rules."[10]

In his 1929 book *The Metropolis of Tomorrow*, Hugh Ferriss described the sense of being overwhelmed by the spectacle of the city—his reference was the view from his New York apartment. Once the mists of dawn had dissipated, Ferriss was able to spot the first pedestrians far below on the sidewalk set between the various buildings, and to ask himself unsparingly: "What is the relation between these two? Are those tiny specks the actual intelligence of the situation and this towered mass something which, as it were, those ants have marvelously excreted?"[11]

The present work too is an attempt to identify causes and to arrive at explanations. Each individual rule presented here—whether it represents an explanation of an urban reality or an urban design instruction—tells a simple truth about our cities. The emphasis lies on the word "simple." Although, viewed holistically, all of the regulations appearing in this book are embedded in an incomprehensively intricate network of relationships, then they nonetheless possess a persuasive operational advantage that makes them practically viable within such multilayered contexts. This comes close to a diagrammatic approach whose advan-

---

9   Christopher Alexander (1965), *A City Is Not a Tree*, 58–62.
10 Quote by Polish-French mathematician Benoît Mandelbrot.
11 Hugh Ferriss (1929), *The Metropolis of Tomorrow*.

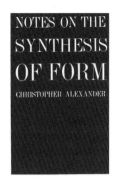

NOTES ON THE
SYNTHESIS
OF FORM
CHRISTOPHER ALEXANDER

tages were characterized by Christopher Alexander in the Foreword to his *Notes on the Synthesis of Form*[12]: "The idea of the diagram, or pattern is very simple. It is an abstract pattern of physical relationships which resolves a small system of interacting and conflicting forces, and is independent of all other forces, and of all other possible diagrams. The idea that it is possible to create such abstract relationships one at a time, and to create designs which are whole by fusing these relationships—this amazingly simple idea is, for me, the most important discovery [...]. Because the diagrams are independent of one another, you can study them and improve them one at a time, so that their evolution can be gradual and cumulative. More important still, because they are abstract and independent, you can use them to create not just one design, but an infinite variety of designs, all of them free combinations of the same set of patterns."[13] Alexander speaks of a method for rendering a design decomposable, qualifiable, in a stepwise fashion, and thereby graspable, and in a way that avoids the danger of operational overload, as well as the danger that the synthesis generates a reductionist and hence deficient result. Patterns or rules are the ingredients of a universal and discrete steering apparatus. The potential inclusiveness of a rule can be useful to the researcher engaging in analysis, to the urban planner engaging in design, as well to the municipal administrator who deploys rules in order to influence spatio-functional interconnections or the interactions between individual and society.

Simply by virtue of the fact that we speak about rules, we automatically mediate between the above-named realms. The distinction between analysis, design, and regulation pales into insignificance in the face of the monotonous use of one in the same tool or method.

Different Kinds of Rules
Rules describe processes. If we conceptualize the city as the momentary state of a process of constant transformation and development, then the processes responsible for change can be described on the basis of a set of abstract rules. These processes possess a certain continuity and inertia in their effects and development; these rules, then, are no mere passive forms of description, but instead also active steering elements for future developments. They define the space of play and the likelihood of impending transformations. Rules form the medium that links the analysis of an existing situation and its projection into the future.

There are, then, various kinds of rules: "Some (standards) refer to form, some to the process of creating it, some to its subsequent performance. Some are legal minimums; others are desirable optimums used as guides in design; some refer to established ways of doing things ('current good practice'); some are predictions (that is, if so many square feet of retail space are provided, that a store will have sufficient business); others are simply (8) arbitrary standardizations that limit unwanted variations in form (screw threads, for example!)."[14]

For this undertaking, two distinctions between kinds of rules are fundamental. First, there is the distinction concerning origin or motivation.

[12]   Christopher Alexander (1974), *Notes on the Synthesis of Form*.
[13]   Ibid., preface to the paperback edition.
[14]   Lynch (1971), 242.

66

Secondly, and more interesting from the point of view of operational urban design, there is the distinction that concerns the capacity to open up a space of possibilities—to create or to permit freedom in the design realm. The question of origins is quickly explained, and is more or less transparent. Is it a question of official codifications, of the way in which building and zoning codes, laws, statutes, and every variety of administrative prescription, attempt to mediate between public and private interests, or instead regulate informal and contextual rules, such as social conventions, cultural or economic forces, traditions, personal maxims, tendencies of the "zeitgeist," of taste, or of "natural law"?

A number of rules are translations of "current best practice" into concrete instructions for urban planning or design. A prominent instance of such instructions are those of Jane Jacobs, who in her book *The Death and Life of Great American Cities* essentially formulated a series of rules—derived from real situations—designed to reverse the deterioration of the American city, or at least avert the repetition of the errors that had, in her view, already been committed. In 1961, she formulated four basic rules for maintaining municipal diversity and vitality: (1) A street or district must serve several primary functions [MFS]. (2) Blocks must be short. (3) Buildings must vary in age, condition and use [DIM]. (4) Population must be dense.[15] These four rules can be viewed, at least initially, as Jane Jacobs' idealized summary description of New York's Greenwich Village as it existed at the time.

Independently of origin, the rules appearing here can also be distinguished in terms of their capacity to open up spaces of possibility. In this context, four fundamental issues must be dealt with:

Decisive to begin with is the realm specified by the respective rule. In order to gain an assessment of possible leeway, an inversion must now take place: which realms are not covered, realms which lie outside of the sphere being regulated?

The second necessary question is whether this underspecified space might not be determined by other, simultaneously valid rules. Accordingly, the degree of determination of certain rules cannot be specified unless they are perceived as being embedded within a specific situation. Formulated in positive terms: control in design terms can be adjusted via the addition and combination of various rules. Example: the round dozen of typical residential standards [BD, CCS, DWW, FAR, FYD, LC, LW, PWH, RYD, SYW, SWL].

A typical set of rules for North American residential areas is found in the *Zoning Handbook*[16] of the *New York City Department of City Planning*. Approximately a dozen formal rules determine the official form and design of New York's residential buildings. These encompass variations in type and size. To some extent, these regulations refer to one another; to some extent they occupy areas that remain underspecified by adjacent regulations. These begin with minimal building lot sizes, the definition of front and side lot lines, the depths of backyards, building heights, and extend all the way to the specification of distances between individual

THE DEATH
AND LIFE
OF GREAT
AMERICAN
CITIES
JANE JACOBS

"Perhaps the most influential single work in the history of town planning... a work of literature."
— The New York Times Book Review

Multi Function Streets
[MFS] §4.01
Difference Max
[DIM] §4.03

Building Distance
[BD] §6.11
Curb Cut Spacing
[CCS] §7.03–2
Driveway Width
[DWW] §7.03–1
Floor Area Ratio
[FAR] §7.01–1
Front Yard Depth
[FYD] §6.04
Lot Coverage
[LC] §6.10
Lot Width
[LW] §6.08
Perimeter Wall Height
[PWH] §7.02–2
Rear Yard Depth
[RYD] §6.05
Side Yard Width
[SYW] §6.12
Street Wall Length
[SWL] §4.12

---

[15]   Jane Jacobs (1961), *The Death and Life of Great American Cities*.
[16]   New York City (2006), *Zoning Handbook*.

Building Distance [BD], **Curb Cut Spacing** [CCS], **Driveway Width** [DWW], **Floor Area Ratio** [FAR], **Front Yard Depth** [FYD], **Lot Coverage** [LC], **Lot Width** [LW], **Perimeter Wall Height** [PWH], **Rear Yard Depth** [RYD], **Street Wall Length** [SWL]

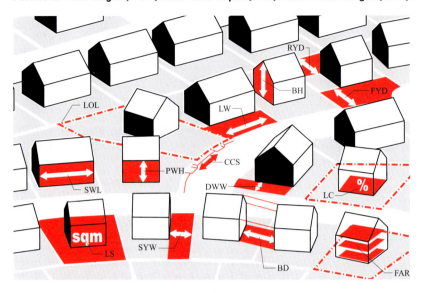

3 Typical Residential Stipulations: **BD** *Building Distance* (min), **CCS** *Curb Cut Spacing* (min), **DWW** *Driveway Width* (min), **FAR** *Floor Area Ratio* (max), **FYD** *Front Yard Depth*, **LC** *Lot Coverage* (max), **LW** *Lot Width* (min), **PWH** *Perimeter Wall Height* (max), **RYD** *Rear Yard Depth*, **SYW** *Side Yard Width*, **SWL** *Street Wall Length* (max).

buildings. With each additional rule, the space of possibilities for New York's residential buildings is further constrained. The series could be extended at will until a—now massive—set of regulations would actually approach a precise description of a specific building type. At this point, rules become a plan.

On the other hand, if a city should seek to guide residential development on the basis of one, or maximally two or three such rules, then the degree of freedom would be correspondingly higher, even approaching total laissez-faire.

The third question with regard to rule-based freedoms is: how strict are the boundaries between the areas defined by the regulations? Is it a question of an absolute standard (for example: maximum building height is 35 feet), or of any relationship (for example: building heights can only surpass 35 feet *provided that...*)?

Fourth and finally, there is the question of *externalities*. Does the rule contribute to guiding areas not explicitly named as objectives of the respective steering mechanism? Might the determination of a maximum floor area ratio [FAR] interfere with certain uses at the location? Is the ban on laundries in wooden houses ultimately an act of discrimination against San Francisco's Chinese community [LL]?

Discussed in the following on the basis of such *precedential cases* is the combination, collision, and collaboration of specific rules within actually existing urban situations and problems:

The following chapter deals specifically with the relation between public and private interests, causing the community to create rules. What is

Floor Area Ratio
[FAR] §7.01–1

Laundry Law
[LL] §7.03–6

public and private interest, how did the public interest emerge and how did it condense into urban regulation?

The third chapter focuses on the power, which is exerted by rules, mainly in their quality of drawing sharp lines between what is allowed and what not. The important discovery that the potential of rules may rather lie in their space of tolerance or interpretation than in sharp fixations is discussed here.

The deployment of rules as controllers of aesthetic quality is dealt with in the fourth chapter. In that sense, one could say that this is the first time rules are considered to be design-tools.

The fifth chapter is about "freedom in bondage", about the rule as a facilitator of freedom(s) or rights. It is also about excessive negotiating conditions caused by extreme proximity.

The sixth chapter juxtaposes official and inofficial codes and the evolutionary, reciprocal influence between them.

The seventh chapter makes explicit for whom rules are made and where they apply. "Externalities" of rules become important in this regard.

The cases in chapter eight demonstrate how urban elements as such are formed by mutual consistency, while at the same time they possess the capacity to facilitate differences to emerge from their context.

Chapter nine tries to explain the design–tool potential of rules.

Whether such a method makes sense can only be judged when we show how rules function within a clearly defined design-task. This is done in the final chapter.

2

The Tightrope Walk of Exercising Control over Private Property

The history of the city is also one of powerful urban visions. Many such visions never make it off the drawing board to become reality—not because they represent inadequate solutions, but instead simply because of the absence of practical instruments capable of inducing private owners to allow a city to be reshaped according to such visions.

The core problem of every urban design action is, to begin with, the definition of the public interest. Derived from a critical quantum of private interests, the public interest is essentially defined as delimited from these. Wherever the public interest has been defined in specific terms, for instance in codifications of what was or was not beneficial to the public health,[1] the following dilemma has been immanent: how to mediate between the two poles, between private and public.

---

[1] A general definition of the idea of *public health* is provided by C. E. A. Winslow (1920): The science and art of preventing disease, prolonging life and promoting health through the organized efforts and informed choices of society, organizations, public and private, communities and individuals.

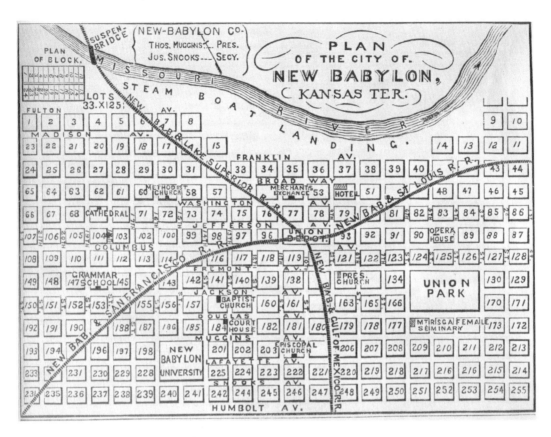

4 The 19th-century City of New Babylon on paper.

5 The 19th-century City of New Babylon in fact.

The American View: the Western Look

Seth Low, former president of Columbia University and the mayor of New York from 1901 to 1903, formulated the task of American urban planning as the solution to the problem of how "to make a great city in a few years out of nothing."[2] This statement was describing the cold start of the American city as a temporally delimited and practical project.

Thus defined, these newly *new towns* thereby escaped the conventional (and above all European) *new town* classification. Discussion became superfluous. All were based more or less on a "preceding plan" or "preconceived frame."

A historical account of American urban development that is far more productive for this investigation resembles the narrative of the classical *Hollywood Western*—both the genre itself and its subdivision into three principal epochs: (1) the conquering of the land (the laying out of grids, subdivision into parcels); (2) basic organization according to ownership (land-use planning, zoning), and (3) the continuing rivalry between neighbors (formerly cattle ranchers). The heroes of the individual stages move between their understanding of the community and their tendency toward individual decisions, toward going it alone. All of this takes place along the mythical boundary between wilderness and civilization, between natural and human law, and most importantly between the two poles of freedom and obligation. In the western, the conflict is between outlaw and law-abiding citizen; in urban design, between private and public interests.

In the 20th century, the Europeans explored and tested totalizing urban planning experiments in order to address the question of whether or not the ideal city could still exist. In contrast the history of the USA beginning in the early part of the same century revolves consistently around the key conflict between private and public interests and the plumbing of that conflict.[3] At least since the nationwide introduction of zoning laws in the first half of the 20th century, methods have been constantly adjusted, and as much administrative control exercised as was necessary, but as little as was possible. This pragmatism not infrequently led to court appearances, and was capable of producing San Francisco's almost palpable over-regulation, but also the almost Wild West conditions prevailing in Houston or Atlanta.

At times, these regulative measures had a positive impact on the physical, cultural, and economic development of urban America, but just as often, outcomes were negative. There was never a shortage of criticism. After being continually refined and endowed with greater sophistication, many of these instruments became export hits—zoning itself having originated in Germany before arriving in the US through its import into New York City.[4] Today, virtually no country lacks building and zoning ordinances.

---

[2] From Seth Low, "An American View of Municipal Government in the United States," James Bryce (1889), *The American Commonwealth*. Quoted by Seymour I. Toll (1969), *Zoned American*, 131.

[3] This highly pragmatic approach is already suggested by the lapidary term "planning." The American planner does not waste time pondering the meaning or indulging in self-doubt vis-à-vis ambiguous and at the same time richly connotative terms like "urban design," nor German expressions like "Städtebau." "Planning" solves problems and is hence a strongly practically oriented discipline.

[4] See Ernst Freund (p.94) and Toll (1969), 130–40.

Also taking place over the past century has been a vigorous transfer of ideologies and styles across the Atlantic, but in the opposite direction.

In short, American urban planning is uniquely well adapted to discussing the question of how public interests are derived from individual ones and vice versa. And even more importantly, how this dynamic impacts urban physiognomy.

The path of this discussion from city to city resembles a laboratory experiment with a number of constants and astonishingly controllable and only gradually altered marginal conditions.

Collective Efforts

In general, municipal administrations and urban planning agencies attain their planning objectives in two different ways: the first involves direct investment in public property. Among other things, this includes the construction of parks, public buildings, and infrastructure. The second and far trickier method involves attempts to exercise control over private property, specifically where a certain public interest, regarded from the perspective of urban design, requires safeguarding. For the most part, this means coordinating certain private actions and decisions on the totality of the surrounding milieu. If the first method is rare and fortuitous, then the second represents one of the greatest difficulties of contemporary urban design. A number of problems await. It is already difficult enough to define the so-called public interest, and at least as difficult to enforce it in the face of private interests. It lies in the nature of the beast that a specific public interest is never as crystal clear as an individual one. This is so because the former is derived from the latter, which renders the weighing of one against the other quite difficult. Over-regulation and arbitrariness are two of many frequently-enunciated reproaches.

Without Us!

[A]
Burnham, Haussmann, Moses and Napoleon III

[L]
New York City

The problematic of collective efforts to define generally valid objectives and rules explains without much difficulty why a *complete makeover* succeeded so well in the 19th century in the case of Baron Haussmann's Paris, while in many respects failing later in 1909 in Daniel Burnham's Chicago.[5] The owners of Chicago's private property successfully evaded being reformed by Burnham's hand. The private uses available through the proposed urban reconfiguration were neither directly recognizable nor effective. In Chicago, Burnham had no Napoleon III at his side, who could offer him unqualified support in his expropriations and the imposition of public debt. Wide-ranging urban restructuring authorized by powerful personalities, however, not solely a European specialty. Just think, for example, of Robert Moses, of how he transformed the city of New York in the 20th century like no other through his expressways, social housing programmes, and the laying out of public parks—with particularly massive impacts on the city's private property. Under the aegis of "public works," existing buildings and those in private ownership were erased, just as

---

5   Daniel Burnham: "It is no attack on private property to argue that society has the inherent right to protect itself against abuses." (*The Plan of Chicago*, 1909, by Daniel Burnham, coauthored with Edward Bennett and produced in collaboration with the Commercial Club of Chicago.

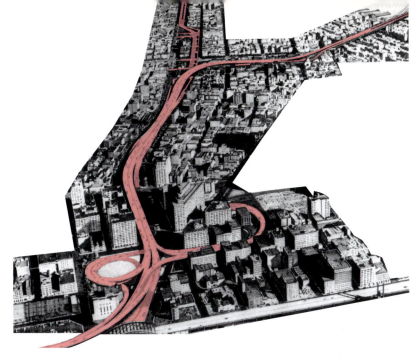

6 Proposed Lower Manhattan Expressway, connecting the Holland Tunnel and the West Side Highway, in the foreground, with the Manhattan Bridge, at upper right, via Broome Street and the Bowery. Rendering of view to the east, 1950.

they had been in 19th-century Paris. The sheer quantity of concrete put into place under Moses' direction alone perhaps makes him one of the most important builders of all time.

But in the 1960s, even Moses had to accept the fact that a number of his projects, including the one for the 8-lane Lower Manhattan Expressway, nicknamed "Lomex," would remain visions. His hovering roadway between the East River and the Hudson would have destroyed 14 blocks in SoHo, eliminating countless historic buildings worthy of preservation and compelling more than 10,000 residents to relocate.[6] And yet the public interest was the overarching concern. Not only would Lomex have decisively relieved New York City's traffic congestion, but additionally (lo and behold) facilitated military defense purposes. How consistent with imperial French arguments! In the end, New York's collective individualism, pressed into block form, did not permit so much continuity.

Unite!

If, in the cases of urban restructurings undertaken by Burnham and Moses, the public interest could only be mediated to a limited degree, then the far smaller town of Circleville, Ohio met with greater success. Things even progressed in the opposite direction: there, the grid was triumphant only subsequently—if all the more decisively. There, no agency with an overarching objective, but instead direct and personal economic profit propelled one of the first comprehensive urban redevelopments (including the street layout)—the so–called "squaring of Circleville."

[A]
The Circleville Squaring Company

[L]
Circleville

---

[6] For the whole history, see Robert A. Caro (1974), *The Power Broker: Robert Moses and the Fall of New York.*

7 Bird's-eye view of Circleville, Ohio, in 1836.

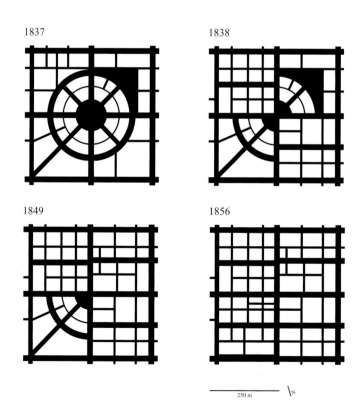

1837

1838

1849

1856

250 m

8 Changing Circleville: 1837–1856.

Within the US, Circleville featured an extremely unusual arrangement: it was laid out on a plan based on concentric circles. The circular form can be traced back to excavations of a settlement of Native North Americans. In 1820, at this location in the vicinity of the Scioto River, Daniel Driesbach was charged with acquiring land to erect a village.

By the end of the year more than 40 families were living there. By that time too the round courthouse stood at the centre of the double octagon in the square with its diameter of 120 m.

Besides this "Circle Square," of course, there was also a "Circle Alley" and a "Circle Street."

A radial-concentric layout, densified with residential buildings—and all this a half-century before Ebenezer Howard attempted to identify such a layout as the ideal plan for his Garden City of Tomorrow.[7]

In any event, things would not remain so for long.

In the late 1830s, the circular alleys quickly made way for a grid of orthogonal streets.

The central building had already been sacrificed, demolished to make way for commercial and residential buildings. The city changed so rapidly "that in half a century, or less, there will be no vestige left of that peculiarity,"[8] as contemporary witness James Silk Buckingham complained when visiting Circleville in 1840.

Dismissed as "a piece of childish sentimentalism,"[9] Circleville's plan was criticized for its peculiarly deformed building sites, while the large central square was said to still be a place for tending pigs.

This discrediting of Circleville's uniqueness was associated with the real motive for this yearning for the rectangular. The main argument was essentially profit-oriented, and held the community responsible for the loss of many hectares of valuable land—first in the center of town, and second in those places where the circle converged with the surrounding orthogonal street grid.

The law resolving to retool Circleville was adopted in 1837. But it contained an important qualification. All of the affected owners of properties had to give their consent before the development petition could enter into force.

Since the requisite unqualified support and consensus from all residents was difficult to acquire at a single stroke, the new statute was subsequently altered by the provision that the change could be initiated by "the owners of real estate in any part of the circular part of the town."[10] In this way, the process of restructuring the town could begin and proceed step-by-step.

Immediately afterward, a second "act of incorporation" was adopted, one that without a doubt formed the foundations for the creation of the first private urban redevelopment company in the US. The utterly appropriate name of this firm, which exists up to the present day, was originally "The Circleville Squaring Company."[11]

---

[7] First published in 1898 under the title *Tomorrow, a peaceful path to real reform*, and in 1902 as *Garden Cities of Tomorrow*. See Ebenezer Howard and Frederic James Osborn (1965), *Garden Cities of Tomorrow*.

[8] John W. Reps (1965), *The Making of Urban America—a History of City Planning in the United States*, 484–87.

[9] Ibid.

[10] Ibid.

[11] The firm still exists, but today bears a different name.

Acting in stages up to the year 1857, the company implemented the first comprehensive urban redevelopment, including the street layout, in the USA.

The circle survived: still detectable today in a few houses are gentle bulges, traces of the former curves of the streets. This putatively more robust element had fulfilled its conditioning task, and has now vanished. Through its annual pumpkin festival, featuring the loveliest and largest squashes anywhere, Circleville continues to specialize in roundness. The Circleville Squaring Company has a new name, but the town logo continues to display a panorama with the formerly round street pattern and the courthouse at the center.

This Land is My Land, This Land is Your Land

Invisible Hand [IH] §1.02

With his "invisible hand,"[12] economist Adam Smith characterizes the social mechanism through which each individual automatically contributes to the welfare of the community solely by pursuing his own private objectives [IH]. Or put differently: "Each sweeps his own doorstep, and the neighborhood stays clean!"[13]

Adam Smith's invisible hand makes do without any definition of the public interest. According to him, a private interest is automatically a public one, and vice versa.[14]

If this notion were accurate, then all public administration would be superfluous. But the reverse is more often the case: the invisible hand of the free market, for example, does not necessarily conform to this altruistic model. Instead, it follows the rational axioms and tendencies of the individual, that of raising profit by exploiting the environment. It is very doubtful, these two invisible hands would ever shake... unless maybe forced by a visible one.

Tendency towards Overexploitation [TOE] §1.08

Biologist Garret Hardin vividly illustrates the reason for the tendency toward exploitation [TOE] using an example of the overuse of the commons, in the process relativizing Adam Smith:

"The tragedy of the commons develops in this way. Picture a pasture open to all. It is to be expected that each herdsman will try to keep as many cattle as possible on the commons. Such an arrangement may work reasonably satisfactorily for centuries because tribal wars, poaching, and disease keep the numbers of both man and beast well below the carrying capacity of the land. Finally, however, comes the day of reckoning, that is, the day when the long-desired goal of social stability becomes a reality. At this point, the inherent logic of the commons remorselessly generates tragedy.

"As a rational being, each herdsman seeks to maximize his gain. Explicitly or implicitly, more or less consciously, he asks, 'What is the utility to me of adding one more animal to my herd?' This utility has one negative and one positive component.

---

[12] Adam Smith (1966), *The Wealth of Nations*.
[13] Quote, originally by Johann Wolfgang von Goethe.
[14] Also compare to the *Common Law of Nuisance* [CLN]: The individual shall comport himself in such a way that his actions do not represent a nuisance to others.

Common Law of Nuisance [CLN] §1.01

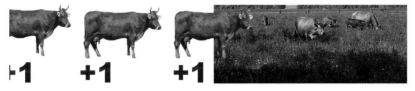

positive component is not shared

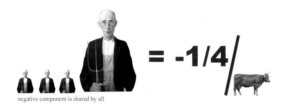

negative component is shared by all

9 The tendency of overexploitation of the commons: The negative component is shared by all, whereas the positive one is not.

"1) The positive component is a function of the increment of one animal. Since the herdsman receives all the proceeds from the sale of the additional animal, the positive utility is nearly +1.

"2) The negative component is a function of the additional overgrazing created by one more animal. Since, however, the effects of overgrazing are shared by all the herdsmen, the negative utility for any particular decision-making herdsman is only a fraction of -1.

"Adding together the component partial utilities, the rational herdsman concludes that the only sensible course for him to pursue is to add another animal to his herd. And another; and another... But this is the conclusion reached by each and every rational herdsman sharing a commons. Therein is the tragedy. Each man is locked into a system that compels him to increase his herd without limit—in a world that is limited. Ruin is the destination toward which all men rush, each pursuing his own best interest in a society that believes in the freedom of the commons. Freedom in a commons brings ruin to all."[15]

Available in principle in order to prevent this tragedy from occurring, says Hardin, are two possibilities: first, we can replace public space for the most part through the institution of private property, thereby surrendering such areas to the responsibility of the individual, or else we can establish generally valid rules which compel the individual to engage in moderate behavior in "public space." We find a combination of the two principles. Formerly existing everywhere in Switzerland, for example (to remain with agriculture), for the use of the *Allmende* was a so-called *Durchwinterungsfuss*, or *wintering feet* standard. This principle coupled the use of the common land directly to the size of the privately owned farm, and allowed farmers to drive only as many cattle onto the commons as he

[15] Garrett Hardin (1968), *The Tragedy of the Commons*, 1243–48.

was able to winter on his own property. Subsequently purchased cattle were excluded from these provisions.

A Private View of the Public

[A]
First Boston, Municipal
Arts Society, Trump

[L]
New York City

In the mid-1980s, the First Boston Bank wanted to build an office tower in Midtown Manhattan. Their plans conformed to the zoning codes then in force. All the same, the bank's activities triggered the interest of an immediate neighbor, namely Donald Trump—one of the most glamorous figures of New York's real estate development scene—and of New York's landmarks preservation group, the *Municipal Arts Society*. Owned by Trump, and sitting across the street on Fifth Avenue, was the eponymous *Trump Apartment Tower*. At that point, Trump made contact with First Boston with the intention of purchasing the intended parcel, or at least of becoming a 50% partner in the project. When First Boston turned him down, the press reported him as saying: "I can't imagine a tower going up on that site that would block the view of the people who bought apartments from me—unless, of course, my name were on the project." After another refusal on the part of the bank, he expressed himself even more bluntly: "I hope you don't have any problem with the Municipal Art Society, and I am telling you I can be of great benefit to seeing that the project goes ahead." And so it came to pass that in 1985, the very same Donald Trump who in 2001 had planned to have his residential tower, then the tallest apartment building in the world, stand an impudent 263 meters tall right next to the UN Secretariat Building,[16] had now transformed himself into a protector of historic monuments. He became a member of the committee of the Municipal Arts Society, now preoccupied with the future of 5th Avenue. And in that capacity, he officially announced his rejection of the First Boston building project, with an explanation that it would rob 5th Avenue of "light and air." Four months later, First Boston definitively lost its bid to build a tower, the *Rizzoli* and *Coty Buildings*, which stood on the intended site, having in the meantime been declared by the commission to be protected historic monuments and an emblem of the city.[17] Interesting as well is the prehistory of these two buildings. Their potential listing as monuments worthy of protection had been pending for 16 years. Already in 1966, 1981, and 1983, the Municipal Arts Society had given explicit consideration to placing them under landmarks protection. It was only on Trump's initiative that the Society took its responsibilities seriously, expanding them in this instance indirectly into the purview of a zoning agency. Now disguised as a historic preservationist, and with help of the Society, Donald Trump, in reality did nothing to defend the public interest, but instead the private panorama of the city shared by his wealthy clients—namely magnificent views they enjoyed from the windows of *Trump Tower* itself.

A public interest is not necessarily just, but instead mirrors—even in the best cases—the opinions of the majority, which in many cases coincides with the public interest, but is also often confused with it.

[16] See *Gentlemen's Agreement* p.223.
[17] From Costonis (1989), 73.

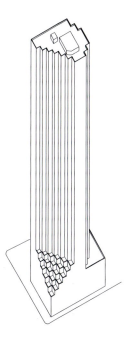

10 The private view to the public: Trump Tower at Fifth Avenue, New York.

A Private Start: Pigs out of their Parlor

The public interest in the introduction of "comprehensive zoning"[18] with methodically codified zones in New York was not the result of a comprehensive planning process by a maximally objective authority, one that defined general urban design goals. Instead, it arose from the initiative of individual, influential business leaders and citizens who were dissatisfied with the trends in real estate development prevailing at the time. [PPI] They feared that their properties would diminish in value and were concerned about loss of profits from their hotels, restaurants, and retailers. Tiffany, Saks, the Waldorf-Astoria and Ritz-Carlton were afraid of losing their customers. Shops specializing in furs and leather goods did not wish to market their wares alongside (their own) odiferous manufacturers. These disturbing facilities also generated obnoxious traffic patterns, involving trucks, pushcarts, and in particular workers, who mixed in an unseemly manner with wealthy customers, diminishing consumer activity. A campaign was initiated by the *Fifth Avenue Association* designed to alter the conditions of economic competition, making it difficult for neighboring property owners to sell or rent to users they regarded as incompatible.

But such intentions cannot be written into generally binding zoning ordinances. The desire for binding regulations concerning commercial buildings in commercial use, in any event, encountered a receptive audience among "good government" activists. With the *New Tenement Law* of 1901, the latter had already successfully established a law which set maximum heights for apartment buildings of 1.5 times the width of the

[A]
Good Government Activists and Fifth Avenue Association

[L]
New York City

Public & Private Interests
[PPI] §1.04

---

[18] Comprehensive zoning refers to the subdivision of a city, county or region into zoning districts within which certain rules apply and which regulate land use in these areas' territories.

SHALL WE SAVE NEW YORK?

A Vital Question To Every One Who Has Pride In This Great City

SHALL we save New York from what? Shall we save it from unnatural and unnecessary crowding, from depopulated sections, from being a city unbeautiful, from high rents, from excessive and illy distributed taxation? We can save it from all of these, so far at least as they are caused by one specified industrial evil—the erection of factories in the residential and famous retail section.

The Factory Invasion of the Shopping District

The factories making clothing, cloaks, suits, furs, petticoats, etc., have forced the large stores from one section and followed them to a new one, depleting it of its normal residents and filling it with big loft buildings displacing homes.

The fate of the sections down town now threatens the fine residential and shopping district of Fifth Avenue, Broadway, upper Sixth and Madison Avenues and the cross streets. It requires concentrated co-operative action to stem this invading tide. The evil is constantly increasing; it is growing more serious and more difficult to handle. It needs instant action.

The Trail of Vacant Buildings

Shall the finest retail and residential sections in the world, from Thirty-third Street north, become blighted the way the old parts of New York have been?

The lower wholesale and retail districts are deserted, and there is now enough vacant space to accommodate many times over the manufacturing plants of the city. *If new modern factory buildings are required, why not encourage the erection of such structures in that section instead of erecting factory buildings in the midst of our homes and fine retail sections.*

How it Affects the City and its Citizens

It is impossible to have a city beautiful, comfortable or safe under such conditions. The unnatural congestion sacrifices fine residence blocks for factories, which remain for a time and then move on to devastate or depreciate another section, leaving ugly scars of blocks of empty buildings unused by business and unadapted for residence: thus unsettling real estate values.

How it Affects the Tax-payer

Every man in the city pays taxes either as owner or tenant. The wide area of vacant or depreciated property in the lower middle part of town means reduced taxes, leaving a deficit made up by extra assessment on other sections. Taxes have grown to startling figures and this affects all interests.

The Need of Co-operative Action

In order that the impending menace to all interests may be checked and to prevent a destruction similar to that which has occurred below Twenty-third Street:

> We ask the co-operation of the various garment associations.
> We ask the co-operation of the associations of organized labor.
> We ask the co-operation of every financial interest.
> We ask the co-operation of every man who owns a home or rents an apartment.
> We ask the co-operation of every man and woman in New York who has pride in the future development of this great city.

NOTICE TO ALL INTERESTED

IN view of the facts herein set forth we wish to give publicity to the following notice:—We, the undersigned merchants and such others as may later join with us, will give the preference in our purchases of suits, cloaks, furs, clothing, petticoats, etc., to firms whose manufacturing plants are located outside of a zone bounded by the upper side of Thirty-third Street, Fifty-ninth Street, Third and Seventh Avenues, also including thirty-second and thirty-third Streets, from Sixth to Seventh Avenues.

February 1st, 1917, is the time that this notice goes into effect, so as to enable manufacturers now located in this zone to secure other quarters. Consideration will be given to those firms that remove their plants from this zone. This plan will ultimately be for the benefit of the different manufacturers in the above mentioned lines, as among other reasons they will have the benefit of lower rentals.

B. ALTMAN & CO.
ARNOLD, CONSTABLE & CO.
BEST & CO.
BONWIT TELLER & CO.

J. M. GIDDING & CO.
GIMBEL BROTHERS
L. P. HOLLANDER & CO.

LORD & TAYLOR.
JAMES McCREERY & CO.
R. H. MACY & CO.

FRANKLIN SIMON & CO.
SAKS & CO.
STERN BROTHERS

The undersigned endorse this movement for the benefit of the City of New York

Vincent Astor	Astor Estate	Astor Trust Co.	Tiffany & Co.	W. & J. Sloane	Brooks Brothers
University Club	Waldorf-Astoria	Columbia Trust Co.	Gorham Co.	Aeolian Company	Knox Hat Co.
Union League Club	St. Regis Hotel	Fifth Avenue Bank	Black, Starr & Frost	C. G. Gunthers' Sons	Theo. Hofstatter & Co.
Criterion Club	Hotel Gotham	Guarantee Trust Co.	Theodore B. Starr, Inc.	A. Jaeckel & Co.	James McCutcheon & Co.
Ritz-Carlton	Hotel Belmont	Harriman National Bank	Dreicer & Co.	Tiffany Studios	Cammeyer
Hotel Biltmore	Hotel Manhattan	M. Knoedler & Co.	Marcus & Co.	Higgins & Seiter	J. & J. Slater, Inc.
Hotel McAlpin	Hotel Netherland	H. W. Johns-Manville Co.	E. M. Gattle & Co.	Davis Collamore & Co.	De Pinna
A. A. Vantine & Co.	Hotel Lorraine	Yale & Towne Mfg. Co.	Charles Scribners' Sons	The Edison Shop.	Kennedy & Company
Mark Cross Co.	Charles Thorley	Scott & Fowles Co.	Maillard's	Frank L. Slazenger	Pratt's Keppel & Co.

We ask Citizens, Merchants and Civic bodies to co-operate and send letters endorsing this plan to the committee, care of J. H. Barton, chairman, 267 Fifth Avenue.

11 ...or shall we save ourselves. A New York Times advertisement by the Fifth Avenue Association in 1916 that promotes action to save the city from incompatible land uses.

widest street they fronted.[19] This success emboldened reformers to turn their attention immediately toward commercial buildings. Calls for public disciplining of such uses were amplified. But it was only after 1915, when the *Equitable Building* rose to a height of 540 feet without interruption that sufficient political support emerged for the introduction of the Zoning Resolution of 1916 [SB]. In order to prevent additional vertical monstrosities from darkening and blocking streets, the ordinance subdivided the city into districts, assigning differing land uses to each and limiting the bulk, height, and placement of the buildings erected there [SSR]. Officially, these measures were intended to benefit the public health and prevent traffic congestion.

Set Back
[SB] §7.02–1

Setback Street Ratio
[SSR] §4.13

[19] Alexander Garvin (1996), *The American City: What Works, What Doesn't*, 434.

82

Set Back [SB], **Base Height** [BAH], **Sky Exposure Plane** [SEP], **Down to Earth** [DTE], **Contextual Base** [CB]

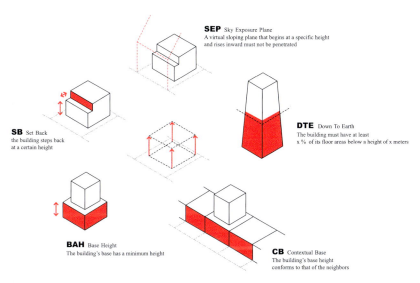

SEP Sky Exposure Plane
A virtual sloping plane that begins at a specific height and rises inward must not be penetrated

SB Set Back
the building steps back at a certain height

DTE Down To Earth
The building must have at least x % of its floor areas below a height of x meters

BAH Base Height
The building's base has a minimum height

CB Contextual Base
The building's base height conforms to that of the neighbors

12 *Anti Equitable Building Rules*—five (still) common ways to administer the *Set Back* by geometric definition. Such rules finally turn urban design from a 2½–dimensional into a 3–dimensional endeavor.

In fact however, the zoning ordinances had "changed private rights into public rights and market decisions into political ones"[20]—although such public rights must be sharply distinguished from the "public interest."

Clash!

Just 10 years later, in 1926, such an ordinance collided with private interests in such a way that only the highest constitutional authority could be of assistance. In the final analysis, it was the members of the *Supreme Court* under Chief Justice William Howard Taft whose decision would make it the invisible puppet master of urban America. The court ruled that as a constitutional practice, a zoning ordinance fell into the province of police powers. A new American institution was born. Now, urban rules took the form of bureaucratic administrative instruments, with no one asking from whence they came, nor which functions they were expected to fulfill. Designed to raise the number of operations that could be executed without reflection, such laws were expected to "civilize" urban development. These rules were observed simply because everyone obeyed them, and so they began, almost imperceptibly, or at least inconspicuously, to determine the form of the built environment. It is a question of those rules which were established and which became necessary only as a consequence of that very built environment—a positive feedback loop, an interplay in which that which is conditioned sets the conditions, and vice versa.

The small town of Euclid, located north of Cleveland, Ohio, served as the

[A]
Ambler Realty Company, Euclid and Taft

[L]
Euclid

20 William C. Wheaton (1989), *Zoning and Land Use Planning: An Economic Perspective*, 12.

Use Groups [UG]

USE GROUPS PERMITTED IN ZONING DISTRICTS

DISTRICTS		RESIDENTIAL	COMMUNITY FACILITIES	RETAIL AND COMMERCIAL								RECREATION				GEN. SERVICE	MANUFACTURING	
		1	2	3	4	5	6	7	8	9	10	11	12	13	14	15	16	17	18
RESIDENCE																			
SINGLE FAMILY DETACHED RESIDENCES	R1 R2																		
GENERAL RESIDENCE	R3-R9																		
COMMERCIAL																			
LOCAL RETAIL	C1																		
LOCAL SERVICE	C2																		
WATERFRONT RECREATION	C3																		
GENERAL COMMERCIAL	C4																		
RESTRICTED CENTRAL COMMERCIAL	C5																		
GENERAL CENTRAL COMMERCIAL	C6																		
COMMERCIAL AMUSEMENT	C7																		
GENERAL SERVICE	C8																		
MANUFACTURING																			
LIGHT MANUFACTURING	M1																		
MEDIUM MANUFACTURING	M2																		
HEAVY MANUFACTURING	M3																		

Use Group 1	Single–family detached residential development
Use Group 2	All other types of residential development designed for permanent occupancy
Use Group 3	Community facilities like schools, libraries, museums, college dormitories, nursing homes and residential facilities for special needs populations
Use Group 4	Community facilities like houses of worship, community centers, hospitals, ambulatory health care facilities and other facilities without sleeping accommodations
Use Group 5	Transient hotels
Use Group 6	Retail and service establishments that serve local shopping needs, like food and small clothing stores, beauty parlors and dry cleaners
Use Group 7	Home maintenance and repair services like plumbing and electrical shops which serve nearby residential areas
Use Group 8	Amusement establishments like small bowling alleys and movie theaters, and service uses like upholstery and appliance repair shops
Use Group 9	Services to business establishments and other services like printers and caterers
Use Group 10	Large retail establishments like department stores and appliance stores which serve a large area
Use Group 11	Custom manufacturing activities like art needlework and jewelry manufacturing
Use Group 12	Large entertainment facilities like arenas and indoor skating rinks which draw large numbers of people
Use Group 13	Low coverage or open uses like golf driving ranges, children's small amusement parks, camps and banquet halls
Use Group 14	Facilities for boating and related activities which are suitable in waterfront recreation areas
Use Group 15	Large commercial amusement establishments, including typical amusement park attractions
Use Group 16	Semi–industrial uses, including automotive uses and other services, such as custom woodworking and welding shops
Use Group 17	Industrial uses that can normally conform to high performance standards
Use Group 18	Industrial Uses

13 Decisions on compatibility—the hygenic nature of comprehensive zoning: use groups and their zoning districts.

setting for a fundamental confrontation. Motivated by the absence of adequate development planning, the community of 10,000, with its two rail lines and three large streets, resolved to introduce a new zoning plan. The reasons were hygienic in nature, namely "to keep Euclid Village as free from unsanitary conditions as possible, and to locate those unsanitary conditions in a segregated district."[21] [UG]

Use Groups
[UG] §3.08

In 1911, the *Ambler Realty Company* began buying up a hitherto undeveloped piece of land measuring 68 ha and located between *Euclid Avenue* and *Nickel Plate Railroad*. In all likelihood, their motives were speculative. Given the parcel's proximity to the railway station and *Main Street*, the land they had pieced together could now be sold for a much higher price to a manufacturing enterprise.

But Euclid's adoption of zoning laws upset their calculations by dividing the property into three different zones. The northern part was virtually unrestricted in terms of use, the southern one was slated for duplex houses, and the narrow strip of land in between would accommodate apartment and public buildings. But its elongated proportions, with the width of only 40 feet, made the erection of such buildings extremely difficult. Ambler Realty Co. went to court, regarding the measures as a grievous curtailment of their anticipated profits without any provisions for adequate monetary compensation. The district judge shared their view, but the verdict was challenged by the town of Euclid and eventually found its way to the Supreme Court. The case attracted national attention, and was regarded as a test case of the constitutionality of zoning concepts and of the ordinances, adopted a decade earlier with the intention of repairing the American city.[22] In addition to highly specific arguments dealing with the structure of the various use zones, basic doubts were expressed about whether a set of laws intended to establish order among a specific population could be used as a standard in other communities. It was also argued that no ordinance could "measure, prophetically, the surging and receding tides by which business evolves and grows, and hence could also not foresee and map exactly the appropriate uses or the amount necessary for each separate use."[23]

In a six-to-three decision, the justices determined that such "comprehensive zoning laws" were in every sense legal and constitutional, not only in the special case of Euclid, but as a general rule.

Through this recognized universality, zoning was rendered capable of being transported and exported. After the verdict, every larger American town—with the exception of Houston, Texas, which lacks zoning codes right up to the present—would eventually introduce its own zoning laws, thereby losing a measure of their former innocence.

---

[21] Charles X. Zimmermann, mayor of Euclid, quoted by Toll (1969), 215.
[22] Garvin (1996), 442.
[23] From *Brief and Argument for Appellee*, 78–79,83, of Case Village of Euclid Vs. Ambler Realty Co (1926), 272 US 365, quoted by Toll (1969), 232–33.

3

Power is Nothing Without Control

Whether directly physical, whether taking the form of a line on a building plan, a zone, or a maximum or minimum value, the setting of thresholds has always been among the problematical core issues of urban planning. To set thresholds in such a way that the city can enforce them as the representative of the public interest without at the same time curtailing private intentions determines whether an urban plan or rule is to be successful, productive, and generally accepted. To set a threshold is by definition an artificial and brutal act that creates sharp borders. Its relevance to its direct context and its flexibility in dealing with subversive behavior determines its potential to generate productive outcomes. What happens when standards are too low, too high, or introduced belatedly?

3.1 The Difficult Act of Setting Thresholds

"The popular mind apparently is intrigued by height, as such. A 60-story tower in New York evokes a 70-story tower in Chicago. What is more serious, a 60-story tower in New York evokes a 70-story tower directly across the street."[1]

Demotivation

[A]
San Gimignano's Nobility

[L]
Chicago, New York City, San Gimignano

In the year 1255, the Italian town of San Gimignano resolved that any new tower erected within the city limits should be no taller than the existing tower of the town hall.

This decision put an end at a single stroke to the town's development boom, and its spectacle of prestige in the form of more than 70 slender towers that were visible from afar on the Tuscan hillside.

Standing there today are only 15.

What happened?

In previous years, competitiveness between ambitious noble families had spurred the construction of ever taller towers. Each additional meter of height was a manifestation of the owner's superior social status—and the only limit was the sky itself.

Under the still popular pretext of protecting the public health, the right of the individual to storm the heavens was curtailed. The intention was to prevent the stones belonging to these bold homeowners from falling onto the heads of citizens walking below. Which did indeed occur regularly, since given the then current state of building technology, maximum safe building heights did not yet extend quite so far into the heavens.

Still, to select the height of the *town hall* as the uppermost allowable threshold was both arbitrary and careless: mainly because this standard was far too low! Any halfway affluent aristocrat was in a position to erect a tower easily surpassing it. All at once, the decision disqualified a common aristocratic motivation, namely to outdo their neighbors in the art of tower construction.

And so, the building craze was brought to a halt.

In subsequent years, building budgets were devoured by the plague anyway. Meanwhile, the town was for the most part deprived of its political relevance by Florence.[2]

Engineering Height [EEH] §7.01–5

The context of the height limit set was the maximum engineering height possible at the time, one certainly higher than that permitted, if in all likelihood not by much. *Engineering Height* [EEH] is the maximum height attainable for a structure given the current state of building technology. Remaining a matter of speculation (albeit of considerable interest) is the question of whether it might have been wiser to set penalties for allowing construction material to fall from one's house rather than setting an absolute height limit. Such a regulation may even have provided impulses for innovations in the field of building technology—the steel frame could have been an Italian discovery, not an American one.

---

[1] Ferriss (1929).
[2] From Alexander Lehnerer (2007), *Tit for Tat and Urban Rules*, 376–79.

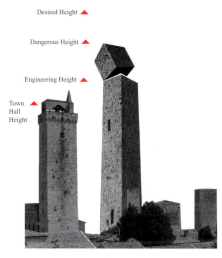

Desired Height ▲

Dangerous Height ▲

Engineering Height ▲

Town Hall Height ▲

14 Speculative San Gimignano and its relevant heights.

It is extremely unlikely that the clinical sounding term "engineering height" was used back then in San Gimignano. In fact, it was a product of the American high-rise debate taking place in early 20th-century New York and Chicago. Soon coming to play a role alongside issues of constructive possibility and feasibility were economic perspectives. After the invention of the steel frame and its code approval (beginning in 1889 in New York), the maximum height was no longer limited by the load-bearing capacities and thickness of the supporting masonry. Now, high-rises transgressed new and unprecedented thresholds in the airy heights: coming into force at a certain point was the "law of diminishing returns" (*Economic Height* [EH], i.e., the point at which the addition of further stories could no longer cover costs, and instead would substantially lower profits).[3] Critically important above all are the efficiency and costs of vertical accesses. In 1915, even before the authorities began regulating the height of New York's buildings in explicit and comprehensive form, the height of the elevators would in the end determine the height of New York's *Equitable Building*, which had 38 stories.

Economic Height [EH] §7.01–6

Laggards in Boom & Height Cycles

At that time, Chicago could only dream of the possibility of more-or-less freely choosing building heights. It was in 1893 that the city underwent the explosive irruption of the issue of high-rise building. The real estate development crisis prevailing at the time was the unavoidable response to the fanatical building activity of the preceding years, which had far exceeded demand. The municipal administration responded immediately:

[A]
Real Estate Developers

[L]
Chicago, New York City

[3]   Carol Willis (1995), *Form Follows Finance: Skyscrapers and Skylines in New York and Chicago*, 46.

controlled growth was to be secured by a height limit of 130 ft (40 m) —a maximum of 10 to 11 stories would cool down the speculative and over-heated real estate market, leading the city out of the crisis. At the time, many deduced that the new height restrictions owed something to skill-ful lobbying of the owners of existing high-rises, who had an interest in maintaining their monopoly on tall buildings. But the city of Chicago quickly came to realize that their *Flat Cap* [FC] was serving to inhibit urban development, so they relaxed the emergency brake slightly: in 1902, the height limit was raised to 260 ft (79 m), and later, after a renewed over-supply of offices, reduced against to 200 ft (61 m).[4]

Flat Cap
[FC] §5.06

Regarded in retrospect, this *temporally irregular standardization* [RC] repre-sents a highly interesting strategy for differentiating urban morphology. The temporal limitation of height standards, that is to say, their perpet-ual modification during a long-term period of development, led to the immediate superimposition locally of a series of brief building phases, almost inevitably giving rise to a heterogeneous urban structure. A post-1902 building stands directly alongside a pre-1893 tower, which in turn stands alongside an office building from 1895 having only 10 stories, and so forth.

Revision Cycles
[RC] §1.05

But in conjunction with constantly changing economic pressures, the ex-ample of Chicago also illustrates the great regulatory difficulties encoun-tered when a universal one-size-fits-all standard converges with temporally highly differentiated contexts. Their brutal force is always belated.

In fact, the tallest buildings tend to appear only toward the end of a real estate development boom [BOB].[5] In the latter part of such a phase, build-ing lot prices have risen so far that developers can only guarantee a re-turn on investment by multiplying the surface of a building parcel via rising up into the heights. At this point, the speculative fever afflicting developers and backers generates a quantity of office buildings far ex-ceeding actual demand.

Boom Behavior
[BOB] §3.05

The three-dimensional graph of the skyline showing the height and den-sity of a central business district does not coincide temporally with the rise and fall of an economic boom cycle. As a result, regulative meas-ures—themselves in fact only triggered by changes of morphology—be-tray an even greater asynchronicity in relation to economic booms and busts, at times making them completely superfluous, or in the worst cases, even counterproductive for real estate development.

This phase displacement not only existed in Chicago in 1893. In New York as well, the comprehensively regulated height limits of the first zon-ing ordinance came into force only in the early phase of the approaching real estate crisis of 1916.

These zoning ordinances, the first height restrictions to be introduced anywhere in the United States, provided critics of zoning with a taste of what awaited the American city once the entire bundle of zoning ordinances was adopted. Rapid change meets continuous regulation—a perma-nently critical interrelationship.

---

4   Larry R. Ford (1994), *Cities and Buildings, Skyscrapers, Skid Rows, and Suburbs*, 31.
5   Willis (1995), 155.

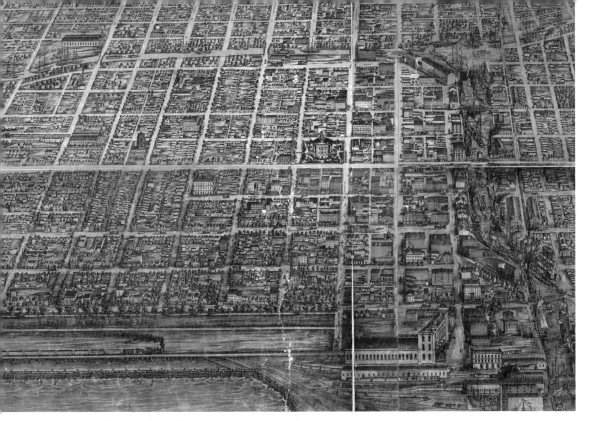

15 Flatland. Bird's-eye view of Chicago's downtown area in 1857.

16 Common Height. Bird's-eye view of Chicago's downtown area in 1874.

17 Height Palimpsest. Bird's-eye view of Chicago's downtown area in 1916.

Flat Cap [FC]

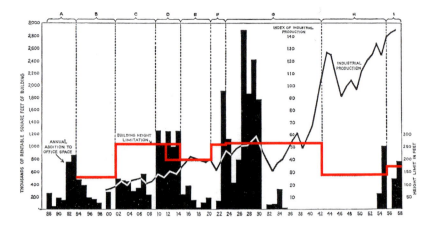

(A) No Limit.
(B) Limit 130 feet (39 m).
(C) Limit raised to 260 feet (79 m).
(D) Agitation to reduce limit causes flood of building permits; limit reduced to 200 feet in 1911, but construction under 260-foot permits continues to 1914.
(E) Building falls off with 200-foot limit.
(F) Limit restored to 260 feet.
(G) Limit raised to 264 feet plus tower, construction booms until hit by depression.
(H) Limit of volume to 14 times the lot area.
(I) Limit 16 FAR.

18 Frequent and often belated changes of the building height limitations in Chicago (1888–1958).

Critique: Mister Freund from Germany

[A]
Freund

[L]
Frankfurt, New York City

Ernst Freund had studied law in Heidelberg before emigrating to the US, where in 1902, he became a professor at the recently founded Chicago Law School.

He spoke twice in the US at the National Conference on City Planning, in 1911 and 1913. On each occasion, his message was the same: America and Germany were different, and it would be best to heed this difference. He took this position in reaction to the growing chorus of calls on the part of colleagues for the adoption in the United States of zoning codes after German prototypes. He strongly doubted that America could be tamed in this way. He used Frankfurt as a comparative example for New York City, whose population level was comparable to the German city at that time. "In Frankfurt the business district is now exactly where it was; no neighborhood, no quarter of Frankfurt has changed its character—excepting of course the quarter that has been added to the city. New York, as you all know, has profoundly changed. Residence districts have first become business districts; and now they have become factory districts. In other words, in Germany property is conservative, and in this country it is not. Therefore, the districting power in Germany means that it simply registers conditions that are more or less permanent; in this country, it would mean that the city would impose a character upon a neighborhood which that neighborhood, in the course of time, would throw off.

"The development of property of a neighborhood in this country, it seems to me, is beyond the wit of man to foresee. It seems capricious;

and I don't believe it is within the wisdom or the foresight of a city council to attempt to control developments of that kind. If this observation is true, it is better that a districting power should not be given to a city at the present time."[6]

Avant-garde, Pioneers and Escapees

With its above average land prices, downtown is on the move! And when not, then only because it is held in place by dotted red lines and zones. Whether as mavericks or as pioneers, it is thanks to a few developers and their projects that downtown has a tendency to change in size, to wander, to initiate new spaces. Often detectable in large projects is an apparent drive to occupy marginal locations in a spectacular manner. In the 1930s, *Rockefeller Center* lived up to its avant-garde role, effecting such a displacement of focus, and one that would have a sustained influence on its newly created context in Midtown Manhattan.[7]

Such a maverick attempt that miscarried, at least initially, was the *Empire State Building*. It failed in the early 1930s to establish a new commercial center on 33rd St between Midtown and Wall Street.

It was the author F. Scott Fitzgerald—himself an American outsider during this period—who conquered the 102 stories of this equally prominent loner that stands between 33rd and 34th Streets. From its roof, he characterizes the condition of the Empire State Building, located between the triumph and the demise of the metropolis:[8]

"From the ruins (of the stock market crash), lonely and inexplicable as the sphinx, rises the Empire State Building and, just as it had been a tradition of mine to climb to the Plaza Roof to take leave of the beautiful city, extending as far as the eyes could reach, so now I went to the roof of the last and most magnificent of towers. Then I understood—everything was explained: I had discovered the crowning error of the city, its Pandora's box. Full of jaunty pride the New Yorker had climbed here and seen with dismay what he had never suspected, that the city was not the endless succession of canyons that he had supposed but that it had limits—from the tallest structure he saw for the first time that it faded out into the country on all sides, into an expanse of green and blue that alone was limitless. And with the awful realization that New York was a city after all and not a universe, the whole shining edifice that he had reared in his imagination came crashing to the ground."[9]

Even without a crowd of imitators thronging around it, the effect of the Empire State Building at this marginal location was enormous for the city's self-image—and perhaps also enormously sobering. By opening up a view from the outside onto Midtown, onto its boundaries, and in particular onto a vicinity characterized by the phenomenon of intensive proximity, the Empire State Building destroyed New York's preoccupation with self-reference. The building guides the gaze toward something within which the Empire State Building is of course itself mirrored. To-

[A]
Empire State Building,
Fitzgerald,
Jacobs and Rockefeller
Center

[L]
Chicago, New York City

---

[6] Ernst Freund (1911), *Discussion*.
[7] Willis (1995), 168.
[8] Robert A. M. Stern, Gregory Gilmartin, and Thomas Mellins (1987), *New York 1930: Architecture and Urbanism between the Two World Wars*, 615.
[9] F. Scott Fitzgerald (1956), *My Lost City*, 37.

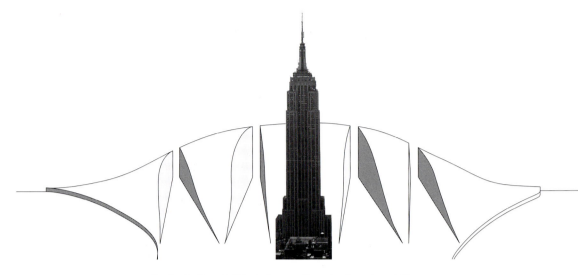

19 The Empire State Building is first to offer a view from the outside.

ward places beyond the narrow canyons of Broadway and Wall Street, beyond the great infrastructural nodal points. This awareness is as interesting for the writer as it is for the developer or land speculator of the post crash and war eras. The decentralism of office buildings and spatial inconsistency were now conceivable, not least because a spectacular instance of it now existed.

There existed and exist in New York extreme divergences in property value into the greatest proximity [CAN]. In some cases, maximum values and far lower average values are separated by only a couple of hundred feet. This temporal and geographic alterability makes the critique of an Ernst Freund understandable, but it is strongly dependent upon underlying regulative and administrative steering mechanisms.

Canyoning Land Value Peaks
[CAN] §3.11

In dealing with temporal and spatial inconsistencies, this notorious belatedness and a conservative drive toward permanence are not necessarily welcome, but are nonetheless immanent properties of standards—of all multifunctional urban planning tools.

As formal statements, they are concerned with the stable characteristics of a vicinity, which are generally regarded as being desirable. These involve strict standards for the widths of sidewalks, the layouts of escape routes, and extend all the way to standardized heights for working surfaces in kitchens.

But such standardized steering instruments are ensnared in a dilemma as soon as the vicinity with which they are concerned and from which they were born is no longer stable. Chicago's indecisiveness when it came to setting height limits is symptomatic of this vicious circle.

Inherent in standards based on controlling interests is a certain reluctance to take account of local exceptions to the average. New York and other cities have racked their brains over this issue up to the present, and have discovered a series of alternative approaches in the process. These rest consistently upon the principle of the general fixing of thresholds. Special treatment of these thresholds then determines the degree of determinable uniformity.

On the one hand, cities regularly transgress their own regulatory obsti-

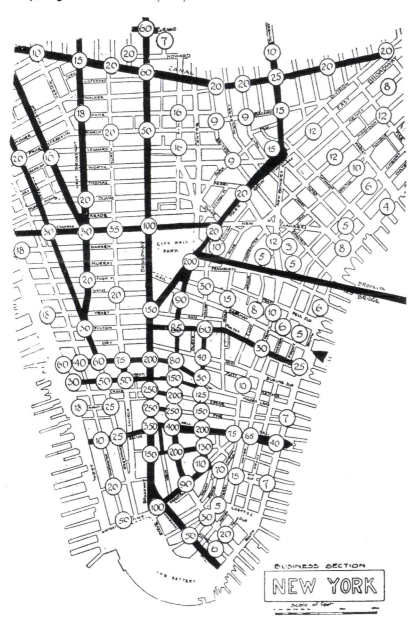

20 Canyoning Land Values in Lower Manhattan, 1903. Dollars per square foot.

nacy through geographically defined special zones—the so-called *Special Districts* [SD]. The local exceptions determine the city's singular character: districts devoted to art, culture, preservation, and business are the special features of each metropolis.

Moreover, thresholds are negotiable, and are thereby endowed with a certain indistinctness. Upper and lower limits are converted into mere

Special Districts
[SD] §3.01

reference magnitudes. For builders, they are now hurdles to be overcome. Absolute limits become relational. In the form of ratios, abstract relations are established between elements or attributes having nothing immediately to do with one another. Numbers of stories are linked to the parcel size and building heights surpassing the allowed height are artificially related to offering subway entrances for the public.

Underdetermination—Overzoning

[A]
FAR and Zoning

[L]
Atlanta, New York City

Not infrequently, thresholds in the form of limits are set so high that there is built-in leeway for the "unanticipatable value"—in a way that resembles the hope that a recently purchased item of clothing two sizes too large will still fit in 10 years, even if one has gained weight.

This happened in New York in 1916, and is observable today in Atlanta.

In many areas, Atlanta's CBD is set at an astonishing FAR of 80.

This means that on each plot 80 times its size can be stacked, one story above the next [FAR]. In the end, this figure serves less to limit density and instead functions as public relations, emphasizing Atlanta's friendly attitude toward investors.

Floor Area Ratio
[FAR] §7.01–1

By comparison, Midtown Manhattan today has a maximum floor area ratio of times 10, and in exceptional cases, 20. Earlier, in 1916, on the other hand, when New York's first zoning resolutions were introduced, little thought was given (at least according to critics) to existing or future development patterns. With the complete utilization and filling out of the zoning envelopes (according to the calculations and the critiques provided by New York's planners), the 1916 ordinances would have allowed the city to grow to 55 million inhabitants, plus an additional 250 million commuters. Utilization zones and building mass ceilings, moreover, often failed to correspond to that which already existed on the ground. More than half of the population lived in areas not explicitly designated as residential districts.[10]

Regarding a number of concerns, New York at that time remained unspecific, retaining—whether consciously or unconsciously—a certain leeway in its steering mechanisms.

In principle, the closer the economic motivations of builders bring them to municipal limits, the higher the level of control exercised by the city on private development. The greater the exertions of developers engaged in this limbo dance, the greater the city's leverage, and the greater the receptivity of builders entering into productive negotiations with the city concerning urban qualities. Force generates counterforce.

Essentially, when it comes to the question of the appropriate maximum of value limits or thresholds, opposed effects are possible and critical. Take for example the utilization figures for building parcels: how high should the basic utilization maximum be set as a limit value? If the FAR is too low, it cannot be guaranteed that all building parcels, regardless of their sizes and locations, can be developed.

If, on the other hand, it is set too high, that is to say, beyond the ambitions of developers, or higher than market demands, then this forecloses the give-and-take negotiations made possible by bonus systems [PB]. In this

Plaza Bonus
[PB] §7.01–4

---

[10] Garvin (1996), 436.

case, the limit value lacks any guiding or determinative force. In such a situation, a city can wait a long time before seeing any public amenities provided by private owners. When thresholds are no longer critical, they immediately become superfluous. Hence the problem manifested for example in the astonishment over the sudden appearance of gas stations or parking lots within otherwise highly densified contexts. These putatively programmatic exceptions comply entirely with all formal zoning standards, yet remain far lower than the limit values specified.

"The problem has sometimes been acute in urban renewal projects, which are attacked by would-be filling station developers who seek some of the best sites before the entrepreneurship and capital resources for a more intensive development can be mobilized. Some of the same problems may occur in special incentive zones in which realization of goals requires the commitment of substantial capital at risks that are greater than normal."[11]

21 Potential reduced: the filling station problem.

3.2 Attempts and Realizations of Control

"The best way to save land is to buy it!"[12] [LP]

Land Preservation
[LP] §2.04

William H. Whyte's attitude would doubtless have encountered unqualified agreement from Daniel Burnham in Chicago, Robert Moses in New York, Baron Haussmann in Paris, and James Hobrecht in Berlin. Whyte's maxim would probably not be contradicted by any architect–urban planner of functionalist Modernism, where the forms of expression would be different, but the presumption is the same.

Others had already had such experiences: In his attempt to grace American Chicago with French avenues, rond-points, and palace architecture, Daniel Burnham was only moderately successful. The only portions of his "blood-stirring" plans[13] that became reality were those that could be executed directly by the city itself, and were owned by it. Among these were several public buildings and the extensive park system. Everything that involved remodeling or exercising control over private property failed. The application of a simple boolean operation on Chicago's contemporary aerial view with Burnham's plan of 1909 would disclose the city's recalcitrant private mass, and would mark out then publicly owned properties. That Chicago's officials built a highway crossing at Burnham's central junction instead of a city hall is a further and highly instructive revelation. Originally conceived as a publicly accessible square, it is the meeting place of the Kennedy, Ryan, and Eisenhower Expressways and the Congress Parkway, which converge and mingle in the so-called Circle Interchange in place of Burnham's axes. There is hardly a less pedestrian-friendly area in all of Chicago.

---

[11] Daniel R. Mandelker (1970), *The Basic Philosophy of Zoning*, 18.
[12] William Hollingsworth Whyte (1968), *The Last Landscape*, 54.
[13] Daniel Burnham (1907).

Agents of Change

A look at the volume of investment is enough to make clear who the actual agents of urban change are. And that the actual task of the discipline of urban planning is to exercise control on these private agents was eloquently expressed in 1914 by New York's *Committee on the City Plan*.

"With or without a comprehensive city plan, the City will probably spend hundreds of millions of dollars on public improvements during the next thirty years. In addition, during the same period property owners will spend some billions of dollars in improvement of their holdings. To lay down the lines of city development so that these expenditures when made will in the greatest possible measure contribute to the solid and permanent upbuilding of a great and ever greater city—strong commercially, industrially, and in the comfort and health of its people—furnishes the opportunity and inspiration for city planning."[14]

Break

But when it comes to such comprehensive planning, the gridded layout of the American city is not terribly helpful. Structurally, the grid ruptures the cybernetic principle of the city [VSR]. It lacks the continuous block perimeter development which relates one building to its neighbor, as well as axes along which a kind of visual coherence can emerge, and even crooked streets, whose geometry dominates a development and brings buildings into relationship with one another.

The number of reciprocal relationships between blocks and buildings is reduced to a minimum. The cybernetic dream of the engineer is dashed against the sharp edges of the block: if all variables were closely coordinated with one another, and one of these variables could be controlled with total freedom, then one would be in a position to control everything indirectly.[15]

Virgin Site Rule
[VSR] §5.02

Through the Backdoor

If in Chicago, Burnham and like-minded supporters had to engage in expropriation and pay high levels of compensation in order to achieve continuous setback lines, then in 1926, in the context of the adjudication of Euclid's planning measures, the mere mention of public health, security, and social welfare was deemed sufficient.

The operative force is the same, only the rhetoric is different. Now, *comprehensive zoning*, backed up by police powers, counteracts the cybernetic weakness of the grid.

The degree to which the American block thereby lost its innocence and autonomy is shown by a look at the development along New York's Fifth Avenue with its orientation toward Central Park. Here, zoning ordinances marked the design of an entire avenue—their vehemence strongly resembling the autocratic visions of the Parisian Baron Haussmann.

The knowledge gained concerning the visionary power of an apparently unwilled or at least authorless administrative instrument jars against the cliché subdivision into various kinds of planning categories. These categor-

---

[14] The City of New York (1914), *Development and Present Status of City Planning in New York City*, 12.
[15] Kevin Kelly (1994), *Out of Control: The New Biology of Machines, Social Systems and the Economic World*, 121.

100

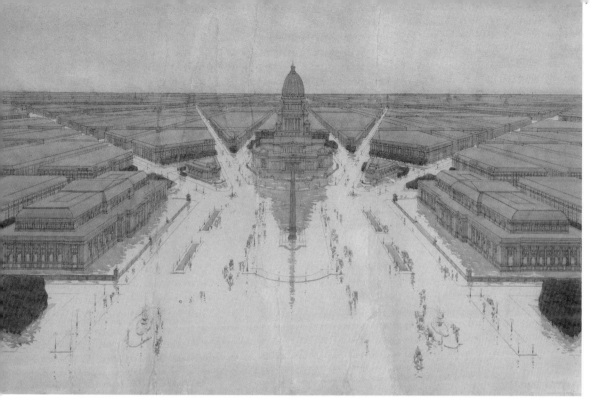

22 Burnham's envisioned Chicago's Civic Center and public plaza, 1909.

23 Same location, today: Chicago's Circle Interchange.

24 Zoning's will-to-form at Fifth Avenue.

25 Fox and hedgehog.

izations are generally closely associated with the traits and temperament of their creators. A division into visionaries and bookkeepers:

On the one hand, there are the strong personalities—some of them even architects—who present compelling visions. We know them by name—even their first names are generally familiar. There is Daniel Burnham, Edmund Bacon, Le Corbusier, Frank Lloyd Wright, and Ludwig Hilbersheimer. If one thinks of Colin Rowe's *fox–hedgehog* analogy, then it is a question of a *hedgehog*, who "is knowledgeable about one great subject, in contrast to the *fox*, who knows about many different things."[16] Apparently, *hedgehogs* act with freedom, and the plan is their medium: "Make no little plans; they have no magic to stir men's blood and will not be realized. Make big plans; aim high in hope and work; remembering that a noble, logical diagram once recorded will never die, but long after we are gone will be a living thing, asserting itself with ever-growing insistency."[17]

On the other hand, there are bureaucrats who present no visions, but instead attempt to see through politically conceived resolutions. As a rule, we do not know them by name. One example is the above-cited Committee on the City Plan of New York in 1914.

They hardly possess independent, historical personalities. They sacrifice their personal identities in favor of a seemingly urban one. Nevertheless, these are the puppet masters of an urban architecture. Standards, norms, and ordinances are their invisible threads. Almost without being noticed, they transform entire cities into *hedgehogs*. Manhattan is a hedgehog, and so is California's Santa Barbara.

---

[16] Colin Rowe citing Isaiah Berlin, Der Igel und der Fuchs, p.51 in Colin Rowe and Fred Koetter (1978), *Collage City*, 132.

[17] Despite the fact that there is no known source for this quotation, it is always attributed to Daniel Burnham. It is quoted in a 1918 Christmas card from Willis Polk to Edward Bennett as a statement made by Burnham in 1907. See Garvin (1996), 504.

Refrain: Santa Barbara!

This city, set 2 hours north of Los Angeles on the Pacific Ocean, has a relatively short albeit highly contrasting history: the *Mission Period* was succeeded by the *Rancho Period*, then came the *Victorian period*, and in 1925, a powerful earthquake.

A visit to Santa Barbara today leaves the impression that the last three phases might never have even occurred. [CMO]

The Christian mission and the Spanish military post *El Presidio Real de Santa Barbara* were erected in the 1780s. These were followed by the colonization and Christianization of the indigenous *Chumash*. The Spanish ruled until 1822, when California became a Mexican territory until 1846, when Colonel John Freemont won Santa Barbara for the United States.[18] Increasing in importance during this period were agriculture and ranching. But the Rancho Period did not permanently alter the urban lifestyles of residents. Horses, grazing lands, and cattle pens took precedence over the show and ostentations of town life.

After the Civil War, Santa Barbara gradually began to change. Soon, there were more Victorian buildings than those in Spanish Colonial style. Via sea lanes and growing harbors, increasing numbers of people arrived in the city from the east. Agriculturalists soon learned that nearly anything could be grown in this climate. The period's mood of upheaval and experimentation resulted in heedless disorder.

A typically dusty piece of American clutter began to emerge.

The 1925 earthquake destroyed the city. But not entirely. Residents realized that most of the Victorian houses and sheds, built of wood, had burned, while just a few stone Spanish colonial buildings had been left standing. Suddenly, an appealing chapter of the city's history had been revealed once again.

After this natural fire clearing, zoning ordinances were adopted which endowed downtown Santa Barbara with a distinctly Spanish Colonial identity. Each newly erected structure was subject to specifications concerning form and material that were based on missionary prototypes. Reappearing (or perpetuating itself) after a century-long interregnum on the American Riviera was a piece of Santa Barbara's Mission Style urbanism. Santa Barbara installed additional preventative measures designed to counteract non-colonial visual contamination. Town ordinances banned billboards—a rarity up to the present for a US American city.

For decades now, an explicit urban vision has taken form camouflaged in the costume of administrative concerns. In a travel guide, we read: "The Spanish influence remains noticeable up to the present, in particular in Santa Barbara's architecture." Remains, or has become? Further, under the category of attractions, it continues: "The courthouse of Santa Barbara: built in 1929, this splendid white building resembles a Spanish palace. Its old world elegance exemplifies Santa Barbara's architectural style. Found inside are details such as sculptured iron lamps, tiled hallways, and fascinating murals which narrate the history of the town. For

[A]
Earthquake and Zoning

[L]
Santa Barbara

City Make Over
[CMO] §7.04–1

---

[18] Benjamin Brooks, C. M. Gidney, Edwin M. Sheridan (1917), *History of Santa Barbara, San Luis Obispo and Ventura Counties, California.*

26 Dustbowl Town, Santa Barbara in 1914.

a marvelous view, climb up to the clock tower."[19] ... This singular architectural style is described exhaustively in Santa Barbara's real chronicle—its building code!

First Strophe: Almost Parallel

[A]
Burnham, Earthquake,
Fire and Wren

[L]
San Francisco, London Nineteen years earlier, in 1906, another and equally massive earthquake struck 330 miles to the north of Santa Barbara, laying waste to a comparable portion of San Francisco. The destruction was enormous. Just one year earlier, no less a personality than Chicago's "blood-stirring" Burnham had also offered a vision for this West Coast city, making it into a graspable, urban planning project. Once again, entirely in the style of Haussmann, and that which he had envisioned for Chicago in 1909. And of course, not without comparable resistance on the part of the population. In this case, however, San Francisco's presumably resistive proprietors had seen their properties for the most part destroyed by the earthquake not long before the publication of Burnham's plans. A tabula rasa—not unlike the later history of Santa Barbara! After this sweeping natural disaster, the path was free for a hilly Paris on the Bay. Lobbying for the implementation of the plan had already included the printing of 3000 copies of Burnham's 1905 report. But the fates were against him. Most of the 3000 copies would burn in the fires of the natural catastrophe that struck on 18 April 1906. For adequate lobbying, moreover, 8 months was simply too little time. Also decisive was the fact that the requisite legal and political mechanisms were not yet in place at the time. A *comprehensive zoning* into which this *comprehensive plan* could have been transformed, did not yet exist. As a self-evident and generally

---

[19]   The City of Santa Barbara (2008), *Attractions Guide—the Courthouse*.

27 Refrain: Santa Barbara Court House.

recognized institution, such a zoning structure could have canalized Burnham's vision into universal rules; rewritten more or less overnight, it might have served as a guideline for the imminent reconstruction of the 28,000 buildings that had been destroyed.[20] If San Francisco's earthquake had arrived 20 years later, we might today have a French-style city on California's Pacific Coast alongside a Spanish one.

In the San Francisco of 1906, Daniel Burnham faced a situation similar to one faced by Christopher Wren in London in 1667. After the great fire of that year, London's authorities decided on rapid reconstruction along the lines of the earlier, medieval street layout instead of adopting Wren's comprehensive reorganization and his master plan. Nor was the city's subsequent and decisive physical transformation in the third dimension effected by a plan, but instead by the introduction of the *Building Acts* of 1667. The form-giving and character-conditioning power of the Acts rested on the restricted use of easily flammable construction materials and the introduction of a general height limit of four stories throughout the city of London. Until far into the 19th century, only official buildings rose higher—and in the absence of a special metropolitan sanction [MS], only to a maximum height of 30 m.

Metropolitan Sanction [MS] §5.05

Homogenizers

Not all of the rules which strive toward visual homogeneity in urban space are primarily motivated by this aim. In this respect, Paris—Burnham's French model—is more than just Haussmann and Napoleon. It is also the city of Louis XVI. In the Paris of his era, builders and developers rarely surpassed the heights their clientele were prepared to reach by

[A] Louis XVI, Ludwig MvdR Baupolizeiordnung

[L] Berlin, Paris, Stuttgart

[20] Mel Scott (1985), *The San Francisco Bay Area: A Metropolis in Perspective.*

climbing the stairs [5SP]. Over the years, this limit vacillated between five and six stories. In 1784, this practically motivated height was made divine and absolute. *Flat Cap Louis* codified it with an ordinance that prescribed that Parisian eaves heights could not surpass 17.5 m. In fact, buildings could surpass this threshold up to an additional 4.9 m, but were then compelled to spring back at this point at a 45° angle [SB].[21]

Two centuries later, in the context of the ideologically-conceived urban design principles featured at the Stuttgart Weissenhofsiedlung (and in the tradition of the 1893 Chicago World's Fair, with its striving for external homogeneity), German architect Ludwig Mies van der Rohe made use of two fundamental rules: all buildings had to be white [CS, CW], and each have a flat roof [FR].[22] These two rules sufficed for the controlled contrast between outer standardization and a creative inner freedom. White outside, colorful within.

Berlin, meanwhile, settled on 22 meters [BB]. This was the maximum eaves height of the German city's courtyard blocks—the so-called *Berliner Mietskaserne* (tenements). This height limit is the essential trait which endows Berlin's urban morphology with coherence. As a portion of the *Baupolizeiverordnung* (Police Building Ordinance) of 1853, the setting of a maximum building height was primarily motivated by the concerns of the fire department. In this instance, the management of potential overpopulation or of the overexploitation of Berlin's developable land, and the associated hygienic considerations, were apparently not a factor. The drawings and explanations of Werner Hegemann confirm this. The plans, elevations, and perspectives illustrate Prussia's building ordinances of 1853–1897. They delineate a potential tenement block with a façade height of 22 m facing the courtyard, 3 minimal courtyards of 29 sqm each (5.34 m x 5.34 m, corresponding to the necessary minimum width for the fire hoses of the time), a lateral wing with windowless firewalls 56 m in length, and seven stories. At 1.5 residents per room, and not taking kitchens into consideration, Hegemann calculated that a typical Berlin apartment building could accommodate 325 people. Since occupancy rates of 3 people per room were common, occupancy of a thousand people was possible. The deeper building parcels introduced in James Hobrecht's development plan of 1862 made possible even higher occupancy rates. Evolving from these apartment buildings in an interplay with building ordinances and development planning (with the standardization of parcel size and building line) were the celebrated and notorious *Berliner Mietskaserne*.

With reference to street façades, Hegemann spoke of *Fassadenprahlerei* (façade ostentation): in contrast to the courtyard interiors, the 1853 building ordinances and associated street widths of more than 15 m meant that it was possible to build up to heights of 15 m. Where street widths were narrower than 15 m, it was still possible to build up to a height of 1 1/4 times the width of the street. In most cases, however, constructive considerations meant that the eaves heights of the inner courtyards also deter-

---

[21] François Loyer (1988), *Paris Nineteenth Century: Architecture and Urbanism*, 129, 234, 407–08.
[22] Richard Pommer and Christian F. Otto (1991), *Weissenhof 1927 and the Modern Movement in Architecture*.

106

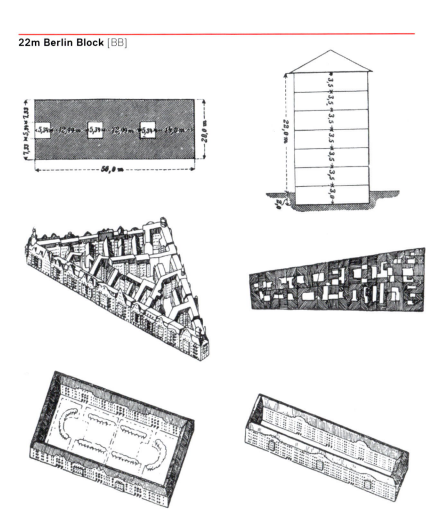

28 Evolution of the *Berliner Mietskasernenblock*, 1853–1925.

mined those of the street side. Still, the theoretical relationship between the width of the street and the height of the façade is no New York invention [SSR], but had in fact been codified already in Prussia 80 years earlier. Although conditioned by divergent motives, Paris, Stuttgart, and Berlin are all examples of the homogenization of urban form. In the first instance, if was a question of codifying comfort levels, in the second, of exaggerating an architectonic-aesthetic drive, while in Berlin, it was a question of the maximum reach of fire hoses.

Setback Street Ratio
[SSR] §4.13

4

Codified Aesthetics

To issue judgments about what is beautiful and what is ugly is difficult enough. To then formulate generally valid rules based on such judgments is virtually impossible without generating new problems. The concept of beauty is characterized by a number of explicit individual judgments, and these are in turn confronted by an only potentially available and strongly diffuse public stance.

Problematized in the following is the attempt to arrive at a visual order for the built environment. The second part concentrates in particular on the visual order of central inner-city districts and their aesthetic maxims.

29 Order, repetition, continuous and discontinuous architecture.

4.1 Control and (Visual) Order

Visually Ordered City

The city is a stage for a perpetual comedy of mistaken identities, one whose themes are control, unity and order. An urban design vision is a picture puzzle of this confusion: unified order, controlled unity, unified control... The close semantic proximity between these terms makes it all the more difficult to distinguish between them. "Order," meanwhile, refers simultaneously to a process and to an outcome.

Actively exercised urban planning control arises from a diversity of motivations. At times, such control harbors an autocratic desire to manifest power. At times, there is the educative intention of designing a modern society in functional equilibrium and within a usable urban organization. A building order shall also create a social order! In some cases, it is a question of the obligation to protect the public interest and the public health. In others, it expresses the need for an overarching identity, for a concrete image of self and other (Santa Barbara). Still others emerge from the desire to satisfy a drive for artistic expression.

But no matter which motivation is responsible, such attempts at control strive for visual representation in the form of recognizably formal orders. Almost of necessity, the result is a causal connection.

As a monostructural ordering principle, the North American grid has never accepted a second, manifestly dominant formal order existing alongside it.

Emerging surreptitiously nonetheless were claims for an *orderly* planning treatment. If necessary, the grid must vanish—at the very least, this orthogonal "urban desert"[1] must be crisscrossed. As an inherent and recognizable trait of the discipline of urban planning, visual order was introduced to the US in model form at the Chicago Fair of 1893, and by the City Beautiful Movement associated with it.

In fact, the World's Fair was an immaculately ordered miniature city. It was a showcase of modern urban development, and was endowed with all the attributes that would number among the standardized infrastructural elements of the city of the future. On an area measuring just 2 1/2 square kilometers were complete water supply and sewerage systems and fire and police departments. Each of the approximately 200 buildings was furnished with electricity.[2] There were telephones, and even an elevated train. In the end, the individual buildings disappeared into a coherent ensemble. All buildings were given a uniform façade color, and not just along the French axis. For the *cour d'honneurs*, the architects settled on a unified eaves height of 18 m [SB].

Visitors to the exhibition did not abstract this unified urban image and its architectural language from the gleaming technical achievements whose display cases the buildings in fact were. The message was: a modern city is an ordered one.

As it happens, Burnham had never actually seen the above-ground world

[A]
Burnham and Co

[L]
Chicago
1893's World Fair

Set Back
[SB] §7.02–1

---

[1]   Leslie Martin and Lionel March (1972), *Urban Space and Structures*, 14.
[2]   Garvin (1996), 507.

30 Visually ordered city: The Chicago's 1893 World's Columbian Exposition.

of Haussmann with his own eyes, to say nothing of the subterranean one.[3] Back then, the congruence between a building structure, however ordered, and an ordered (meaning effectively functioning, and also invisible) infrastructure was regarded as an indissoluble connection—and would in the end become a compulsory aspect of the city and its visions.

Beautiful Personality Disorder

It is not especially difficult to attribute a behavioral disturbance to a city. Frequently, this rests on an obsessive compulsive personality disorder. In a heightened global situation of competition, cities today suffer increasingly from a histrionic disturbance. The clinical picture involved can be characterized by dramatized self-presentation, suggestibility, a tendency toward the theatrical, a perpetual search for thrilling experiences, and the excessive preoccupation with being regarded as outwardly attractive.

In most cases, such compulsive behavior expresses itself in excessive conscientiousness and scrupulousness, coupled with profound doubt, exaggerated caution, the unfounded conviction that others submit to the same routines, and a resistance to allowing anyone else to do anything. The compulsion to be outwardly attractive at all costs is distinctly observable in Santa Barbara. The ugly duckling summons the strength to become a classy Spanish beauty. Seldom have the codified consequences and the perfectionism associated with the complete makeover ever been as distinctly manifest within an urban redevelopment project. Of particular interest is the consensus achieved there, the shared recognition of an ideal of beauty. Spanish beauty now becomes a universal axiom [CMO].

In his book *God's Own Junkyard*, Peter Blake cites the U.S. Supreme Court of 1954 on this theme: "It is within the power of the legislature to determine that the community should be beautiful... [RTB]"[4]

Remaining unresolved, however, was the question of who exactly de-

City Make Over
[CMO] §7.04–1

Rights to Beauty
[RTB] §1.03

---

3   Haussmann also used his new avenues in order to install functional canal systems beneath them. In a Paris that had already been built, this congruence between above-ground and subterranean worlds was an almost practical, even necessary relationship. This was not necessarily the case with the new planning of the Chicago Fair.

4   Peter Blake (1964), *God's Own Junkyard: The Planned Deterioration of America's Landscape*, 140.

cides what is "beautiful" and what "ugly," and whether it is worthwhile to consider attempting to codify a specific ideal of beauty.

Many guardians of law today agree that the criteria of beauty cannot be established via jurisprudence. The reasons for this are readily apparent: beauty is never amenable to consensus, and can rarely be objectified or generalized. It is a relative concept, one dependent upon personal taste and point of view.

The word "beautiful" is not actually found in building codes. Instead, it is alluded to adroitly via circumlocution. Not seldom, such expressions of taste are found as derivations or externalities in documents pertaining to a specific ordinance.

In 1960, on the other hand, Kevin Lynch approved of urban planning under the aegis of an aesthetic perspective:

"These shapings or reshapings should be guided by what might be called a 'visual plan' for the city or metropolitan region: a set of recommendations and controls which would be concerned with visual form on the urban scale. The preparations of such a plan might begin with an analysis of the existing form and public image of the area. (…)

"Substantial physical change may not be justified on this esthetic score alone, except at strategic points. But the visual plan could influence the form of physical changes which occur for other reasons. (…)

"The controls employed to achieve visual form at the city scale could range from general zoning provisions, advisory review and persuasive influence over private design, to strict controls at critical points and to the positive design of public facilities such as highways or civic buildings."[5]

What seemed plausible and legitimate to Kevin Lynch is in fact a matter of enormous difficulty and uncertainty, in particular when public taste seeks to compel the conformity of private expressions.

Gene's Own Junkyard

Beginning in 1972, Gene Crandall ran a recycling business—or to speak plainly, a junkyard—located at Port Byron in the town of Mentz in New York State. Although by no means visible from the street, a town order was issued in 2000 directing Gene to erect a fence designed to block views of his junkyard [JFO]. Otherwise, his license would no longer be renewed. After repeated aggravating episodes with the city, Crandall took his automobile crane and stacked his junked automobiles alongside and on top of one another, specimens of every imaginable make and color, each divested of its tires. Growing little by little along the boundaries of the site was the obligatory view-blocking fence, a colorful wall of old automobiles. This "fence" measured a quarter of a mile in length, and had even been given a fully functional gate at the entrance. The town was furious. But the public felt differently: "They [the cars] got kind of popular, stacked up on the property line all the way out,"[6] said Mr. Crandall. For many passers-by, the stack of automobiles is far more than a simple fence, namely an industrial work of art. According to its owner, his inadvertent art object was even for sale. Considered as a fence, it corresponded

[A]
Crandall and the Dept. of Motor Vehicles (DMV)

[L]
Port Byron

Junkyard Fence Order
[JFO] §6.15

---

5 Kevin Lynch (1960), *The Image of the City*, 116.
6 Gene Crandall, quoted by Carol W. LaGrasse (2002), *The Wall of Cars*.

Junkyard Fence Order [JFO]

31 The inevitable outcome of the Junkyard Fence Order.

to the DMV junkyard law: "When the Town went after me, the State said I qualified."[7] The *Junkyard Fence Law* had failed to specify the precise material to be used. There are beautiful fences and ugly ones, but at least in this instance, the State of New York held itself aloof from this question, providing a certain interpretative leeway via a calculated lack of specificity.

Long-Haired

[A] Kenney

[L] Buffalo

Living in Kenmore, a suburb of the city of Buffalo, also located in New York State, were Stephen Kenney and his wife. Early one September morning in 1984, he strolled through the tall grass of his front yard to his mailbox. A mailbox similar to the others found in this middle-class neighborhood in a middle-class district. Inside, he found a summons to attend a hearing at the local district court, to take place the following week.

A year earlier, he had received a similar letter. He had been cited because the vegetation growing in his garden, or more precisely his unmown lawn, apparently contravened a paragraph contained in the village housing code [YM]. The section in question explicitly surveyed the planting of varieties of scrub that could be "noxious or detrimental to the health." Shortly thereafter, he set up a sign at the center of his small blossoming meadow, which bore the inscription: "This lawn is not an example of sloth. It is a natural yard growing the way God intended. It is not a breeding place for mosquitoes or other obnoxious pests. It will never be a source of noise pollution from lawn mowers, weed eaters or big trucks pumping petrochemicals; nor will the reduction in run-off contain toxic pesticides."[8]

At that time, the then 30-year-old Stephen Kenney wore his hair long. At least officially, however, neighbors were not concerned with Kenney's personal appearance, but instead with the state of his property. They were also concerned about potential security risks, and were worried

Yard Maintenance [YM] § 5.12

7 Ibid.
8 The New York Times Metropolitan Desk (1984), *Man to Defend His Unmown Lawn in Court.*

about the possibility that the lawn, three feet in height, might provide a refuge for rodents and insects. Paradoxically, not a few of the neighbors expressing such fears were members of the local chapter of the *Audubon Society*, which regularly published articles on the advantages of allowing gardens to grow wild.

Growing in Kenney's garden, measuring 6 x 6 m, were three dozen different types of wild flowers, whose seeds threatened to contaminate the toxic green, immaculately manicured surfaces of his neighbors' lawns. Concerning his property's appearance, Kenney was charged with transgressing the paragraphs which specified that residential buildings be maintained in such a condition that they "assume the desirable residential character of the property."[9]

But what exactly are we to understand by "desirable residential character"? "Appearances are a major part of this case," commented the village's attorney, Mr. Viksjo, continuing: "The property does not fit in with the residential community."[10]

Despite many letters of support, Stephen Kenney lost his case in the end. At least the judge had reduced the nearly $ 30,000 in monetary fines that had accumulated to his account to a mere $100.

Shortly before the decision was announced, a neighbor remarked to the *New York Times*: "I just hope they do not send him to jail or anything! Then he'd be a martyr, and these environmentalists would probably erect a weed in his honor."[11]

Artificial Underbrush

Santa Barbara simply banned these artificial "weeds." For Venturi, they are "almost all right," while for Reyner Banham, they are the positive embodiment of the absence of control. We are referring of course to that quintessentially American creation, the billboard.

[A]
Banham, Blake and Stover

[L]
Passaic, St. Louis, Massachusetts

In 1966, during a visit to Van Nuys in Los Angeles, Banham referred to them as "the only symbols of vitality on a scabrous stucco desert."[12]

And billboards are the ingredients from which it is possible to concoct either a withering critique or instead a euphoric acclamation of the singular aesthetic of urban America. Photographer Ed Ruscha portrayed billboards in series, and the very same images could easily have appeared as illustrations of tawdriness in Peter Blake's *God's Own Junkyard*. Raging in the 1960s was a vigorous dispute over America's "*Art Gallery of the Public*".[13] Opponents chopped billboards down, while others felled perfectly legal trees in order to preserve unobstructed views of the slogans appearing on the billboards set behind them.

That which Banham perceived through his euphoric British eyeglasses as an instance of charming, untamed growth is in fact the result of a controversy that raged for over a century, one that often had to be settled in the courtroom. The disagreement revolved around the question of

---

9   Ibid.
10 Ibid.
11 Ibid.
12 Banham quoted by Art Seidenbaum, in a 1966 *Los Angeles Times* article.
13 Burr L. Robbins, who was president of the General Outdoor Advertising Co. Inc. in the 1960s, quoted by Blake (1964), 11.

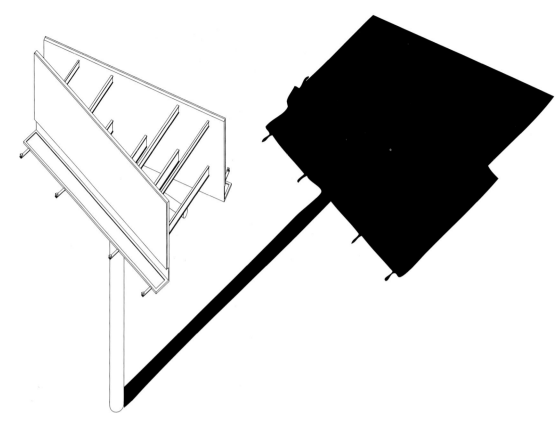

32 Shady art gallery of the public.

whether purely aesthetic considerations were sufficient to justify controlling private commercial interests through binding rules. In many cases, ancillary arguments had to be devised in order to effectively enforce aesthetic objectives.

The general attitude of the American court system has changed frequently over the past century.

In the early years of the 20th century, billboards were in no danger of being judged according to their aesthetic qualities.

In 1903, the city of Passaic, New Jersey intended to do so, and was immediately halted by a court ruling. In response to the adoption of a three-meter setback law and a height limit of 2 1/2 meters for billboards, the court countered: "Aesthetic considerations are a matter of luxury and indulgence rather than of necessity, and it is necessity alone which justifies the exercise of police power to take private property without compensation."[14]

The message was clear enough: looking good is a luxury!

In subsequent years, growing numbers of complaints led to a heightened latitude in assessments of what looked good and what did not. Still, such assessments were restrained in the extreme. Threadbare rationales were put forward instead. In St. Louis in 1913, a *Billboard Control Ordinance* was adopted, but not with the justification of promoting the

[14]   City of Passic Vs. Patterson Bill Posting (1905), 72 NJL 285.

town's beauty, instead—it was claimed—to secure the public health, security, and morality. Besides representing an elevated fire hazard, billboards also served as hiding places for illicit behavior, while criminals were said to lay in wait for victims behind them.[15]

Only 20 years later, in 1935, did the state of Massachusetts spell things out, resolving on the ban of all signboards less than 300 feet (90 m) from public parks, and 50 feet (15 m) from public roadways: "We think that the preservation of scenic beauty and places of historical interest would be of sufficient support. Consideration of taste and fitness may be a proper basis for action in granting and denying permits for locations for advertising devices."[16]

All rather vague! In 1963, Mrs. Webster Stover was forced to confront the fact that she failed to adhere to the generally prevailing ideal of beauty. In protest against the municipal authorities, Mrs. Stover strung up a clothes line in her front yard, along with hanging racks, old uniforms, underwear, and scarecrows. Clothes lines were forbidden in front yards for aesthetic reasons. But that didn't bother the Stovers in the least— during the next five years, they even added an additional line.

In the end, the Stover's invocation of their constitutional freedom of speech and opinion availed them nothing. The clothes line would have to go. The court waved aside their defense, explaining that purely aesthetic considerations were sufficient, and that the regulation "simply prescribes conduct that is unnecessarily offensive to the visual sensibilities of the average person and tends to debase the community, and reduces real estate values."[17]

Again, quite explicit: the law possesses general validity, and it counts for something!

There seems to exist a statistically verifiable threshold, a mean value for distinguishing between the attributes "ugly" and "beautiful." And when something falls below that threshold, the community's socio-visual unity is at risk.

In many locations today, such scenic view protection ordinances serve to protect against this type of visual pollution. Billboards—referred to almost lovingly as "sky trash, litter on a stick, or the junk mail of the American highway"[18]—simply don't stand a chance. Still, in a city like Houston, for example, such zones affect a mere 10% of the total surface area.

Upside Down

Accompanying drivers through the Nevada desert along *Interstate 15* is a series of enormous billboards. Set at intervals of 250 m and casting their enormous shadows onto the landscape, they guide travelers into a town whose architectonic quality is owed to signboards the size of buildings.[19] Las Vegas is the world's largest billboard flower bed. The town pursues an ideal of beauty that differs radically from those of the cities discussed

[A]
Billboards

[L]
Las Vegas

[15] St. Louis Gunning Advertising Co. Vs. City of St. Louis (1911), 235 MO 99. Appeal dismissed, 231 US 761 (1913).
[16] General Outdoor Advertising Co. Vs. Department of Public Works (1936), 289 MA 149.
[17] People Vs. Stover (1963), 12 NY 2d 462. Appeal dismissed, 375 US 48 (1963).
[18] Scenic America (2008), *Background on Billboards*.
[19] From Tom Wolfe (1969), *Electrographic Architecture*, 380–82.

above. That which is regarded as ugly elsewhere is perceived as beautiful here. Arriving in Las Vegas, one might well think to oneself: finally, Banham's hippie fantasy of a total control vacuum.[20] That would be a false assumption. Here as well, unity is threatened by lack of compliance to a common rule based on an averaged standard. The Las Vegas Building and Zoning Code is as comprehensive as any.

Everyone is familiar with Figure 33, Robert Venturi's sketch entitled "I AM A MONUMENT," which bears the subtitle: "Recommendations for a Monument."[21] Anyone planning to erect a monument in Las Vegas will need to consult the 70-page "Sign Standard Chapter 19.14." The guidelines it contains are anything else but recommendations.

Vegas' Lighting
[VL] § 7.04–3

At first glance, it is a question of quite normal standards. Upon closer examination, maximum values seem to have been confused with minimum ones [VL]. Instead of a maximum possible upper limit of fluorescent lighting, we read that *at least* 75% of the total surface of a building's façades must be taken up by neon signs!

In this town, it would be literally against the law to erect a moderate looking building.

Things are no different with the advertising signs that line the streets. There are maximum and minimum setbacks, heights, and prescribed strengths of illumination. Cheerfulness by command!

As secondary literature to accompany Venturi and Scott Brown's *Learning from Las Vegas*, the Las Vegas building code is highly recommended. It is a potent antidote to their unbridled enthusiasm.

1-866-Adopt-a-Highway

[A]
Corporations and Individuals

[L]
Along the U.S. Freeways

Sponsoring volunteers: there is a certain type of billboard that stands even in national parks and other advertising-free protected zones, i.e. where private roadside advertising is explicitly forbidden. These are the signs of the federal "Adopt a Highway" programme [AAH]. This campaign combines the public interest in clean American highways with private broadcasting and advertising needs. Private individuals and organizations either collect the trash lying along a roadway themselves, or else contract with a cleaning firm to maintain a specific segment of highway, the average length being 2 miles. By way of compensation, such contributors to the public good are rewarded with the presence of a blue or green sign displayed publicly along the highway.

Adopt a Highway
[AAH] § 4.04

Tendency towards Overexploitation
[TOE] § 1.08

Detectable—as always when it is a question of private actions in the public realm—is a tendency toward overexploitation à la Garret Hardin's *Tragedy of the Commons* [TOE]. Acting as highway patrons alongside private citizens are local firms. In the meantime, large corporations as well, including Disney, Verizon, and Sony are mentioned on these signs. An association with a cleaner environment and a proximity to a government institution make the presence of a firm's logo on such an official sign doubly impressive and valuable. Middlemen such as the *Adopt a Highway Corporation* openly advertise sales to businesses and commercial sign advertising on interstates and other major highways in various states for adopt-a-highway programmes.

---

[20] Reyner Banham et al. (2000), *Non-Plan: An Experiment in Freedom.*
[21] Robert Venturi, Denise Scott Brown and Steven Izenour (1972), *Learning from Las Vegas*, 156.

33 How to build monuments according to Venturi and Scott Brown.

Vegas' Lighting [VL]

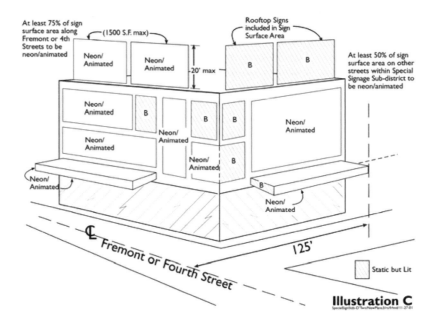

At least 75% of sign surface area along Fremont or 4th Streets to be neon/animated

(1500 S.F. max)

Neon/Animated

Neon/Animated

20' max

Rooftop Signs included in Sign Surface Area

B

B

At least 50% of sign surface area on other streets within Special Signage Sub-district to be neon/animated

Neon/Animated

B

Neon/Animated

B

B

Neon/Animated

Neon/Animated

B

Neon/Animated

Neon/Animated

B

Neon/Animated

₵ Fremont or Fourth Street

125'

Static but Lit

Illustration C

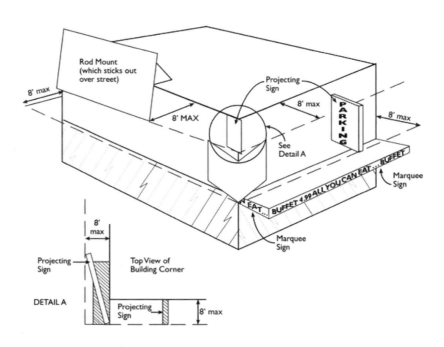

Rod Mount (which sticks out over street)

8' max

8' MAX

Projecting Sign

8' max

8' max

See Detail A

PARKING

Marquee Sign

EAT...BUFFET 4.99 ALL YOU CAN EAT...BUFFET

8' max

Marquee Sign

Projecting Sign

Top View of Building Corner

DETAIL A

Projecting Sign

8' max

34 ... and how to build monuments according to the Las Vegas Zoning Code.

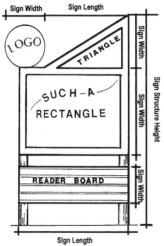

Signs constructed of individual elements shall measure the overall sign display by determining the sum of the area of each square, rectangle, triangle, portion of a circle or any combination thereof to create the smallest single continuous perimeter enclosing the extreme limits of each word, written representation (including any series of letters), emblems or figures of similar character including all frames, face plates, nonstructural trim or other component parts not otherwise used for support.

The smallest continuous perimeter that encompasses the entire coherent message is used, in this case, the words making up the message are intentionally spread far apart.

The smallest continuous perimeter is used that encompasses the entire message, in this case the perimeter is adjusted for the smaller height letters.

35 Channel Letters.

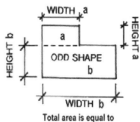

Total area is equal to area a plus area b.

In the case of an odd shape, calculate the smallest regular geometric shape (triangle, rectangle or circle) that encompasses the perimeter of the sign and add the areas together for the total area.

CIRCLE

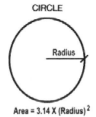

Area = 3.14 X (Radius)^2

Spherical Sign

Spherical signs areas are calculated as if they are circles: $3.14 \times (radius)^2$

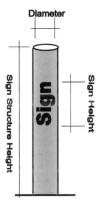

The area of a cylindrical sign shall be the diameter multiplied by the height of the cylinder.

36 Measurement of specific sign areas.

Figure 4   Incidental Signs

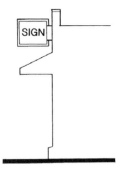

Figure 8   Projecting Sign

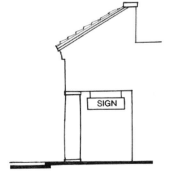

Figure 5. Arcade Sign

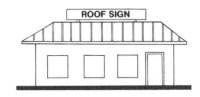

Figure 9   Roof Sign

Figure 7   Monument Sign

Figure 10   Wall Sign

Figure 6   Awning Sign

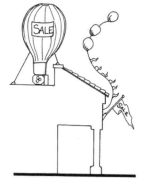

Figure 12   Special Event Sign

37 Las Vegas Sign Standards.

38 Adopt a mile of public infrastructure!

And this although the programme is, at least officially, "not a forum for advertising or public discourse."[22] Given this development, the Federal Highway Administration felt itself obliged in a memorandum of 2001[23] to state that commercial trade logos, slogans, telephone numbers, internet addresses, and similar forms of commercial promotion were not in keeping with the inconspicuous display intended by the programme's founders. Despite this, the programme has been so successful that it is only a matter of time before we see the arrival of adopt-a-beach, adopt-a-bridge, adopt-a-city, etc. programmes.

4.2 Downtown's Will to Form

Every self-respecting North American city needs one—including San Francisco, of course. One simply can no longer do without a high-profile financial or central business district. Finally by the 1960s, the "inspiring drama of the free enterprise"[24] required a suitable and solid representation in every larger US American city.

When it came to the development of a typical American downtown, San Francisco in this period was among the most sensitive and hesitant communities. Tall buildings stood in direct competition with tall hills, with the outstanding landscape qualities of the Bay Area and its fine-grained development contradicting the image the citizenry had of their town. And so San Francisco took its sweet time before allowing its high-rises to go forward. Between 1930 and 1958, only a single tall office building was constructed, and only in 1959 did the city acquire its first modern high-rise, the *Crown Zellerbach Building* on Market Street.

---

[22] From California Department of Transportation (2008), *The Adopt-a-Highway Programme.*
[23] U.S. Department of Transportation (Deputy Executive Director Vincent F. Schimmoller) (April 27, 2001), Memorandum: Adopt-a-Highway Signs—Interpretation (Ii-477(I)—"Advertising on Adopt-a-Highway Signs").
[24] Earle Shultz and Walter Simmons (1959), *Offices in the Sky*, 7.

Policemen and Trouble Makers

[A]
Anti-High-rise Movement

[L]
San Francisco

Without criminals, there would be no police—and the same is true of fires and the fire department. Both institutions work simultaneously preventively as well as via intervention. Precedential cases originated by these troublemakers are constantly necessary, as they lead to sensitization.

Such villains then compel the introduction of preventive measures designed to eliminate the emergent problem for the wider community once and for all.

In the San Francisco of the 1960s, a quartet of such troublemakers suddenly stood together in close proximity, generating public annoyance in the financial and business district: the *Holiday Inn* and the *Transamerica Building* were regarded as "too bizarre," the *Embarcadero Center* as "too large and too bulky "and the *Bank of America Building* as "too big and too dark." Nonetheless, it seemed almost impossible to charge the Bank of America with ignorance of its context—contradicting such an argument were the 1500 bay windows on its façade.

The anti high-rise movement then active in San Francisco had definitively lost the battle against the four offenders. All that remained was public defamation. The Transamerica Building had an especially hard time of it. Its appearance was said to be incompatible with an attractive downtown. Regarded as embarrassing, uneconomical, it was soon nicknamed "The Egyptian Embassy," and was illustrated in newspapers and magazines wearing a dunce's cap.

In the late 1960s and early 1970s, the wrath of activists was directed principally against purportedly ugly, unwieldy, excessively tall and poorly sited office buildings.[25] One recipient of ill favor was US Steel, when it proposed erecting a 150 meter tower on the waters of the Bay. Newspaper articles caricatured the building as an ungainly "steel giraffe," one that palpably disturbed the site's sense of balance and proportion.[26]

But the controversy gave rise to a remarkable tool. Since the ranks of the high-rise's opponents contained a few architects proficient in drafting, so-called *Opposition Drawings*[27] could be prepared [OD]. On the basis of a bird's-eye view seen from the direction of Bay Bridge, architects and supporters of the *US Steel Building* attempted to demonstrate just how well the structure was adapted to the existing urban context. The building's opponents now provided a perspective from the opposite direction, from Telegraph Hill. These images showed how strongly the US Steel Building would plunge the proud Bay Bridge into shadow—that is to say, how a private office building would blight a public icon.

In the end, in 1971, the *San Francisco Supervisors* (SUPES) granted permission for the construction of the US Steel Building on this site, stipulating that it would have a height of only 175 ft (53 m) at most.

This deployment of counter-perspectives functioned as well in the case of the 20-story *Haas Towers* project—against which no objections were raised until the lawyer had it immortalized from a number of different

Opposition Drawing
[OD] § 5.16

---

[25] Chester W. Hartman (1984), *The Transformation of San Francisco*, 269.
[26] Donald Appleyard and Lois Fishman (1977), *High Rise Buildings Versus San Francisco*, 87.
[27] Ibid., 99.

124

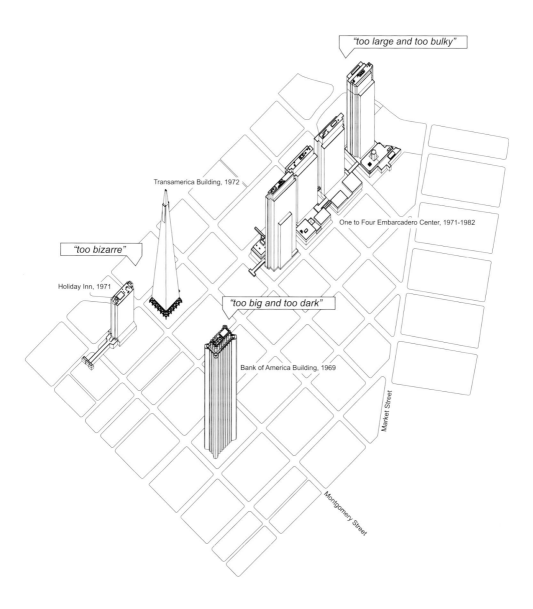

"too large and too bulky"

Transamerica Building, 1972

One to Four Embarcadero Center, 1971-1982

"too bizarre"

Holiday Inn, 1971

"too big and too dark"

Bank of America Building, 1969

Market Street

Montgomery Street

39 San Francisco troublemakers.

perspectives from Russian Hill. Virtual buildings were now regarded as having evidentiary status, and the discipline of urban simulation was launched. The more scientific and the more complex the methods used to generate these anamorphic images, the greater the public's prepared-ness to regard them as objective. The first setting for such activities was located directly behind San Francisco's Bay Bridge, at the *Environmental Simulation Laboratory* at UC Berkeley, founded by Donald Appleyard in 1972 and containing fabulous apparatuses, gigantic city models, and swiveling endoscopes by means of which one could navigate at eye level through models of the city.

40 *Environmental Simulation Laboratory*: simulating the street-level view within the San Francisco Central Business District.

Real Simulation

[A]
Swiss Prime Tower

[L]
Zürich

Even such an ingenious simulation cannot replace a personal or real interaction, that is to say, a 1:1 experience of the critical object in urban space. Switzerland and its cities are well aware of this fact. Ideally, one drives or moves through the city physically and in real-time.

In 2007, it was possible to contemplate a 126 m tall steel scaffolding that had been erected in the former industrial quarter of the Swiss town of Zürich (Kreis 5) from close up. Next to the Hardbrücke, its quartet of steel profiles marked out the edges and complete height of the future *Swiss Prime Tower*. According to law, each Swiss building project must be rendered beforehand in its actual planned dimensions through a so-called *Baugespann* (structural mockup). The ordinance includes the construction of dormer windows, tool sheds, but also of high-rise buildings. For a specified period of time (2 months), the citizenry, assuming it is willing to exercise a minimum of imagination, has the opportunity to visualize the project within its three-dimensional boundaries and to discuss its urban integrity. Thereafter follows an act of participatory democracy, the voting in a referendum. In the case of the *Swiss Prime Tower*, however, the full 126 meter tall scaffolding would not have been necessary. For reasons of proportionality and safety, the city would have preferred a "preview" measuring just a fraction of that height. Since they were planning to erect the tallest building in Switzerland to date, the clients spared no expense and effort in erecting this spectacular simulation, spending more than 100,000 Swiss francs for purposes of prestige and advertising.

Little Big Plan

[A]
San Francisco Plan

[L]
San Francisco

The desire not only to simulate visual qualities, but to actively and preventively guide them as well was manifested beginning in the 1970s in San Francisco's *General Plan*, and finally in the same city's 1983 *Downtown*

126

41 The virtual envelope becomes reality for immediate public review: 126 m tall "Baugespann" of the future Swiss Prime Tower, Zürich.

Plan, which was the work of planning director Dean Macris.[28] The plan reduced building heights and building bulk on the basis of a floor area ratio and geometric bulk definition [BBK]. It envisioned landmark protection status for 266 important buildings, and required the preparation of a shadow study in order to ensure that new buildings would permit adequate sun and light to reach the surrounding streets. Whole streets and their views acquired quasi landmark status [QSV].

All of this is familiar already from New York. Of interest is this manifestation of San Francisco's collective taste and the yearning for visual attractiveness. This approach called for the architectural treatment of high-rise roofs with hat-style structures in order to avoid the so-called "refrigerator look" (i.e., a monotonous sequence of androgynous glass-fronted crates [ARL]).[29]

Cynical commentators soon join the fray. Allan Temko, architecture critic with the *San Francisco Chronicle*, commented that the plan was more concerned with aesthetic matters than with the effective restriction of growth and density in San Francisco's downtown:

"Nor would I trust Macris' chief assistant on design matters... His contributions on the Plan would not require architects but milliners. So we'd put these party hats on buildings, as if we didn't have the most colossal dunce cap in the world on the Transamerica Building."[30]

It was calculated that by the year 2000, the plan would in principle permit the construction of more than 24 million sqft (2.2 mio sqm) of new office surface, in particular to the south of Market Street. This meant growth rates similar to those registered in the years prior to the plan's adoption. Such figures recall the reproach of "over-zoning" that had been leveled against New York's 1916 resolution. As far as San Francisco's citizenry were concerned, Dean Macris' plan was simply too weak, and represented an inadequate planning for exercising control over the "*vertical earthquake*" taking place in San Francisco's downtown. Resistance was so great that in 1985, the city's *Board of Supervisors* (the municipal governing body) endowed the plan with the force of law, but with an addendum, a limit on the maximum building volume per annum. To begin with, this was set at a maximum of 950,000 sqft for the entire city—a "growth cap" lower than the square meters covered by certain individual high-rises in New York City.

What San Francisco was proposing here was definitively "the first quota system for city planning [DQ]."[31] Alongside the "beauty contest," designed to determine whether the "hat" on the high-rise tower corresponded to the prevailing ideal of beauty, decisions would be yielded to the discretion of a review panel, which granted building permits to the numerous applicants and filled the annual quota. Administratively, it is only possible to get a handle on this process when a multiplicity of additional guidelines are introduced, for example those regarding the economic relevance of a specific project for the city. One year later, in 1987, *Proposition M* reduced the annual quota by 50% to 475,000 square feet,

---

28 Hartman (1984), 274.
29 Ibid., 273.
30 The City of San Francisco (1983), *The Downtown Plan—Proposal for Citizen Review*.
31 Paul Goldberger (1987), *When Planning Can Be Too Much of a Good Thing*.

Building Bulk [BBK]

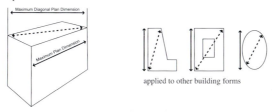

Maximum Diagonal Plan Dimension

Maximum Plan Dimension

applied to other building forms

Maximum Plan Dimension:
The greatest horizontal dimension along any wall
of the building, measured at a height corresponding
to the prevailing height of other development in the area.

42a Method of measuring bulk.

☐ Bulk Regulations By Height Controls
▨ OPEN SPACE (Any Development Subject To Review)
▨ See Chinatown Area Plan, Downtown Plan, Rincon Hill Plan

42b San Francisco's specific bulk areas.

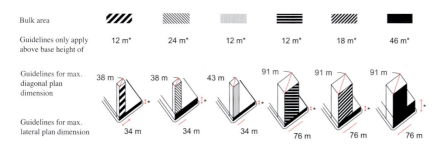

Bulk area						
Guidelines only apply above base height of	12 m*	24 m*	12 m*	12 m*	18 m*	46 m*
Guidelines for max. diagonal plan dimension	38 m	38 m	43 m	91 m	91 m	91 m
Guidelines for max. lateral plan dimension	34 m	34 m	34 m	76 m	76 m	76 m

42c Guidelines for each bulk area: a tower's max. diagonal and lateral dimensions.

129

Quality of Street Views [QSV]

43 Map of streets with excellent views that deserve protection, San Francisco.

Anti Refrigerator Look [ARL]

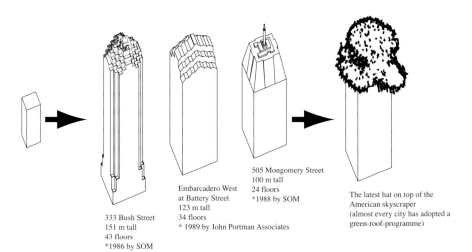

333 Bush Street
151 m tall
43 floors
*1986 by SOM

Embarcadero West
at Battery Street
123 m tall
34 floors
* 1989 by John Portman Associates

505 Mongomery Street
100 m tall
24 floors
*1988 by SOM

The latest hat on top of the
American skyscraper
(almost every city has adopted a
green-roof-programme)

44 Methods.

Skyline Wall Syndrome [SWS]

45 CBD San Francisco.

making high-rise development in San Francisco virtually impossible. Even where this was not the case, it was charged that (to cite *New York Times* critic Paul Goldberger) "they have all turned out to be tame examples of the post-modern style, cautious little buildings that struggle not to offend." Goldberger goes on to criticize the high degree of determination exercised through the required review process:

"San Francisco no longer has planners, it has design czars. The city government through its planning department and the public through referendums have become the controlling forces in determining what happens in downtown San Francisco. They go far beyond the normal mandate of setting out the basic outlines of growth through zoning laws, as planners do everywhere else; here, they determine the specific design of individual projects, and ultimately decide whether or not projects can go ahead at all."[32]

The "hats" set on the towers, however, were intended to counteract another downtown tendency familiar under the term *Skyline Wall Syndrome* [SWS]. As speculative projects controlled by similar marginal conditions and land costs, office high-rises tend to have similar numbers of stories, and hence similar heights. In many cases, such utilization does not approach the potential legal limit, but instead corresponds to a purely economic calculus: how many times must the building lot be multiplied into the heights in order to be profitable while avoiding excessive costs, for example, for vertical accesses? This *Economic Height* [EH] often lies well below the maximum utilization set by law, and by falling below it, disempowers the potential for architectonic shaping offered by such legislation. And the developer of a neighboring parcel determines the height of his tower on the basis of similar calculations. The height differences

Skyline Wall Syndrome
[SWS] § 3.04

Economic Height
[EH] §7.01–6

---

[32] Ibid.

between buildings deemed desirable on the basis of aesthetic criteria, then, can be administered on the basis of general rules only with great difficulty. And if the maximum possible utilization is set somewhat below the economic height that prevails in a particular period, then that standard functions as a height limit, once again generating a uniform sequence of buildings.

A genuine predicament for the city. A successful, that is to say, interesting and dramatic skyline with its peaks, valleys, and jagged canyons, is very difficult to shape consciously. Lowered height limits, once again, generate uniformity, while also restraining inner-city growth in undesirable ways.

Helpful instead is a constant radical revision of building laws [RC], and maximally turbulent pricing developments in the land and real estate markets. One indispensable ingredient, of course, is a local, egocentric corporate headquarters that functions like a mountaintop cross, so to speak; another is a collective architectonic expression on the part of office towers that shifts rapidly over the years.

Revision Cycles
[RC] §1.05

Backdrop Preservation

[A]
High-rises

[L]
Vancouver, San Francisco,
Hong Kong

Like San Francisco, and like very few other cities, Canada's Vancouver possesses a clearly rendered, holistic image of its future physical development. Both cities share the desire to secure their historical aesthetic qualities for the future in a sensible fashion.

Instead of diagrammatically and actively determining where the highest buildings in the city should stand, Vancouver has adopted the reverse approach of specifying where they are prohibited. Responsible for this approach are its three-dimensional view corridors. These axes slice through urban space, keeping views onto the surrounding *North Shore Mountains* from specific points in the city unimpeded by (high-rise) development [BP]. Thereby objectified and personalized with individual names, there are 27 different "view cones" in place along the *False Creek Shoreline* alone. The public demand for unobstructed views is thereby expressed in positive and spatial terms rather than being regulatively restricted. Determining private space indirectly and hence in an inverted fashion, the city actively defines in the first place its originary public space. A spatial figure-ground relationship in a quasi-equilibrium emerges. A public airspace that is shaped in this way creates citywide continuity of a kind that a low-lying gridded street space would be incapable of achieving. In a fully asynchronous way, the view cones are thereby free to behave in relation to block and street structures in a way that generates new spatial relationships. From the perspective of such an approach, which encompasses entire blocks and urban districts, instruments such as a maximum floor area ratio or general height limits in specific zones, for example, are too shortsighted, and too bound up with only local conditions and their specific locations.

Backdrop Preservation
[BP] §2.08

Surrounded on several sides by water, both San Francisco and Vancouver have realized that the maximum allowable heights of buildings must be lowered in proportion to proximity to the water [TDS]. On the one hand, this gradation produces a visually spectacular mountain range character in the skyline, at the same time maintaining exquisite views of the development lying behind it and set against bayside waters. Initially this ap-

**Taper Down to
Shoreline**
[TDS] § 3.02

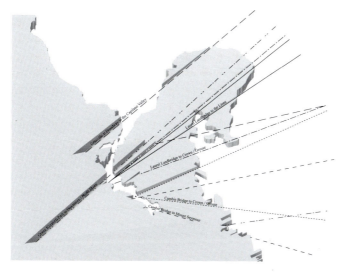

46a False Creek view cones towards the North Shore Mountains, Vancouver.

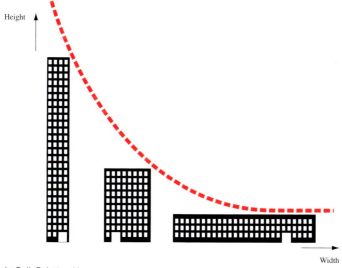

46b *Height Bulk Relation*, Vancouver.

proach seemed plausible, although the degree of practical compliance with this rule does not always enlarge the horizon. That which developers cannot build vertically, they often build horizontally. In San Francisco today, the Fontana Towers of 1965 block views of the Bay, not because they are too tall, but instead for the opposite reason: here, we have a pair of massive, elongated buildings set alongside one another, squashed flat by the height limits in effect along the waterside. One or two tall, slender towers would not have drawn such a thick curtain across the view. In the absence of still higher buildings set behind them and rising out of their shadows, or at least a correspondingly steep topography looming up in

47 The Fontana Towers crouch down, with the effect of blocking views even more, San Francisco.

the background, the rule makes little sense.

A sectional view of Vancouver's skyline shows clearly how building heights ascend as one moves away from the waterside [TDS]. This not only has a positive impact on the views available from the inner downtown toward the water, but also takes advantage of the external appearance of the downtown as a whole, for example in the form of photographs shot from Stanley Park.

Taper Down to Shoreline
[TDS] § 3.02

This kind of urban vanity is not a rarity. The way in which it can become a regulatory obsession is exemplified by a view of Hong Kong—specifically the view from Kowloon's cultural center *Tsim Sha Tsui* across the water of *Victoria Harbor* in the direction of *Hong Kong Island*—a view of the skyline, and in particular of the ridgeline [RLP]. For some time now, the city has been especially concerned with the latter. Increasingly, a progressively heightened skyline blocks the green slopes, including Victoria Peak, that are visible from Kowloon.

Ridge Line Protection
[RLP] § 2.06

Should Hong Kong Island block this background backdrop with buildings, it would suddenly cease to be a city featuring a breathtaking skyline set at the feet of mountains, and would run the risk of sacrificing its topographic specialty, this panoramic tourist destination. The *Urban Design Guidelines*[33] of Hong Kong's Planning Department deal with this theme as follows:

"Hong Kong Island has a magnificent natural setting with the spectacular Victoria Peak overlooking Victoria Harbour and Kowloon Peninsula. Developments on the north shore of Hong Kong Island should respect

[33] The City of Hong Kong (2005), *Guidelines on Specific Major Urban Design Issues—Heritage and View Corridors.*

48a The visual importance of Hong Kong's ridgeline.

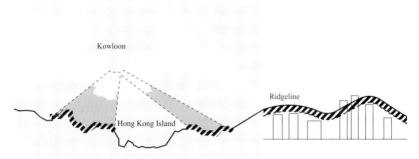

48b View corridors across Victoria Harbor to protect a 20% offset of the ridgeline.

the dominance of Victoria Peak and other ridgelines / peaks when viewing from Kowloon side, in particular from the proposed West Kowloon Cultural District; Cultural Complex, Tsim Sha Tsui; and the proposed promenade at South East Kowloon Development. Uncontrolled building height for developments within the view corridors which may breach the building free zone should be avoided. Other suitable vantage points in a more local context could also be considered on a case-by-case basis.

"The fascinating juxtaposition of the mountains, sky and sea combines to form ever lasting images. Being one of the five most beautiful harbor cities in the world: Sydney, Vancouver, San Francisco, Rio de Janeiro and Hong Kong, panoramic view from Victoria Peak to Victoria Harbour should be preserved. Protecting views to Victoria Peak and the ridgelines from the waterfronts help protect the opposite view from Victoria Peak and other ridgeline areas towards the harbor and the city."

Here is a city fully aware of its own magnificence!

The practical approach to enforcing these objectives can be read in the *Executive Summary—Urban Design Guidelines for Hong Kong*[34] of November 2002. Seven vantage points are determined which allow magnificent views of Hong Kong from all sides—from the Peak down to the harborside and vice versa. From these vantage points, view cones pass in the di-

[34] The City of Hong Kong (2002), *Urban Design Guidelines for Hong Kong—Preservation of Views to Ridgelines/Peaks—Executive Summary.*

rection of the protected ridgeline, including a 20% offset, leaving an adequately large green surface (or "Building Free Zone") of the slope visibly undeveloped. In a way that resembles a well-executed group photograph, the rising sightlines from the harborside automatically guarantee that buildings along the water's edge will not be large enough to stand in front of the towers behind them (nor to block views of the water from the latter). This rule does not exclude the "punctuation" of the ridgeline at appropriate points by buildings—which must however be characterized by "exceptionally good architectural" standards.

The building which in 2002 came to interrupt such a protected sightline, its entire bulk, moreover, standing directly on the waterside, is the *IFC One Tower* (International Finance Center), which looms above everything else. And in the very same year when the guidelines—intended to prevent more such "dragon killers"—were adopted. In keeping with the myth of a recumbent landscape dragon, many residents regard the *IFC Tower* as stabbing through its green spine. Often perceived as visually destabilizing the skyline, it had been approved for construction already in 1996.

Perfect Hideout

[A]
St. Paul's Cathedral

[L]
London

London View
Management
[LVM] § 2.10

In Great Britain's capital city of London as well, the authorities do less to guide high-rise construction than to "manage" views of it [LVM]. For this city, visually unattractive buildings are no scandal as long as they are well concealed. In this context, Christopher Wren's *St. Paul's Cathedral* assumes a key role: London's narrow, winding streets afford hardly any views of St. Paul's in its monumental totality. Small wonder, then, that in most images of the cupola (whether in oils, on celluloid, or stored digitally), we see the building from a remote southwestern perspective set on the opposite bank of the Thames River. Paintings by Antonio Canaletto, John O'Connor, and countless tourist photos confirm this.

The entire city of London is affected by this prioritization of distant views: in the mid-1970s, an office tower was planned for *Broadgate*, right in the vicinity of Liverpool Street Station—and hence more than a mile from St. Paul's. This building would have intruded into views of St. Paul's from the lookout point set on *Henry VIII's Mound* in Richmond Park, 10 miles away. Given the circumstances, the tower was refused a building permit, and was in the end tipped over onto its side to become a long, flat building: now it could be built.

In 1991, a series of additional studies led to the definition of a dozen strategic views worthy of protection, eight of which included St. Paul's, as well as the *Palace of Westminster*, and the Tower of London. Within these imaginary view corridors, no tall building could enter into competition with the silhouette of either of these national monuments. Airspace would be kept free of any visual pollution.

A number of additional studies on this theme were prepared in subsequent years. But much uncertainty remained concerning just exactly how the *London Plan* was to be implemented with regard to the safeguarding of important view axes. That views from specified locations onto Wren's Cathedral would be unimpeded seemed practicable. But how did things stand with the background? Did St. Paul's cupola neces-

49 View towards St. Paul's from King Henry VIII's Mound in Richmond Park.

sarily require a background of undisturbed sky, or might it perhaps not tolerate a pair of "background singers" in the form of exceptionally good-looking and closely positioned high-rises? Might even less successful buildings have a chance provided they conceal themselves discreetly in the shadows behind the cupola? At a certain distance from St. Paul's, towers over a hundred meters in height would be permitted to stand—wholly undetected by any tourist camera. But what happens when a tourist shoots his photos from a position slightly to the left or to the right of London's "Kodak Points?"[35] In that case, you can reckon with having your picture ruined by an intrusive aerial or a shiny expanse of façade. A botched photograph of a normally decontextualized historic monument, or office space worth millions, whose sheer size could provide a new context for St. Paul's monumentality: difficult to weigh the one against the other—and certainly not when "as-of-right"[36] within an intrinsically tasteless building ordinance!

Villains and Victims
That which transpired in London in terms of succession or juxtaposition, happened in New York via superposition. This can be best illus-

[A]
Breuer and Grand Central Station

[L]
New York City

[35] Freely adopted from Disneyworld.
[36] As-of-right development does not mandate review by community boards, the City Planning Commission or City Council. No public hearings are required.

137

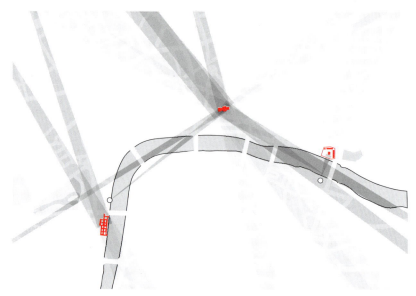

50 Views on London's key monuments—Palace of Westminster, St. Paul's Cathedral and Tower of London.

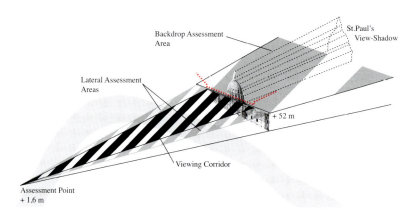

51 Management of protected vistas by geometric definition.

Assessment Point 4A.1

Camera Location
At orientation board
National Grid Reference
527658 183891, height
66.50m AOD [RPG3a]
Height of camera 1.60m
Date of photograph
18/03/2005 15:46:51

Assessment Point 7A.1

Camera Location
Outside information centre
National Grid Reference
533666 180313, height
15.10m AOD [Estimated]
Height of camera 1.60m

Date and time of photograph
16/09/2004 09:43

Assessment Point 8A.1

Camera Location
Southwestern end of bridge,
over river edge
National Grid Reference
532769 180395, height
14.60m AOD [Estimated]
Height of camera 1.60m

Date and time of photograph
06/07/2004 11:00

Assessment Point 10A.2

Camera Location
Axial to St Pauls (GA 8)
National Grid Reference
532111 180549, height 6.60m
AOD [Estimated]
Height of camera 1.60m

Date and time of photograph
02/09/2004 12:43

52a Exact photographic assessment at a height of 1.6m above street level.

52b Hiding behind St. Paul's Cathedral, London.

trated on the basis of an exceptional case. It is the story of a former
rogue, one who in the end became a pitiful victim. Indirectly, this incident once again concerns external appearance. And all of this only because time had passed.

The rogue's name is Marcel Breuer. And everything began with *Grand
Central Station*—or more precisely, above it.

Grand Central Station: its actual greatness resides in its superficial
smallness. In contrast to *Pennsylvania Station*, its far more modest above-
ground dimensions have kept it alive until the present. "If Penn Station
was built mainly to send a message about the splendor of arrival, then
Grand Central was conceived to make clear the choreography of connection."[37] Pennsylvania Station was demolished in 1965, while Grand Central Terminal has to date survived all such air battles unscathed. A direct
and rule-related relationship exists between the two stations: it was
Penn Station's sacrifice that led to the formation of the *New York City
Landmarks Preservation Commission*, which was responsible for the decision to safeguard Grand Central Terminal 18 years later.

[37] Paul Goldberger (1998), *The Skyline, Now Arriving*, 92.

53 Grand potential in Midtown Manhattan.

"Very few parcels of land in our largest cities... have had as many as three different structures on them in the last hundred years." For reasons of economic pressure, that which Richard Nelson characterized in 1955 as the "rule of three"[38] would also be valid for Grand Central [ROT]. Standing first on the parcel on 42nd Street was the *Grand Central Depot* of 1871. This building was replaced in 1913 by the Grand Central Terminal, designed by architects Reed & Stem and Warren & Wetmore. Already in 1910, one could read in the *New York Times* about the foresighted construction plans of the railroad:

"The station, when finished a few years hence, will rise 150 feet above the Level of Forty-second Street. But the railroad company is missing no opportunities. It realizes the future value of the air space above this building. In order to utilize this air space when the time is ripe, the columns and beams which are being put in the station now in course of construction are of sufficient strength to carry an additional structure which will tower twenty-two stories above the roof of the new station."[39]

It was in this newspaper article that the first drawings of this phantom tower were illustrated.

Very soon after the completion of the 45 m tall terminal building, clearly, the time quickly became ripe for additional stories. Yet neither Reed & Stem nor Warren & Wetmore would build this tower. In 1954, William Zeckendorf proposed replacing Grand Central with a building 80 stories tall and containing 4.8 million sqft (450,000 sqm)—a tower that would claim the title of world's tallest building. Also unrealized was I.M.Pei's wasp-waisted glass cylinder. In 1955, after the failure of Erwin S. Wolfson's initial plan for a tower in place of the six-story office building on the north side, a reworked design was granted a permit, and in 1963, the *Pan Am Building* (known today as the *MetLife Building*) went up. Of course, this did nothing to fill in the potential airspace above Grand Central.

In 1968, it was the turn of architect Marcel Breuer. The financially stricken *Penn Central Railroad Company* commissioned him to convert this profit-devouring train station into a real estate gold mine. Breuer, a self-declared modernist, designed a slender tower in accordance with the then up-to-date design maxims of the *Seagram Building*. Its glazed metallic 52-story structure complied with the relevant zoning ordinances, and attempted by means of a shadow gap to maintain a respectful distance from the Beaux Arts hulk set below it—even though Breuer's desire for renewal meant a preference on his part for total demolition.

For the *Landmarks Preservation Commission*, on the other hand, this "shoehorning" [SH] of the terminal through Breuer's commercial modernist addition came close to demolition—it would reduce the old building to a ludicrous status, distorting it to the point of unrecognizability.

At the time, the problem was not necessarily the contrast between modern glass and venerable stone, but instead the fact that the new building was to have sat *on top of* the old one.

In the event, the complaint on the part of Penn Central that the refusal of

---

[38] Richard Nelson in 1955 in the *Appraisal Journal*, quoted by Costonis (1989), 107.
[39] The New York Times Editorial (1910), *First Detailed Official Plans of the New York Central's Improvements.*

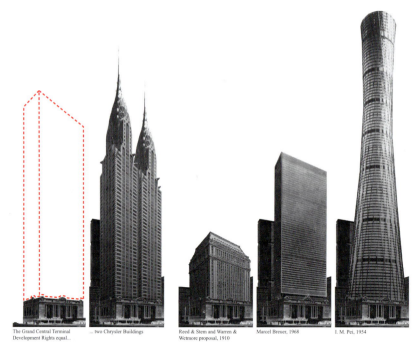

The Grand Central Terminal Development Rights equal... ... two Chrysler Buildings Reed & Stem and Warren & Wetmore proposal, 1910 Marcel Breuer, 1968 I. M. Pei, 1954

54 Variation within stability: the air above Grand Central Terminal in Midtown Manhattan.

a building permit would amount to an unconstitutional "taking" was not accepted by the Supreme Court in 1978. According to the court, a city most certainly has the right to protect its most culturally and historically valuable buildings—even in cases where the lands lying beneath them could be exploited more profitably by their owners.

In 1978, this verdict made little Grand Central Station—which makes a dwarf-like impression in its surroundings—a figurehead of the American resistance on the part of inefficient older buildings. The greatest luxury of Grand Central remains the invisible phantom tower rising above it—perhaps putting in an appearance as a steel and glass fata morgana designed to tempt ambitious developers and the owners of the terminal building.

Beginning in the 1980s, it was Marcel Breuer himself who was threatened with being saddled with an upper addition. His *Whitney Museum* was exploring options for expansion—and where else if not above the present building! The "new brutalist" museum was to have been expanded by Michael Graves' postmodern extension. Suddenly, the roles were reversed: in this affair, Breuer—the former villain—was cast as a hero, simply because his building was now threatened by the same fate he had threatened to inflict on Grand Central, that of being outstripped by an obviously foreign presence.[40]

New York's shoehorning is a not uncommon method for rendering lucrative parcels already occupied by protected landmark buildings. The precondition for this approach is that the present building does not occupy the legal maximum of airspace, and that this potential volume has not yet been sold to a neighbor. Instead of filling in this potential con-

[40] Costonis (1989), 109.

struction volume, the owner of the underutilized parcel has the option of selling the rights to do so permanently to a neighbor, where it will be materialized [TDR]. At that time, this option was not available to Grand Central Terminal; there existed no demand by neighboring buildings for unused air rights, that is to say, neighboring parcels were already fully utilized, making such a purchase pointless. Only later, when the *Grand Central Subdistrict* was extended, could its rights travel further away.

In general, these rules were intended to prevent collisions between profit and preservation, at the very least attenuating them, and in the best cases preventing them altogether.

In cases where no such deals were possible, and where the Landmarks Preservation Commission was able to give its assent without compromising its duties, or was in a position to protect the older building only through the addition of a compromising annex, we find incidences of the vertical assemblage. This was the case with the *Villard Houses* located at 455 Madison Avenue. Since 1980, they have carried a backpack of steel and glass, just as the *Hearst Magazine Building* on Eighth Avenue has been saddled with a Norman Foster since 2006.

The mechanisms of these vertical displacements or annexations, of course, also take place in the horizontal dimension. And the results of such constructive processes are strikingly conspicuous only in rare cases. Which is precisely why they take place: for New York's land speculators and developers, the assembly of numerous smaller parcels into a single large one is more profitable by a wide margin than the sum of the individual parts [LA].

As a tall building located at 40 Wall Street (one that in 1930 was involved for a period of many weeks in a bitter competition with the Chrysler Building for the status of world's tallest building), the *Bank of Manhattan Company Building* (as it came to be known) required a correspondingly large parcel. In principle, a commensurate surface was available. Unfortunately, it was divided among seven different parcels with various owners. In 1930, *Fortune Magazine* described in exemplary and striking terms the process by which a broker, concealed by means of the names of various corporations, gradually assembled the parcels into one:

"The property is attacked from the principal front, and the lots facing the street—say Wall Street—are first secured. Then the secondary lots are taken. And by the time the gentlemen in possession of the rear lots have begun to suspect that their properties have key value to a great scheme, they find themselves cut off from the sun and with only one possible profitable movement—backwards and out."[41]

Once this process has been completed, spectacular architectural drawings are prepared envisioning the site's potential development, and a purchaser is quickly found.

Transfer of Development Rights
[TDR] § 5.14

Lot Assembly
[LA] § 6.07

---

[41] Fortune Magazine (1930), *Skyscrapers: Pyramids in Steel and Stock*, 60–61, 73–75. Quoted by Willis (1995), 161.

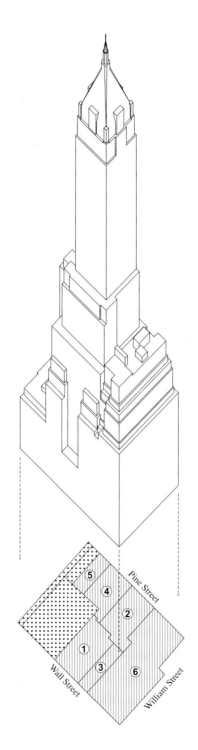

55 *Lot Assembly* from the inside out at 40 Wall Street for the Bank of Manhattan Company Building (numbers indicate the order of assembly).

5

Connected Isolation
—Neighborhood

A history of the city can be understood as the persistent problematic of close proximity between *neighbors* [NH]. [1] The myopic examination of direct and indirect relationships of proximity suffices to characterize an urban texture. What is exclusively decisive is the intensity of such proximity. A special relation of proximity, one generated for example by a high degree of density, always means an increasing degree of constraints for the parties involved. In general, when direct neighbors are present, individual freedoms are constricted—and this is true whether we are dealing with a Midtown Manhattan high-rise that casts shadows onto its neighbors or generates excessive traffic, or with the nuisance of loud music in a Berlin apartment block, or instead with the height of the hedges surrounding a neighbor's property in a residential zone. The kind and scale of the neighboring units are secondary. Their mutual relationship is always of the same kind. Individual interests collide with those prevailing in the adjacent context—even to the point of becoming unbearable. Seldom have such unbearable conditions been so manifest and dramatically crystallized as in the trivial design-guidelines for hedges between adjacent parcels in an American suburb.

Neighbor
[NH] § 5.01

[1] The term "neighbor" as used here contains no implication of "neighborhood," but instead refers literally to a direct relationship between two or more adjacent structures.

56 H. Ferriss' envelope crystallization.

5.1 Prologue: Loss of Autonomy—A Neighborhood Paradigm

"But with continually increasing dimensions, it became apparent that the large structure could no longer be regarded as an isolated instance; it was definitely affecting adjoining buildings, the neighborhood and even the city as a whole. It became increasingly evident that the large project was a concern not only of an individual, but of the community and that some form of restriction must be adopted [PC]."[2]

Proximity Coercion
[PC] § 1.07

In his *Metropolis of Tomorrow* of 1929, Hugh Ferriss describes the evolution of the setback building in New York, and the introduction of zoning laws associated with it (in 1916). In fact, it furnishes a general prologue to urban density: first, scale generates boundaries, and hence a neighboring public domain—individual autonomy is reduced in proportion to growing size. Secondly, universal rules are reactions to an exaggeration that has become evident; they are designed to reduce the excessive influence of neighboring properties. Third, the quantities are decisive when it comes to mutual influence. Fourth, reciprocal influences generate new dependencies, and hence new rules. Fifth, freedom of movement to begin with is limited by direct neighbors—administrative instruments are merely formal derivations thereof.

Myopic Neighborhoods

[A]
Hedges

[L]
Santa Monica

"Fences, walls, or hedges shall not exceed eight feet (2.4 m) in height when located in a required side yard or rear yard. Fences, walls or hedges shall not exceed forty-two inches (1 m) in height when located in a required front yard."[3]

Hedge Height
[HH] § 5.13

A site hedge has three sides, or three evaluative criteria [HH]: the owner plants a hedge in order to gain protection from undesired gazes onto his property, or to block views from it onto unattractive surroundings. In most cases, as far as the owner is concerned, a hedge cannot be dense or high enough—the height limit has been reached when the hedge casts an excessive amount of shadow. For the most part, a hedge is adapted in its dimensions and proportions to the size of the property it surrounds. Important for the owner, finally, are ecological or natural-aesthetic desiderata. Green areas should never be truncated!

---

2   Ferriss (1929).
3   The City of Santa Monica (2007), *Planning and Zoning—Fence, Wall, Hedge, Flagpole.*

(4) – – – – – – – – – Owner's Desired Height

(3) – – – – – – – – – Ideal Plant Growth

(2) – – – – – – – – Height Prescribed By Municipality

(1) – – – – – – Neighbor's Desired Height

57 The hedge and its four ideal heights.

At the same time, however, the hedge adjoins a neighbor's property. And it affects that property in all of the ways listed above, with one decisive difference: lacking the requisite property rights, a neighbor cannot control or actively shape the hedge's growth. The resultant visual shield may not only be undesirable, it may even block all views into the distance; due to its disadvantageous orientation, a hedge's shadow may darken an entire neighboring property, or it may be taller than that property is wide. Depending upon which side of the hedge the evaluator happens to occupy, evaluations of one and the same hedge can be diametrically opposed. Then too, there is the perspective of the public—the view from the street, as represented by the responsible authorities. In most cases, the community has a responsibility to shape the character of private gardens within a residential district. While individual residents may wish to close themselves off by means of hedges, the community may pursue the ideal of a light and air flooded quarter featuring open view axes, maximum opportunities for "street and neighborhood watches,"[4] and good visibility at intersections. And finally, there is the perspective of the natural rate of growth peculiar to the hedge itself.

In this way, a simple hedge quickly comes to possess four virtual and ideal dimensions. If these depart markedly from one another, conflict is inevitable, and a hierarchization of heights becomes necessary.

The law is the law! The more controversial the opposed claims being issued, the more horizontal neighborly relationships are supplemented or even supplanted by vertical, administrative steering instruments. Decentralized control is taken over by a central authority. If maximum and codified heights are in force, one need no longer come to an agreement with neighbors. Control sacrifices its "self" and neighborly relations become hygienic, that is to say, continuity vanishes while the context acquires a kind of care-free status.

5.2 Immaterial Intruder—The Right to Light

The Dark Side

[A]
Shadow and Daylight

[L]
New York City

Shadows move. And in the worst cases, they shift in the course of the day onto a neighbor's property, interfering with its enjoyment. The longer such shadows linger there, the more they restrict such enjoyment, elevating the probability of annoyance on the part of the neighbor. Foreign shadows are regarded as an attack on one's private property. Once again, contextual independence has been eliminated!

The natural relationship between building dimensions and cast shadows represents a strong connection between constructive volume and the two-dimensional layout of a parcel. With increasing volume and height, a building necessarily loses its innocence, and becomes an offender—even where the orthogonal grid promises perpetual independence and virginity. The New York of the early 20th century is only one example among many of shadows becoming an explicit subject of public and private contention. Shadows falling on pedestrian routes were attacked just as sharply as the blocking out of sunlight envisioned for the illumination of office and residential surfaces. Once again, we encounter the presumption that natural light and sunshine in particular are indispensable for public health.

Anywhere we look, we find that every conceivable instrument is deployed in order to minimize the disturbance caused by a neighbor's shadows.

---

4   Jane Jacobs mentioned the term "eyes on the streets," referring to a type of self-evident do-it-yourself surveillance on the part of residents for the prevention of acts of violence on streets. See also Jacobs (1961), *The Use of Sidewalks: Safety*, 29–54.

But not all shadows are equal! One and the same quantum of shadow can be disadvantageous to differing degrees depending upon location. As a rule, residential utilizations and private gardens can suffer less shadow than office or service areas. This evaluative distinction was heightened by the introduction in the mid-20th century of uniform artificial ceiling illumination for offices.

Beginning with the setting of unimaginative minimum distances, going on to setbacks, and continuing all the way to New York's *Sky Plane* [SEP] principle, attempts to rein in the generally dark, unwelcome guests entering from nearby properties can be divided into two categories: the first type directly addresses the origin of light deprivation, that is to say, the dimensions, height, and distances of the structures causing it (as a rule, with consideration given to utilization) are fixed absolutely. The second type of steering instrument addresses the impact itself, i.e. allows or forbids specified degrees of shadowing under certain conditions, in this way only indirectly conditioning the forms and dimensions of shadow-casting structures. Building forms are not specified in terms of boundary limits, that is to say: there are no height maximums or similar standards. The main concern is to prevent the transgression of a specified degree of light blockage.

Such *performance standards* permit a higher degree of design freedom, since it is the owner who in the best cases chooses the means through which he sets out to achieve the required performance: by means of a setback, that is to say, through the total displacement of the building from the site boundary, or by means of a specially tailored volume, or simply by building a flat structure…

Sky Exposure Plane
[SEP] §7.02–6

Two Hours of Shadow

A rule contained in the *Kantonalen Planungs- und Baugesetz* (cantonal planning and building law) of the city of Zürich is an exemplary instance of performance standards. It compels owners to take neighboring buildings into consideration: *par. §284, line 4* specifies that neighboring buildings may not be substantially inconvenienced, in particular by the shadows cast by high-rises,[5] particularly on residential buildings or those located in residential zones. A "substantial shadow nuisance" is specified as a wintertime light blockage of the buildable surfaces of a neighboring site lasting more than two hours [2H].[6]

An introduction taking the form of a leaflet explains how this magnitude of a two-hour long shadow interval is to be determined and construed in relation to the site.

The rule establishes close neighborly linkages in the form of an obligatory consideration. This rule's superficial utilitarianism is striking, yet at the same time it harbors enormous steering potential through its intimate interconnection of morphology, density, and programme.

[A]
Building Shadows

[L]
London, North America, Zürich

2h Shadow
[2H] § 5.08

[5] [LH] Important in this context is the rule's area of application: it applies exclusively to high-rises, which in Switzerland means buildings taller than 25 m. In London, by comparison, a high-rise is at least 50 m tall, and in Germany, a mere 22 m tall (for example, "Landesbauordnung Nordrheinwestfalen," §2 Abs. 3 Satz 2)
[6] Kanton Zürich (1967), *Anleitung Zur Bestimmung Des Schattenverlaufes Von Hohen Gebäuden, Die 2-Stunden-Schattenkurve.*

Lowest Highrise
[LH] §7.01–2

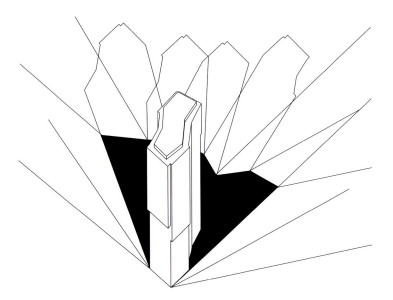

58a The *2-Hour Shadow* of the Swiss Prime Tower's building mass.

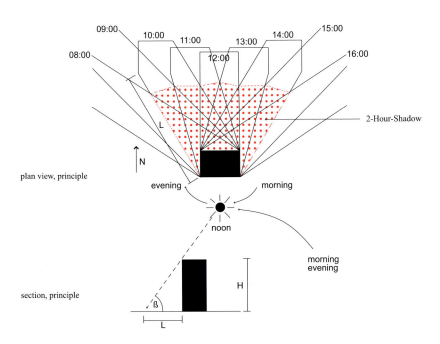

58b Shadow Construction: Draw a field from the intersection of the 8 am shadow and the 10 am shadow to the intersection of the 9 am shadow to the 11 am shadow to the intersection of the 10 am shadow...

Remixed: Zürich's shadow rule applies exclusively to residential buildings, and thereby almost automatically becomes and instrument for mixing uses: In order to achieve a certain level of constructive density while at the same time complying with the rules, housing development is necessarily mixed in with other (less sensitive) programmes including offices, service areas, shops, parking facilities, etc.. A stubborn rule concerning lighting requirements thereby realizes the social dream of mixed-use urban quarters—and even makes these obligatory.

Rephased: granted, this two-hour shadow rule is the sole valid standard, and functions on a trial basis only first, within existing urban quarters having the requisite density, and second as a guiding principle for the development of hitherto undeveloped districts.

In the first case, depending on the existing density of residential utilization, the rule is capable of hindering all new building activity and additional specification.

In the second case, the rule means that whoever arrives first has the license to build as high as and large as he wants. For all subsequent buildings, the degree of consideration required rises, reducing size options correspondingly.

The operational use of such a rule as a phasing instrument in planning comes close to generating a real and quasi unguided temporal development: it is only the contingent sequence of project development that determines the degree of freedom or determination conditioning each. This occurs at the cost of a comprehensive planning perspective, one that would grant all protagonists equal opportunities, no matter how quickly they manage to build. But perhaps this egalitarian claim is also the reason why such utilitarian planning approach continually leads to artificial results. Cities are intrinsically inequitable. And definitely so in the production and hierarchy of their forms.

The rights and freedoms of first comers is manifested in England's *Ancient Lights Doctrine* [ALD]. If an English building has enjoyed uninterrupted sunlight through its windows for a period of 20 years, then the owner has the right to enjoy such undisturbed sunshine in perpetuum[7] —and this holds true even if the sunlight must pass through another property in order to reach his, thereby restricting or altogether blocking its future development.

Ancient Lights Doctrine [ALD] § 5.11

Of course, an owner can enlarge his windows or insert new ones, but in such cases, his right to enjoy permanent and unobstructed sunlight through them comes into effect only after an additional period of 20 years following such modifications.

Things became difficult in British cities like London after the enormous destruction of World War II. New buildings wholly lacked these accumulated rights to light access. Of course, the building sites were still there, but the walls and windows laying claim to unobstructed sunlight,

---

[7] Prescription Act 1832, Section 3: "When the access and use of light to and for any dwelling house, workshop, or other building shall have been actually enjoyed therewith for the full period of twenty years without interruption, the right thereto shall be deemed absolute and indefeasible, any local usage or custom to the contrary notwithstanding, unless it shall appear that the same was enjoyed by some consent or agreement expressly made or given for that purpose by deed or writing."

59 Hints of abandonment—the state of the brick reveals indicates whether the right to light can still be deemed as effective for the respective window: a) broken reveals, with brick infill bonded into the wall, indicate the likely absence of any intention to use the window in the future.
b) straight reveals, and brick infilling panel, suggest the possible intention to reopen the window at some further date.

and hence capable of preventing adjacent development, no longer existed. In the short term, property owners were able to re-secure these rights by registering, while the effective waiting period was now extended from 20 to 27 years.

In this comprehensive form, the English rule never traveled across the Atlantic. Not even in the 1980s, when the Americans could quantify the loss of sunlight objectively in terms of the reduced performance of their solar collectors. In 1980, the *New York Times* reported numerous cases in which the proud owners of solar collectors were unable to take advantage of these devices because a nearby tree had grown too tall, or because a new, multistory apartment building cast an enormous shadow across it. It was in this period that many cities and communities began to consider their options for sensibly administering such *Solar Access* [SC]. Given the experiences of the last oil crisis and the explosive rise of oil prices, such considerations had become unavoidable.

Solar Access [SC] § 5.10

But here too, the sequence of development is essential: already in the early 1980s, a number of North American states introduced solar access rules. New Mexico was among them. At the time, New Mexico guaranteed unrestricted and permanent access to sunshine to anyone with a new solar collector, provided no existing building blocked it already. But this pre-emptive legal move was amenable to misuse, as characterized vividly by David Engel of the US *Department of Housing and Urban Development* (HUD) in the *New York Times* article "Rights-to-light legislation can lead to absurdities". "Imagine: some developer plans a multi-million dollar building and a guy buys a small lot next door, parks his mobile home and puts up a solar collector. You've got a perfect set-up for bribery."[8]

Also cited was Melvin Eisenstadt, a solar power adviser to the state of New Mexico, who mentioned another unintended consequence of the

8   Suzanne Charle (1980), *New Laws Protect Rights to Unblocked Sunshine*.

first-come-first-serve rule: "A while back, we were all holding our breath (...). A developer in Albuquerque wanted to put up a six or seven-story hotel on land abutting a residential section. The residents tried to stop the project, but the zoning commission decided in favor of the developer. Really, all they needed to stop the project was to pass around the hat, get several thousand dollars, and install a solar collector on one of the homes that would be shaded by the hotel."[9]

On the model of New Mexico, residents of Zürich can bring about the downfall of any undesirable high-rise development—and not necessarily by rejecting it via referendum. All they have to do is to find a developer capable of erecting a residential building quickly and directly adjacent to the future high-rise, that is to say, falling somewhere within its true two-hour shadow.

Waldram: The Light Expert, The Right To Light and The Sky Factor

Englishman Percy J. Waldram and his colleagues are experts in the field of natural lighting. They are intensively preoccupied with the illumination of interiors, desk surfaces, and the sidewalks of narrow street canyons. Waldram himself was the inventor of the so-called "Daylight Diagramme," which is a part of New York City's zoning ordinance,[10] among others. The diagram determines whether a given street receives light that is adequate for pedestrians, and whether those indoors receive sufficient light through windows.

[A] Waldram

[L] New York City

Natural light suffers from the disadvantage that it cannot be described and standardized in a similarly explicit way compared with its counterpart, namely shadow. The latter is digital in character: it is either 100% present, or entirely absent. Daylight, on the other hand, shifts gradually according to atmospheric conditions, and so, hence, does its suitability for specific activities. Moreover, the human eye is all too capable of adapting quickly to changing lighting conditions, so that the threshold separating inadequate from adequate lighting conditions is relative.

Now, lighting experts have a problem: the presence of shadow, which is relatively easily quantified, cannot serve as the sole standard for evaluating the daylight situation, for needless to say, rooms and buildings that are not directly in shadow can also be afflicted by daylight problems. In addition, the direct measurement of light incidence is not necessarily informative, since lux measurement alters continually with atmospheric conditions. In order to get around this impractical uncertainty, Waldram considers the available daylight in relation to the portion of unrestricted sky visible through critical windows, a factor that is precisely measurable.[11] The Sky Factor [SF] is the contemporary term for this ratio, and it extends from 100% on the roofs of the building to 0% at the rear portion of a room whose horizon line, visible from the window, has been built up. In this way, scientists and consultants regain precise quantifiability in their evaluations of diffuse daylight.

Sky Factor
[SF] §7.02-15

9 Ibid.
10 The City of New York (2007), Zoning Resolution. Article VIII: Special Purpose Districts.
11 Percy J. Waldram (1909), The Measurement of Illumination; Daylight and Artificial: With Special Reference to Ancient Light Disputes, 131–40.

Sky Factor [SF]

60 Measuring the sky from inside through the window.

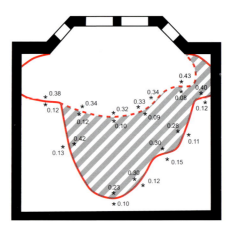

61 Grumble line—before and after a new building is erected in front of the window.

In specially developed diagrams involving the rendering and subtraction of the buildings involved, it is possible to determine the visible area of sky in relation to the maximum visible sky, thereby defining the relevant sky factor. In 1923, after a series of empirical investigations, the now enlightened engineer Waldram proposed a sky factor of 0.2 % as representing adequate lighting "for ordinary purposes, comparable with clerical work."[12] He went on to remark that below the threshold, the point is reached at which "average reasonable persons would consistently grumble."[13] Ever since, this value has been referred to as the "grumble point." Alongside this point exists the so-called "grumble line." This is the imaginary line

[12]   P.J. Waldram and J.M. Waldram (1923), *Window Design and the Measurement and Predetermination of Daylight Illumination*, 96.
[13]   Ibid.

lying along the floor of a room behind which less than 0.2 % of sky is visible, and where a shortage of daylight can lead to grumbling.

In subsequent years, after numerous court decisions Great Britain had permitted the sky factor as a standard for determining adequate illumination, it became a generally recognized method among "rights to light" appraisers.

With the help of the city of New York, Waldram's standard made it across the Atlantic. His diagrams are fixed components of the *New York Zoning Ordinance*, and are familiar well beyond the city's boundaries as the *Daylight Evaluation Chart* [DEC]. "The daylight evaluation chart is a graphic representation of a pedestrian's field of view as he or she looks down a street and sweeps his view 90 degrees to the left or to the right."[14] For Midtown Manhattan, there exist three such charts for streets of varying widths (street widths of 60, 75, and 80 feet are equivalent to those measuring 18m, 23m, and 25m). Measurements are taken from a point of view at the center of the street, at a distance of 250 feet (ca. 76m) from the building under investigation.

Daylight Evaluation Chart [DEC] § 7.02–5

The building in question is now rendered within a matrix of horizontal and vertical sightlines, and thereby shown to cover a certain number of *daylight squares* within the grid of the matrix. The more of these that are covered, the lower the level of light incidence. Critical, however, are the daylight squares above a certain height. Within this matrix, New York has its very own grumble line. Referred to as the *seventy degree line*, this line is drawn from the measuring point at the street center (described above), and follows an angle of 70° through the mass of the building. Its use is justified as follows:

"Research shows that, as an average, 70 degrees is the elevation angle at which buildings in the Special Midtown District are set back from the street line. Most of the daylight below 70 degrees is blocked by such buildings. Slabs, towers or other setback portions of buildings rise to block an average of 25 percent of the available daylight squares above 70 degrees. In building evaluation, the DEC measures the blocked sky above 70 degrees. Below 70 degrees, buildings are given credit for unblocked daylight."[15]

Waldram's empirical investigations correspond in New York to a general average, one that is then used to define a threshold.

The general, statistical average manifests itself through such rules as a general axiom, thereby again legitimating itself.

The Passing Score

Still, this *seventy degree line* does not constitute an absolute point for the height of a setback. It simply determines the value of that portion of blocked-out sky within the total accounting and estimation of the degree to which the light is interfered with. But this is calculated only afterwards! Below this line, unblocked daylight squares receive a positive value of 0.3, and above it, a negative value of −1.0.[16]

---

[14] The City of New York (2007), 81–272 *Alternative Height and Setback Regulations—Daylight Evaluation—Features of the Daylight Evaluation Chart.*

[15] Ibid.

[16] The City of New York (2007), 81–274 *Alternative Height and Setback Regulations—Daylight Evaluation—Rules for Determining the Daylight Evaluation Score.*

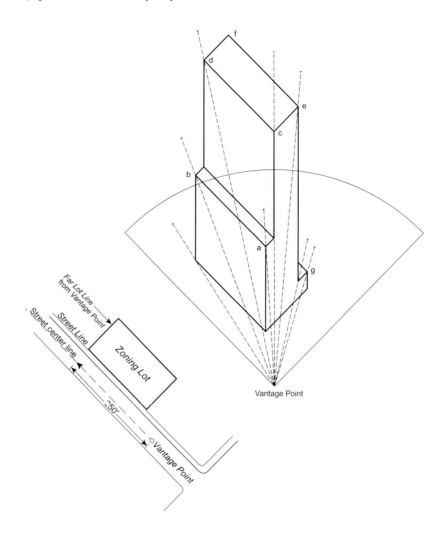

62a Vantage point in the middle of the street.

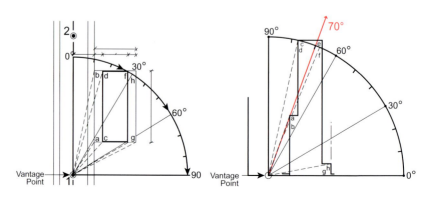

62b Horizontal and vertical angles of view.

Daylight Evaluation Chart [DEC]

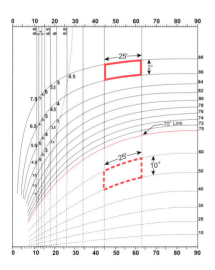

62c Only daylight squares above the 70° line block daylight.

62d1 Vertical and horizontal axes of the daylight evaluation chart (plan view)—with a further subdivision of the daylight squares (above the 70° line).

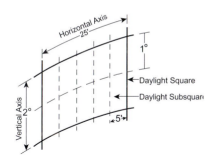

62d2 A further subdivision of the daylight squares (above the 70° line).

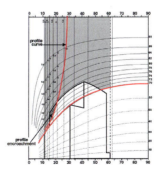

62e The building is rendered into the *Daylight Evaluation Chart*.

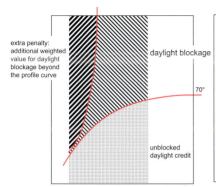

62f In which area are the daylight squares blocked?

62g Example of daylight scores balance (for one vantage point).

Squares above 70° blocked	- 20.5
Squares below 70° open	+ 0.0
Add. Profile encroachment penalty	- 0.45
Total Blockage	**- 20.95**
Available daylight squares	89.9
Remaining daylight	68.95
DAYLIGHT SCORE 68.95 / 89.90 =	**76.70 %**

The ratio between the total number of blocked and unblocked daylight squares, together with their valuation from a variety of viewing points (where more than one street is involved) results in the percentage of available daylight. This rate cannot be less than 75% for the building as a whole, and no less than 66% seen from the individual streets. If these values are slightly low, then the owner has a number of options. One of these is contained in *Section 81-276* of the ordinance: *Modification of Score of Reflectivity*. By choosing a strongly reflective façade material, the owner can ensure that sufficient light is mirrored onto the street canyon, thereby finally creating an urban canyon *as-of-right* building in conformity with the law.

These regulations are relatively new. In 1961, they supplanted the 1916 resolution through which New York set the maximum heights of setbacks in relation to street widths on the basis of *height districts*. At that time, there were three such districts in Manhattan, and depending on location, a building was permitted to rise from the street edge either once, 1 1/2 times, or twice the width of the street [SSR]. [17] Daylight scores of 75% or 66 % correspond to the street illumination required within the 1916 "two times" district.

Setback Street Ratio [SSR] §4.13

But why introduce this procedural complication in 1961?

The reasoning underlying an altered approach is laid out in the 1961 resolution itself: "However, if any one frontage is less than 75 percent, other frontages must be greater than 75 percent to reach the passing overall daylight score. This allows flexibility in building design while maintaining daylight standards within the levels established by buildings built as-of-right under the 1916 and 1961 Zoning Resolution." [18]

Here, New York created a situation with possibilities for variation, and one offering leeway for individual differentiation in a way that goes beyond homogenizing, explicitly and geometrically defined limits, yet without additionally heightening administrative discretion and necessitating the involvement of commissions, thereby generating insecurity and causing planning delays.

In this case, the dilemma between a steering ordering and compulsory, formal aesthetic order affecting buildings and streets seems to have been effortlessly overcome. The relevant passages of the code read like the instructions to a game whose gaming pieces are referred to as "daylight squares," with the building constituting a three-dimensional playing field. Beginning with the 1961 resolution, the New York high-rise begins to negotiate with itself. A little less on one side of the building, a little bit more somewhere else. Perhaps a bit taller, and hence somewhat narrower... absolute form is replaced by an absolute number. *Minimal scores* instead of *minimal setbacks*.

[17]   Willis (1995), 71.
[18]   The City of New York (2007), *81–274 Alternative Height and Setback Regulations—Daylight Evaluation—Rules for Determining the Daylight Evaluation Score*.

Setback Street Ratio [SSR]

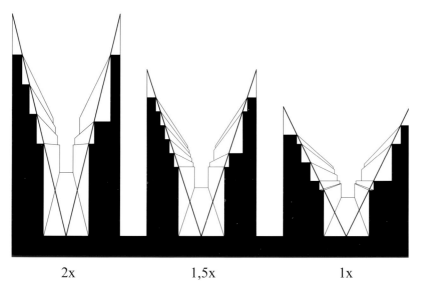

2x   1,5x   1x

63 Street canyons according to *Setback Street Ratio*—height of first setback depending on street width.

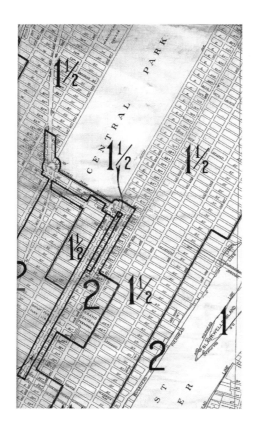

64 *Height District Map* of Midtown Manhattan—specifying the *Setback Street Ratio* (fig.63).

5.3 How Big Is your Neighborhood

Traveling Rights

[A]
Air Rights and Neighbors

[L]
Grand Central Subdistrict,
New York City

Proximity can only really be experienced via reciprocal influence. Running everywhere—along streets, inside of buildings, on façades— are imaginary lines that define zones and are constituted in dependency upon immediate neighbors. This influence is guided by superordinate rules. They specify how far dependencies between neighbors may go, but being defined geographically, are themselves limited in scope. An additional line, an additional zone.

Geographically delimited zones connect specific rights and duties to definite locations. In New York as well, such districting is a much-favored tool of urban regulation. Height, utilization, mutual consideration between neighbors, permitted use, etc., these constitute a packet of rules applying to a specific area. At a specific location, each building has certain expansion rights. In such zones, the neighboring parcel and its development are not only burdened by undesired features such as blocked views or disturbing cast shadows. In many cases, it also has traits coveted by its neighbor: a parcel in Midtown Manhattan that has been developed to the allowable limits gazes with envy and irritation at its neighbor, whose land is far from having been filled in to the maximum permissible degree. The owner of this underutilized parcel has the right to cash in at any time by filling in his unused airspace with office levels. At a certain level of economic pressure, and given high land prices, not a bad idea.

**Transfer of
Development Rights
[TDR] § 5.14**

In New York City (and not only there), underutilized parcels are presented with another option: they can sell the right to fully exploit their remaining airspace to covetous neighbors [TDR]. The potential volume then materializes inside of the neighboring property. Rights of use are now transferred permanently. The question is: what kind of distance can such rights travel? To a directly adjacent property? Across the street? To a distance of two city blocks? And who counts as a "neighbor"?

1992—nearly 15 years after Penn Central's defeat before the Supreme Court, Grand Central Terminal continues to stand, wedged like a dwarf between its tall neighbors in the middle of Midtown Manhattan. The Terminal still has enormous potential.[19] Suspended above it are *air rights* amounting to the volume of two Chrysler Buildings—nearly 200,000 square meters of additional usable space.[20] But where should it go? The owner Penn Central would be delighted to make a lucrative sale of these rights to neighbors of Grand Central, but those in the immediate vicinity do not represent anything like the necessary market for additional construction volume on this scale. By virtue of the effect of zoning limits alone. What to do?

**Special Districts
[SD] §3.01**

Although it has long since ceased to be possible to depart on long trips from this station, Grand Central is attempting to ship its *air rights* to remote destinations. And not just across the street, but to distances of many blocks. In Penn Central's view, an expanded *Grand Central Subdistrict* [SD], one approximately 29 blocks larger than the one proposed by the

---

[19] See fig. 54, p. 142.
[20] David W. Dunlap (1992), *Grand Central Owner Seeks Broader Use of Air Rights*.

Transfer of Development Rights [TDR]

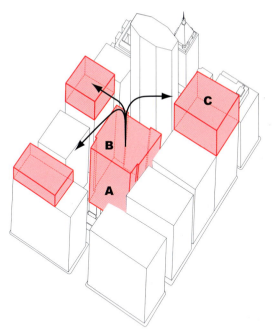

65 Potential transfer of development rights.
The transferable rights (B) of a historic landmark (A) can be transferred to other sites and appear as density bonuses (C) on other buildings.

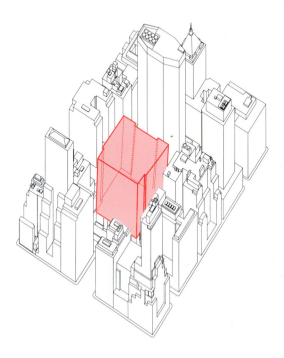

66 Grand Central Terminal's air rights: actually there is no place available within the Terminal's immediate vicinity.

city's planning department, would provide a sufficient travel freedom for its unused *air rights*. The proposal was immediately refused by the planning department: blocked from embarking on a long journey—and at the very same time as the waiting room of the terminal was being elaborately restored!

In the preceding years, it had become increasingly evident that Penn Central would never be able to sell its air rights in the absence of the establishment of a special district within which such rights could be transferred without restriction—even to those not directly adjacent to the terminal building itself. Ultimately, the subdistrict extended from East 41st to 48th and from Madison Avenue to Lexington Avenue.

With the help of the Grand Central air rights, utilization at the center can have a floor area ratio of 21.6, and at the edge of the subdistrict, it was raised from 15 to 16. Fifteen potential locations for densification were identified by the planning department. Stipulated additionally was the provision of "public amenities" in conjunction with each development. By formulating as an objective that the new district would generate improved public space in the vicinity around the terminal building, the planning department was thereby able to save face in relation to the public. This objective deftly concealed its having yielded to pressure from the Penn Central Corporation, which had shown itself, as ever, prepared to do battle: had the firm been denied the right to sell and distribute its air rights freely, then it would use them in order to erect a tower as quickly as possible directly above the terminal building.[21]

And although the *Grand Central Subdistrict* turned out to be smaller than the one envisioned by Penn Central, the results brought about a rather peculiar situation in this artificially enlarged neighborhood: along the outer edge of the Grand Central District, parcels require air rights from the terminal building, thereby heightening their utilization, although no perceptible relationship existed to the contributing building—the one not being visible at all from the other.

With such a rule, the planning authorities found themselves in a genuine dilemma. Originally, this *air rights transfer* had been introduced for the sake of preservationists' requirements: sites occupied by buildings worthy of historic preservation but having lower levels of utilization were to have been relieved of economic pressure in order to safeguard them from profit-oriented redevelopment. Despite such underutilization, owners would now have the option of deriving profit from their properties. Should the resulting development rights be restricted to the immediate vicinity, this would entail the danger that "you cut down the potential market for such rights and can create enormous piggyback monsters too close to the landmarks..."[22] In the process, one simply transports "the pig from one parlor to the other,"[23] in the words of Norman Marcus, at that time counsel to the *New York City Planning Commission*, cited by the *New York Times* in 1979. On the other hand, Marcus pointed out that "the legal nexus of rationality might be lacking"[24] which

[21] Ibid.
[22] John Costonis quoted by Carter B. Horsley (1979), *In the Air over Midtown: Builders' New Arena*.
[23] Norman Marcus quoted in Ibid.

would allow air rights to be transferred across greater distances. In the *New York Times* article he made reference to the possibility which existed at the time for having air rights travel from the *Staten Island Greenbelt* across New York Harbor to Lower Manhattan. "An overly wide radius of transferability risks loss of the planning connection linking and rationalizing the underutilization of the landmark lot with the measure of overbuilding tolerated on the receiving lot."[25]

Perhaps real neighborhoods extend indeed only as far as the reciprocal impact of their buildings' shadows?

Traveling Obligations: UK's Involuntary Do-Gooders

Not only rights embark on journeys, but also obligations. Great Britain's developers often commit themselves to contributing to the quality of urban life by integrating affordable housing units into their projects. Ever controversial is the question of whether such units must necessarily occupy the same site as the main development.

[A]
Thatcher

[L]
Great Britain

In the 1980s, Margaret Thatcher and her government relieved Britain's municipal administrations of their long-standing obligation to provide adequate and affordable housing. The government's *Affordable Housing Programme*[26] was eliminated without replacement. This need was to be regulated now solely by the market itself. And designed to support and sensitize the markets was *Section 106* of the *Town and Country Planning Act of 1990* [106]:

Section 106 Agreements [106] §5.03

"Agreements regulating development or use of land:

"(1) A local planning authority may enter into an agreement with any person interested in land in their area for the purpose of restricting or regulating the development or use of the land, either permanently or during such period as may be prescribed by the agreement.

"(2) Any such agreement may contain such incidental and consequential provisions (including financial ones) as appear to the local planning authority to be necessary or expedient for the purposes of the agreement.[27]"

Such *Section 106* agreements were envisioned as becoming the main instigators of urgently needed affordable housing. In the event that a certain construction project surpassed a given scale or utilization, then such agreements stipulated that it must contain a substantial portion of affordable housing. In the course of heated public debate, proposals ranged from 30 to 50% for all private residential developments planned for the city of London. The then mayor of London Ken Livingstone explicitly advocated the adoption of the higher figure. Given that the cheaper units would have to be integrated directly on site, the mayor hoped for a desirable side effect, namely the growth of mixed and socially balanced residential districts.[28] Nonetheless, there was criticism. In the first place, the consistent integration of the required affordable units into the respective project was not always adhered to. Accompanied by the ra-

---

[24] Norman Marcus quoted in Ibid.
[25] Norman Marcus quoted in Ibid.
[26] A major reason for offering affordable housing is to keep key workers (those in public service: teachers, bus drivers, etc.) in town.
[27] United Kingdom Legislation (1990), *Town and Country Planning Act 1990, Chapter 8: Section 106.*
[28] See Mayor of London (2005), *Housing—the London Plan Supplementary Planning Guidance (SPG),* 59.

tionale that their presence would necessarily involve unacceptable re-
ductions of quality, the cheaper apartments were shifted kilometers
away to distant locations, to stand "off-site," clear at the other end of a
given district. This put an end to talk about the desirability of mixed areas.
Second, developers and landlords were reluctant to assume all costs
while surrendering the benefits of such projects to the public. For the
most part, the additional costs involved in a Section 106 agreement had
to be shouldered by the purchasers of already extremely expensive apartments. The result was an almost paradoxical situation: precisely
through the private production of affordable apartments, the prices of
private residential units now rose, which only widened the gulf separating those able to enter the private real estate market, and those continu-
ously dependent on government support.

6

Codes, Conventions and Maxims: Official and Informal Regimes, Rules of Place in 1960s New York

Official urban regulations collide with informal regimes, economic constraints, rules of the zeitgeist, and local peculiarities. Such local and temporary circumstances lead to adaptations within the official rules of a given city. Such mechanisms are observable when municipal rules are subjected to revisions. For this reason, the New York City of the 1960s is taken up in this chapter as a prominent case study—as the relevant date flips from 1916 to 1961 and the city's zoning resolution was comprehensively revised for the first time.

Anywhere But New York

Edward M. Bassett could lean back and wait and see how his zoning ordinance would begin to alter New York City. In 1916, his Zoning Resolution is adopted—a resounding success for him and for his colleagues on the commission. But he has a problem. Bassett is aware of the great danger faced by the novelty he has introduced: sooner or later will come the day when his new regulations must survive a court challenge. In the absence of parallel regulations in other cities, or at least some precedential case, it will be difficult to argue.

Only one thing can help: the impression of newness must be stripped from the New York ordinance as quickly as possible. Ideally, this must happen everywhere, and not solely in New York itself. Other cities must adopt their own zoning ordinances as quickly as possible. Then, if New York's zoning ordinance should come before the court, its advocates could at least point out that similar zoning laws had met with approval in many other cities throughout the country. [1]

In order to effectively safeguard New York's 1916 resolution, Bassett would have to travel to Chicago, San Francisco, Boston, Los Angeles, etc. If they are to survive in New York, the new zoning laws must be converted into mass commodities.

And that is how Mr. Bassett became the ultimate zoning crusader in US America.

"During the next twenty years I visited every state and all the large cities of the country. (...) On these trips I made talks before boards of trade, legislative bodies, both state and city, assisted in drawing zoning ordinances and state enabling acts for zoning, tried zoning cases, and argued test cases before appellate courts." [2]

Throughout the land, he praised the advantages of zoning. In a speech delivered on 13 November 1922 before the *Chicago Real Estate Board*, he asserts with satisfaction that New York's architects and owners had come to genuinely like and appreciate the new pyramidal forms generated by setback controls. [3] What a revelation: rules govern stylistic taste!

Standards make possible a mass-produced style, one that in turn itself becomes an accepted, regularized standard. In the end, high-rises without setbacks were no longer conceivable—not even for a public that remains wholly unaware of the ordinances and bulk districts that necessitated them. The wedding cake architecture of New York City's towers became a popular bestseller.

In the 1920s, the setback style became the prevailing form of expression for tall buildings, and formal differences between them were marginal. Distinctive traits were restricted to façades—their materiality, fenestration pattern, and ornamentation. Favorite materials included limestone, brick, terracotta, metal, and after changes introduced to the code in 1937, glass as well. Otherwise, there was little to contribute to a building's individuality. "The logic of the setback solution was so strong that few architects made an effort to manipulate the formula." [4]

[1] Toll (1969), 195.
[2] Edward Murray Bassett (1939), *Autobiography of Edward M. Bassett*, 122.
[3] Toll (1969), 196.
[4] Willis (1995), 102.

67 Two uneven twins from East 54th Street.

Two Uneven Twins

Approaching New York's Park Avenue on East 54th Street against the traffic flow, one encounters a pair of buildings standing opposite one another which seem to wholly contradict the above discussion: two high-rises with more or less identical façades, but entirely different in form and volumetry, have faced each other since 1958, when the 1916 ordinance was still in force. On the left, 390 Park Avenue, popularly known as Gordon Bunshaft's *Lever House* of 1952. A pioneer with glass façades, a superstar of architectural books from the start.

And on the right?

Here is the building known simply as "400 Park Avenue"—and nothing else. Not named after a global concern, it sits there blankly, with its shameless green glazing. Built in 1958, it is an instance of pure speculation, the ultimate cash cow, a profit machine. Overbred, it stands on Park Avenue, heavy and greasy. With a bit of luck, a section of its genetically

[A]
Lever and 400 Park Ave

[L]
New York City

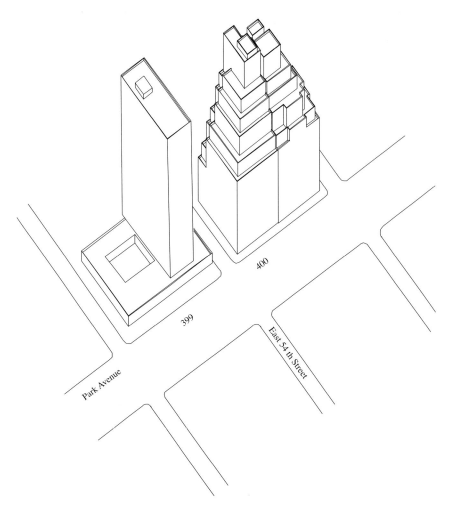

68 Lever House (*1952) and 400 Park Avenue (*1958).

related façade can be found unnoticed in the backgrounds of photographs of its slightly older neighbor taken by tourists with an interest in architecture. 400 Park Avenue appears alongside the Lever House as a portly, anonymous little brother, condemned to the lifelong labor of converting the ground lying beneath it into gold, only to vanish eventually unnoticed. Meanwhile, things are much simpler for the Lever House: it need do nothing more than exist in all of its divine, profligate, and ultimately useless slenderness.

In this regard, 400 Park Avenue has done everything right. It obediently fills out the maximum dimensions allowed by the relevant regulations. Of course, in doing so it fails to correspond to the incipient ideal of beauty of the European high-rise avant-garde, but it does perform its profitable function—not least through the application of modern possibilities of artificial illumination. Only through this technical innovation could buildings such as 400 Park Avenue endure such corporeal distention—only to perish of it in the end.

It was only after World War II that fluorescent lighting, efficient lift sys-

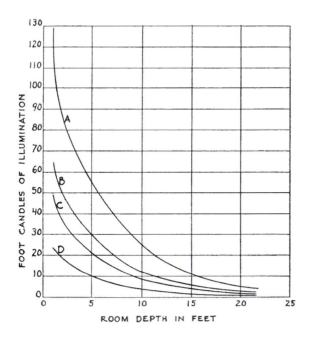

QUALITY OF WINDOW EXPOSURE

A – JUNE DAY-CLEAR.
B – "   "   -CLOUDY.
C – DECEMBER DAY-CLEAR.
D –   "   "   -CLOUDY.

69 *Naturally Lit Office Depth* is dependent on room depth.

tems, and air-conditioning would make possible the full utilization of the laissez-faire 1916 zoning envelopes. Hugh Ferriss' *Metropolis of To-morrow*[5] became materialized reality, and could now dispense with simulated views of the future. The city converted its formerly abstract potential for development into everyday physical reality. Ferriss' "crude clay" became a fine-grained mass for a standardized mold.

Prior to these technical innovations, a tower simply had to become slimmer in order to permit sufficient light to enter [NLD]. The limits of the zoning envelope thereby lay beyond that which was attainable. The 1916 ordinance was based on precisely this division of labor between explicit rules and what it incorrectly regarded as an unrepealable natural law. Technical progress now liberated large office towers from their dependency on nature and location. Ultra-dense, seemingly uncontrollable blocks induced New York's planners to perform calculations whose appalling results were that under such conditions up to 100 million new

Naturally Lit Office Depth
[NLD] §7.02–14

5 Ferriss (1929).

workers could be accommodated within the city.[6]

In this period, a tower nonetheless having slender dimensions indicated nothing about natural or normative constraints, and said much instead about the vanity of its owners.

In the 1950s, floor plates offering leaseholders up to 2300 square meters were no rarity,[7] and without any obligation to offer large window openings or tall ceilings, more of them could be stacked up one above the other. The relatively minimal total heights of such buildings did not exactly endow them with elegant profiles. And only a few buildings took advantage of the additional option offered by the 1916 ordinance allowing a slender tower to then be placed on a bulky base. Still, one quarter of the total parcel surface could rise as high as desired. But the race for maximum heights was a thing of the past. In their 1959 book *Offices in the Sky*, Shultz and Simmons wrote: "Only 20 of the 109 new buildings erected in Manhattan since 1947, are 30 or more stories tall, and of these only five exceed 40 stories."[8]

Almost equal in breadth to height, such anonymous buildings as 100 or 400 Park Avenue nonetheless entered New York City's (building) history as an independent typology. In the 1950s, the *Bulky Block Type* [BBT] was born. By 1952, Robert Curtiss, heading the Management Division of the *Real Estate Board of New York, Inc.*, was able to report that 45 buildings of the block type were finished or under construction in New York City.[9]

Bulky Block Type [BBT] §7.02–16

Forward March!

The inception of the era of the fat meatballs in minimalist international-style façade cladding was marked shortly after the end of World War II by the building at 445 Park Avenue. Completed in 1947, and named the *Universal Building* in honor of its principal tenant, it was the first postwar building—and moreover the first fully climate controlled[10] office building in New York City—characterized by the minimalist aesthetic of the setback style. The 22-story building fills the entire block up to a level of 12 stories before springing back in a series of setbacks. "The design (by the architects Ely Jacques Kahn und Robert Alan Jacobs) combined a traditional sense of tectonic solidity with the liberating dynamism of stressed horizontals and syncopated setbacks."[11] Kahn and Jacobs achieve this through alternating façade bands of limestone and glass, applied to each projecting ceiling. As a result, the building resembles works by Erich Mendelsohn, as well as Mies van der Rohe's *Concrete Office Building Project* of 1922.[12] Given that, in contrast to its predecessors, the external feature is not conditioned by internal structure, expert critics quickly subjected it to the reproach of "impurity."

Its tension, however, probably resides precisely in this schizophrenia.

[6] See *Underdetermination—Overzoning*, p.98.
[7] Shultz (1959), 248.
[8] Ibid., 249.
[9] Ibid.
[10] "These buildings are modern. primarily because they are air conditioned." Lee Thompson Smith, president of the Real Estate Board of New York, 1950. In Willis (1995), 136.
[11] Robert A. M. Stern, Thomas Mellins and David Fishman (1995), *New York 1960: Architecture and Urbanism between the Second World War and the Bicentennial*, 333.
[12] Ibid.

Bulky Block Type [BBT]

70 Universal Pictures Building at 445 Park Avenue (*1947, by Kahn & Jacobs).

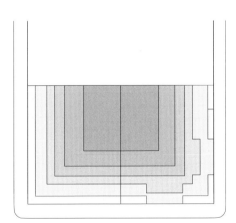

71 400 and 410 Park Avenue with their tree–ring like setbacks depending on the adjacent street width.

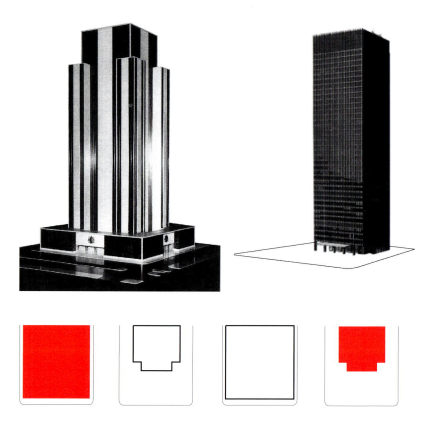

72 Proposed Seagram Building by Pereira & Luckman, 1954. Model. Enormous cigarette lighter or big trophy still following the *Bulky Block Type* paradigm.

Final design by Mies van der Rohe.

On the one hand, 445 Park Avenue strives to give off an aura of elegance and novel dynamism, while on the other, the volumes of this building, with its origins in speculation, are necessarily pressed to the limits of the possible. The fact that this was implemented more or less in the absence of design considerations can be confirmed by examining the point at which the building springs back. Surrounded on three sides by streets of varying widths, the façades on each were subject to differing ordinances concerning the height at which it must spring back and to what extent. These upper limits were now materialized one-to-one—and hence differently on each of the three sides—in the building's total volume.

Kahn and Jacobs designed the façades according to current principles: the volumes emerged directly from the scratching pens of the zoning commission of 1916.

It is no accident that nearly all of the slenderer buildings of this period— still controlled by the authority of the 1916 zoning resolution and predating its revision of 1961—bore the lustrous names of major corporations. Corporate headquarters could afford to be slim. Only their speculatively motivated colleagues were thick and shapeless.

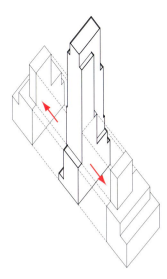

73 The anorexic Daily News Building losing its profitable hips.

In order to safeguard his universal design autonomy, the architect had only one option at that time: it was necessary to depart as far as possible from the maximum allowable upper limits. But this presupposed a client capable of appreciating the value or at least the luxury of voluntarily renouncing the maximum utilization of his property. The Lever brothers and Seagram were among such clients. The luxuriousness of these buildings consists precisely in the space left around them. But even much earlier, buildings had renounced their profitable hips in favor of a more individual and hence more spectacular appearance. New York architect Raymond Hood was involved in two of these. The first was the RCA Building (today the GE Building), the centerfold of Rockefeller Center, dating from 1933; the second was the Daily News Building on 42nd Street built in 1930. Here: "Raymond Hood persuaded him (his client) to erect less office space on the lower floors than zoning would have allowed in order to produce a more dramatic architectural form. Above the ninth floor on the main Forty-second streets façade, the Daily News rose straight up without setbacks (the rear, however stepped up in multiple recessions). The effect of soaring verticality derived both from the lack of recessions and from the bold pattern produced by the piers, which were faced with white glazed brick that altered with dark bands of windows and black and beige spandrels."[13]

But such exceptions could not repress the feeling that with the exception of New York City, elegant, slender high-rises were being erected nearly everywhere.

And the guilty parties were soon identified! On 12 June 1960, Ada Louise Huxtable, the New York Times' future premier architectural critic wrote in a paper: "At present, better design can be achieved only through this kind of financial sacrifice. Lever House, the Seagram, the Pepsi-Cola

[13] Willis (1995), 102.

Building and the new Union Carbide headquarters—all prestige structures on Park Avenue—are exceptional examples in which rentable space has been given up voluntarily by building less than the law allows. More distinguished architectural forms, sun-filled plazas and spacious settings are some of the desirable effects achieved by this deliberate flouting of urban economics."[14]

Ms. Huxtable was not criticizing economic booms and pressures, but instead New York's current zoning ordinance, based structurally for the most part on the ordinance of 1916. Actually, she was not even criticizing that, but instead precisely the obverse of such deterministic rules, namely the freedom ceded to New York's property owners and developers in the badly-formulated envelope of the 1916 ordinance. She called for an ordinance as a one-size-fits-all designer suit labeled MIES and SOM. Not too little, but instead too much freedom was the substance of her critique. In the same article, Victor Gruen formulated this reproach more explicitly: "The developers and architects of the big buildings are only victims of circumstance. The real fault lies in the fact that this largest city in the nation still has no master plan, that we permit hit-or-miss construction, that we are not concerned with the separation of various types of traffic, that legislation offers no encouragement to good developers, but on the contrary, encourages fullest speculative exploitation of the land."[15]

New York would soon receive its master plan, and in a different and more vehement form than Gruen the master planner could possibly have envisioned.

A Numbers' Flip: 1916 and 1961

In the late 1950s, Ada Lousie Huxtable was infatuated with Mies van der Rohe, and waxed ecstatic: "There is cleanness, lightness, serenity and sense in the new buildings. There is elegance, and even opulence, in the use of rare marbles, rich bronzes and exotic woods in combination with steel and concrete, with fine silks, soft carpets and warm colors in luxurious interiors. Even the glass walls, still so coldly offensive to many, provide a desirable lightness and brilliance in their transparency, color and capacity for reflection. (...) The new buildings can lighten the city's canyon-streets physically and psychologically."[16]

Many agreed with this stirring hymn, and in the end so did New York's planning commission. In 1961, it submitted the 1916 ordinance to far-reaching revisions. The image of a sedate, freestanding tower à la the Seagram Building became the accepted and legally binding maxim and ideal of the new ordinance.

Let us recall again what Edward Bassett had said in 1922: "In New York architects and owners now liked the pyramidal shapes emerging from the setback controls."[17]

Emerging from the "Rules Rule Style" of that period were the "Style Rules Rules" of 1961.

[14] Ada Louise Huxtable (1960), *Towering Question: The Skyscraper*.
[15] Ibid.
[16] Ibid.
[17] See also *Anywhere but in New York* (p.166), quote by E. M. Bassett in Toll (1969), 196.

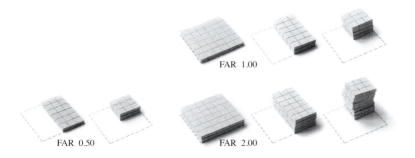

FAR 1.00

FAR 0.50

FAR 2.00

74 Calculation of the *Floor Area Ratio* (FAR).

Group pressure had legitimated and manifested itself in a completely opposed way in the years between 1916 and 1961. In 1961, it became a codified reality, as New York arrived at modernism: A complete inversion of the perception of open space took place. "The old ordinance, with its solid roots in the traditional space making of streets and avenues bounded by walls of buildings that filled up city blocks to near solidity, was abandoned. The new regulations encouraged unmodulated, independently spaced skyscraper tower slabs rising from generously scaled plazas—an "open" city, a city that was space positive rather than mass positive, a city that, were it to be rebuilt completely along the lines of the new code, would become one with the continuous open space of the essential ruralism of the Megalopolis."[18]

This demonstrative departure from the street as dominant element was clearly expressed in the elimination of the direct coupling between setback size and street width [SSR].

Setback Street Ratio
[SSR] §4.13

New Currency: From Form to Number

Density received a name, and urban planning its own universal currency, known as the *Floor Area Ratio* or simply FAR for short [FAR].[19] Mocked by Robert Moses in the *New York Times* as an "alphabetical slogan,"[20] rendered manageable by the New York consulting firm Voorhees, Walker, Smith & Smith, and representing a link between site area and the total floor area of all stories, it constitutes probably the greatest innovation in 20th-century US-American urban planning. At a stroke, utilization became quantifiable, and hence comparable. It was only via this ratio that urban planning became a global event. Finally, the abstract unit of money received a comparably abstract urban counterpart. The effect of this abstract relation, in any event, is anything else but abstract. Sud-

Floor Area Ratio
[FAR] §7.01–1

[18]   Stern (1995), 9–10.
[19]   Also Floor Space Index (FSI). In Germany, this ratio is referred to as the "Geschossflächen-zahl." (GFZ).
[20]   The New York Times Editorial (1960), *Mayor Criticizes Moses on Zoning—Makes Light of Attack on Floor Area Ratio Plan to Prevent Overbuilding.*

denly, Chicago's density could be compared directly with that of New York or Berlin. Now, a marketable resource existed. Urban density was not only comparable to the direct context, but to the entire world.

At the expense of urban continuity: the relevant unit of measure is no longer the neighboring buildings nor the urban context, but instead only the individual parcel itself. In the end, only the dimensions determine the building's height and the number of square meters contained in its interior.

The perspectives of clients and developers were narrowed. This was something embodied explicitly in the Seagram paradigm in relation to the city: each building in its individual pool. And as such, a completely self-referential and anti-urban relation. But such self-referentiality involved certain advantages: "The formula restricts the number of square feet of floor space in buildings for each 100 feet of lot areas and allows, the Planning Commission contends, greater freedom of design."[21]

It is easily understandable that this ratio is not in and of itself, and no matter how high it is set, in a position to automatically generate either a Seagram Building or a 400 Park Avenue tower. In contrast to a formally defined setback envelope as the relevant upper limit, a simple number can never do so—and this necessitates its combination with other rules and constraints.

Over the Top

Beginning in 1961, codified upper limits could be transgressed legally. But not without some sort of compensatory performance. If the previous formal volumetric specifications were still absolute upper limits, then the floor area ratio was reduced to a reference standard. A maximum value of 15 repetitions in height of the parcel surface is no longer a maximum value at all, but instead an initial bid on the part of the city in negotiating urban form with private owners. The latter were by all means able to surpass a FAR of 15, but in that event were obliged to offer the city something in return. In a location like the Manhattan of the 1950s, shortages of public amenities were not difficult to identify. Almost throughout, there was an absence of high-quality public (open) space

Plaza Bonus
[PB] §7.01–4

[PB]. Under the new rules, the provision of such spaces on private parcels legitimated their intensified utilization in the form of the vertical extension of high-rises. In this way, the aesthetic ideal that could be characterized as the tower-within-a-plaza was legitimated economically. "The FAR formula effectively ended the standard setback massing, not because the new code prohibited it, but because sheer-walled towers in open plazas became more profitable."[22]

But the reflexive acceptance of exchanges of valued items between the city and private developers is dependent in the extreme on the setting of the FAR threshold in relation to prevailing economic pressures. And New York was not the first city to codify such incentives in its zoning ordinances, but instead Chicago. Found already in its zoning revision of 1957 were rules according to which: "We'll give you (the developer)

[21] Ibid.
[22] Willis (1995), 141.

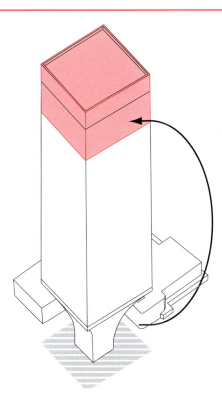

75 Substracted from the ground—added to the top: *Plaza Bonus* at the 157 m tall Ranier Tower, Seattle (*1977 by Yamasaki & Associates).

something more than you are permitted as-of-right if you'll give us something in return."[23]

Nonetheless, the basic allowable density was set so high that it occurred to virtually no one in Chicago at that time to utilize his bonus by offering the city additional public space.

Things were very different in New York: the bonus rules of the New York resolution of 1961 succeeded strikingly in coordinating private economic, aesthetic, and public interests. Suddenly, all were acting in concert. The mayor acquired the long sought-after public spaces, the developer higher profitability, and architectural critic Ada Louise Huxtable her slender, elegant towers.

A happy ending.

That is to say, if this economy of the commons, so to speak (as described by Garret Hardin in 1968 [TOE]), had not tended to encourage overutilization and overexploitation:

Tendency towards Overexploitation [TOE] § 1.08

Economic overexploitation: "The postwar building boom got underway in earnest. On the one hand, the boom was prompted by a speculators' rush to construct as much as possible under the more permissive 1916 code [also a kind of grandfathering and inertia of trends]. But so great

---

[23] Clifford L. Weaver and Richard F. Babcock (1979), *City Zoning—-the Once and Future Frontier*, 58.

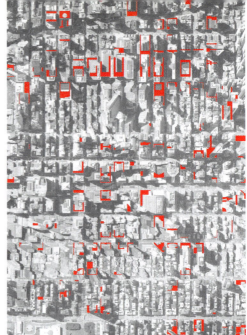

500 m

76 Sugarcoated public spaces in 18th-century Rome (left) and 20th-century New York (right).

was the city's capacity to absorb new office and dwelling space that the new zoning soon enough made its mark—far more quickly than the changes that followed the ratification of the 1916 zoning..."[24]

"In New York City the incentive system led to at least a temporary glut of vacant office space. One researcher, Jerold S. Kayden, concludes that New York's plaza bonus produced 7,940,792 sqft (737,700 sqm) of floor area between 1963 and 1975 and contributed to high vacancy rates and deterioration in rental prices in the New York City office market. No wonder Mr. Helmsley, one of Manhattan's larger developers, is reported to have said he regretted the city's generosity in granting him a whopping 312,000 sqft (29,000 sqm) of bonus floor area in his One Penn Plaza building."[25]

Aesthetic overexploitation: the new zoning opened up New York, and the International Style wave broke upon the city with full force. In subsequent years, the former exceptions entered into mass production. The *haute couture* of the Seagram Building and the Lever House soon became affordable off-the-rack fashions. The "wedding cake" was eventually replaced by the "sliced cake": "As the old New York zoning ordinance produced the wedding cake architecture along Fifth Avenue and Park Avenue, so incentive bonuses have sired what has to be the plaza generation in urban architecture. ... exchanging more open space at ground level for more rentable bulk above."[26]

Overexploitation of public space: "The new urbanism legislated the disintegration of the traditional city; its authors probably did not see clearly

[24] Stern (1995), 9.
[25] Weaver (1979), 58.
[26] Ibid.

178

enough that with the collapse of traditional street architecture would come the collapse of traditional street life and perhaps of the very idea of neighborhood. (...) The year 1960 was an important watershed in another, highly ironic way: just as the new zoning was taking effect, many of the planning notions that had led to its adoption were devastatingly criticized. The new thinking was given shape by Jane Jacobs in her polemical book, *The Death and Life of Great American Cities*, published in 1961. So it could be argued that the collapse of the old order came just at the time when many of its characteristics were being favorably reassessed..."[27]

This coupling of private economic and public interests is reminiscent of the reasons for commissioning G. B. Nolli in 1748 to sketch the reputed public spaces of Rome.[28] In fact, one could draw up a plan of Midtown Manhattan's ground-floor zone whose differentiated presentation of public space would be at least as intriguing as the Roman one revealed by Nolli in 1748. A map showing remarkably numerous apparently public spaces in private ownership, ones not earmarked for the sake of subsequently reducing tax burdens, but instead as an expression of the striving for elevated utilization. And of course also to elevate private use of the respective property.

Frigid Wasteland

In 1969, sociologist (and Jane Jacobs' mentor) William H. Whyte worked for the New York Planning Commission. For the most part, he observed the behavior and movements of individuals within the built environment, how they occupied public spaces, and how, on occasion, they rejected these. According to him, it is with their feet that pedestrians judge whether a public space is successful or not [PSA].

Equipped with cameras (both still and film), and a pair of research assistants, he arrived at conclusions of extraordinary explicitness, many of them borderline platitudes: "This might not strike you as an intellectual bombshell," he liked to say, "but people like to sit where there are places for them to sit."

"Ironically, it was at Seagram, that monument of internationalist style, where Whyte found his most successful plaza and the city found a reason to give incentives for plazas to other builders. Yet what Mies van der Rohe and Philip Johnson had achieved by accident, other architects could not achieve even though they tried. Armed with the information and data he had collected observing the square day after day, Whyte concluded coldly, 'It is difficult to design a place that will not attract people. What is remarkable is how often it's been accomplished.'"[29]

On the other hand, Philip Johnson recalled that "when Mies van der Rohe saw people sitting on the ledges, he was quite surprised. He never dreamt they would."[30]

In 1977, the *New York Times* registered its dissatisfaction for the first time

Public Space Acceptance [PSA] §1.10

---

[27] Stern, (1995), 9.
[28] For explanation see *Sugarcoated Public Space*, p.198.
[29] Rutherford H. Platt and Lincoln Institute of Land Policy (2006), *The Humane Metropolis: People and Nature in the 21st-Century City*, 236.
[30] Quoted by Jerold S. Kayden, The New York Dept. of City Planning and The Municipal Art Society of New York (2000), *Privately Owned Public Space: The New York City Experience*, 11.

with the results of the plaza bonus system: "Unfortunately, what the city has often received in the guise of a plaza in residential construction is a decorated driveway or a bleak northern corner in permanent shadow. The 'public' space has been closed off by walls, planted with token trees that promptly die, or left as ugly cement strips. When such abuses appear, a change in the regulations is called for. [...] Planning Commission today has erred on the side of over regulation. Some specific requirements, such as the nature of decorative paving and the exact distance between trees, have been sensibly loosened. But we still question the desirability of putting rigid controls on such things as shop signs, or the need for 'optional' amenities such as artwork (uncontrollable in terms of quality) and kiosks and game tables. Sunlight, seats, greenery and accessibility can do the job, without the city entering the risky realm of dictating too many details. This genuinely progressive zoning should not be pushed too far into discretionary areas of design. [...] Still, the principle of this kind of regulation is sound and the need for corrective action is clear, if plazas are to be a genuine public amenity rather than a concrete con game."[31]

Privately Owned Public Space,[32] a book authored by Jerold S. Kayden, illustrates more than 500 plazas, parks, and atriums found on private property. According to him, more than 82 acres of public space, distributed throughout the city, were constructed between the introduction of the zoning revision of 1961 and the year 2001. Many of these spaces were of questionable quality, but they did legitimate the production of 16 million additional square feet of doubtless highly profitable office surface.

In those years, New York City was determined to challenge the operative distinction introduced by sociologist Hans Paul Bahrdt between "private" and "public" as characteristic elements of urban form. According to Bahrdt, the city is "a system in which all life, including daily life, reveals a tendency to polarize, to unfold in terms of social aggregations which are either public or private. The public sphere and the private sphere develop in a close relationship without losing their polarization, while sectors of life that cannot be characterized either as 'public' or 'private' lose their meaning. The more strongly the polarization is exerted and the closer the interchange between the public and private spheres, the more 'urban' the life of an urban aggregate is from the sociological viewpoint. In the opposite case, an aggregate will develop the character of a city to a lesser degree."[33] And even if New York did not abolish these polarities, then it did install durable gradients between them.

Reengineering

In 1958, two years after receiving the commission, the New York architecture and planning firm of Voorhees, Walker, Smith & Smith published its comprehensive report *Zoning New York City: A Proposal for a Zoning Resolution for the City of New York*.[34] After public review, a number of subsequently

[31]   The New York Times Editorial (1977), *A Little Zoning Is a Good Thing*.
[32]   Kayden (2000).
[33]   Quoted in: Aldo Rossi (1982), *The Architecture of the City*, 86.
[34]   Voorhees Walker Smith & Smith (1958), *Zoning New York City; a Proposal for a Zoning Resolution for the City of New York*.

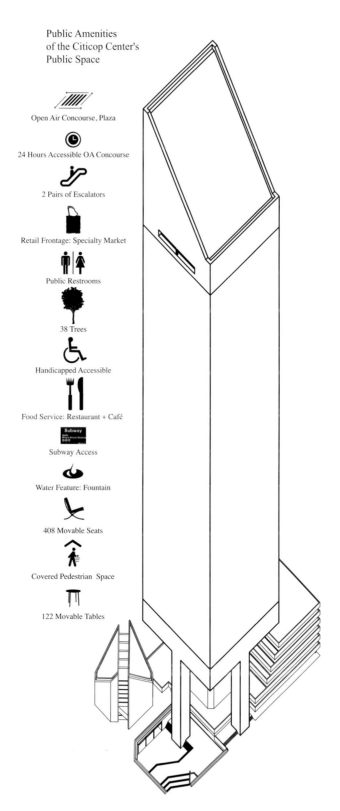

Public Amenities
of the Citicop Center's
Public Space

Open Air Concourse, Plaza

24 Hours Accessible OA Concourse

2 Pairs of Escalators

Retail Frontage: Specialty Market

Public Restrooms

38 Trees

Handicapped Accessible

Food Service: Restaurant + Café

Subway Access

Water Feature: Fountain

408 Movable Seats

Covered Pedestrian Space

122 Movable Tables

77 Stacked public amenities at the 279 m tall Citicorp Center (*1977, by Stubbins Associates and
Emery Roth & Sons, today Citigroup Center).

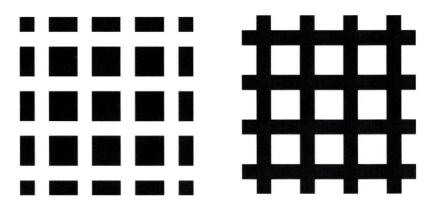

78 Space positive rather than mass positive: New York's 1961 inversion.

enacted changes, and many hours of helicopter tours during which countless experts strained their necks to catch sight of New York City's materialized drawbacks, the report was endowed with the force of law in 1961 as the new zoning resolution of New York City.

The authors presented their proposal as a contrast to the ordinance previously in force, much of which was still based on the 1916 resolution: whereas the earlier rules were based on the fixed geometric setback envelope in order to prevent buildings from robbing their neighbors of the requisite light, the Voorhees report argued solely from a public perspective. The social behavior of buildings was assessed principally from the point of view of the street and of public space. The "proposed regulations are intended to insure that public streets and all portions of buildings fronting on streets have access to light and air, and to provide a general feeling of openness at street level."[35] In 1961, the city of New York was characterized by the urbanistic inversion from an orientation toward individual buildings to a specification of the open space surrounding them. Suddenly, the form of the building was no longer conditioned directly. Instead, only its impact on space had to comply with defined criteria. Initially, this orientation toward public performance freed New York's high-rises of any formal determination or definition. A lack of specification generated a certain leeway.

In the 1920s, the draftsman Hugh Ferriss achieved celebrity by representing in his charcoal drawings the maximum utilization allowed by the 1916 zoning ordinance.[36] He modeled potential architectural volumes on the basis of the existing regulations.

Voorhees and his colleagues did precisely the reverse. They took existing buildings and modeled generative regulations based on them [SR]. As prototypes, they chose Mies van der Rohe's recently completed Seagram Building (1958) and the Lever House by Gordon Bunshaft, SOM (1952). In order to elucidate their setback rules graphically, the Voorhees Report even used photographs of these two public plaza prototypes as models.

[35]   Ibid.
[36]   Commissioned by Harvey Wiley Corbett and first published in Ferriss (1929).

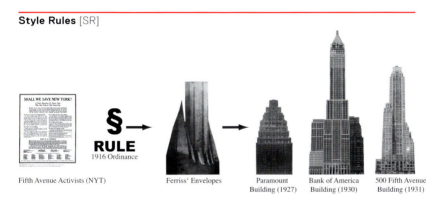

| Fifth Avenue Activists (NYT) | | Ferriss' Envelopes | | Paramount Building (1927) | Bank of America Building (1930) | 500 Fifth Avenue Building (1931) |

79a The 1916 order: codification results in form, produces form.

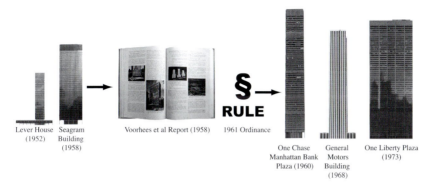

| Lever House (1952) | Seagram Building (1958) | Voorhees et al Report (1958) | 1961 Ordinance | | One Chase Manhattan Bank Plaza (1960) | General Motors Building (1968) | One Liberty Plaza (1973) |

79b The 1961 order: form results in codification, produces form.

If Ferriss had simply filled in the existing regulative architectural mold up to its limits, then Voorhees and his partners fashioned a new, immaterial mold based on the ideal high-rise structures of the time—only to witness the rise of countless Seagram and Lever House replicas. Action instead of and simultaneously as reaction.

In 1922, Ferriss visualized the invisible, while in 1958, Voorhees translated the already visible into invisible regulations. The geometric straitjacket was replaced by a comfortable corset—consisting of setbacks [SB], plaza bonus [PB], floor area ratio [FAR], and the sky exposure plane [SEP], criteria which allowed a great deal of leeway while consistently endowing structures with slender profiles.

Apparently unaware of the determinative impact of this interplay between various rules and the economic pressures of subsequent years, the Voorhees Report advertised itself with the claim that "the proposed regulations offer scope and incentives for original architectural design."[37] Voorhees and partners had designed a visionary mechanism without the visionary consciousness of their own design power.

Hugh Ferriss died in 1962 at the age of 73.

Set Back [SB] §7.02–1
Plaza Bonus [PB] §7.01–4
Floor Area Ratio [FAR] §7.01–1
Sky Exposure Plane [SEP] §7.02–6

---

37 Preface by James Felt in Voorhees Walker Smith & Smith (1958), *Zoning New York City; a Proposal for a Zoning Resolution for the City of New York*, vii.

80 **The idols made explicit: Voorhees Report, 1958, with Mies and Bunshaft as examples.**

Economy

While setback buildings were not exactly forbidden after 1961, the new guidelines did effectively render them impractical and unprofitable. Disappearing for good from the libraries of planning and architectural offices during the 1960s was a hitherto frequently used book. The newfound irrelevance of William Clark and John Kingston's *The Skyscraper—A Study in the Economic Height of Modern Office Buildings*[38] clarified just how intimately urban planning regulations were bound up with economic tendencies.

Clark and Kingston had investigated the "efficiency" of tall buildings with regard to land values, setback provisions, vertical transportation, construction costs, etc [EH]. Based on the design of a hypothetical building on a parcel measuring 200 by 405 ft (19 by 38 m), one similar to the block lying to the south of Grand Central Station), they generated eight buildings of various heights. On the basis of the static form of a maximum utilization with clearly prescribed setbacks, the reduction in volume proceeded simply by the cutting away of horizontal slabs from the perpetually equal shape of the volume. On the basis of common frame conditions (the taller the building, the more expensive the vertical accesses and construction costs), they arrived at the result that a building having exactly 63 stories was the most economically efficient. After 1961, the calculation was no longer valid. Not because the factors determining profits had changed—even today, the price of a building lot continues to determine how much building volume must be constructed in order to

Economic Height
[EH] §7.01–6

---

[38]   William Clifford Clark and John Lyndhurst Kingston (1930), *The Skyscraper—a Study in the Economic Height of Modern Office Buildings*.

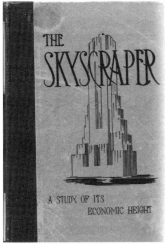

81 Examination of the skyscraper's economy: deemed to be outdated after 1961.

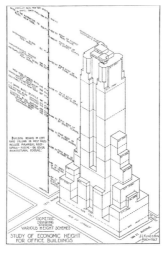

82 Study example of the perpetually equal shape. Volume decreases only by taking away slices from the top in eight steps.

TABLE No. 1

SUMMARY OF INVESTMENT COST, GROSS AND NET INCOME AND RETURN UPON INVESTMENT

(Assuming land value at $200 per square foot)

	8-Story Building	15-Story Building	22-Story Building	30-Story Building	37-Story Building	50-Story Building	63-Story Building	75-Story Building
	(in thousands of dollars)							
INVESTMENT								
A. Land (81,000 sq. ft. @ $200)	$16,200	$16,200	$16,200	$16,200	$16,200	$16,200	$16,200	$16,200
B. Building	4,769	7,307	9,310	11,775	13,808	16,537	19,390	22,558
C. Carrying Charges:								
1. Interest during construction:								
(a) Land (6% on cost for full period)	810	972	1,134	1,296	1,458	1,620	1,780	1,944
(b) Building (6% on cost for half period)	119	219	326	471	622	826	1,065	1,353
2. Taxes during construction—Land	292	350	408	466	524	584	642	700
3. Insurance during construction	3	5	8	12	21	35	65	95
TOTAL CARRYING CHARGES	$1,224	$1,546	$1,876	$2,245	$2,625	$3,065	$3,552	$4,092
D. Grand Total Cost	22,193	25,053	27,386	30,220	32,633	35,802	39,142	42,850
Total assignable to Land	17,302	17,522	17,742	17,962	18,182	18,404	18,622	18,844
Total assignable to Building	4,891	7,531	9,644	12,258	14,451	17,398	20,520	24,006
INCOME								
E. Gross Income	1,819	2,780	3,483	4,181	4,755	5,581	6,302	6,901
F. Expenses:								
1. Operating	311	482	592	723	814	942	1,058	1,213
2. Taxes	479	541	591	653	725	774	846	926
3. Depreciation	95	146	186	235	276	331	388	451
TOTAL EXPENSES	$885	$1,169	$1,369	$1,611	$1,795	$2,047	$2,292	$2,590
G. Net Income	934	1,611	2,114	2,570	2,960	3,534	4,010	4,311
NET RETURN								
H. Net Return on Total Investment	4.22%	6.44%	7.73%	8.50%	9.07%	9.87%	10.25%	10.06%
I. Increase in Investment from Last Addition of Stories	....	$2,860	$2,833	$2,834	$2,413	$3,169	$3,340	$3,708
J. Increase in Net Income Resulting Therefrom	....	677	503	456	390	574	476	301
K. Net Return on Increase in Investment	....	23.69%	21.51%	16.09%	16.15%	18.13%	14.25%	8.12%

Percentage of Net Return — *Net Return Upon Total Investment for Varying Building Heights*

10.00
8.00
6.00
4.00
2.00

LEGEND
A'A' ACTUAL CURVE
B'B' NORMAL CURVE

BUILDING HEIGHT IN STORIES

CHART NO. 2

83 Comparison of the eight volumetric variants. Result: peak profit at 63 stories.

generate a profit. But instead because the regulations no longer automatically produced a three-dimensional template which made the height of the building the sole parameter for increasing the amount of gross surface area.

The fact that finance experts had been able to agree without significant disagreement on a *single* prototypical test building for their calculations demonstrates yet again how little variation and leeway, given the commensurate internal pressure, had been available for determining the volumetry of a pre-1961 speculative office tower. Back then, it was possible to build on one quarter of the parcel as high as desired. This had remained the sole option for variation. Prior to 1961, to build higher than the respective economic height had represented the same degree of luxury as the generous plaza area ceded by the Seagram Building. After this year, understandably, the competition to win prizes for erecting the tallest building in the city was over. From now on, the building with the largest plaza in front of its main entrance would receive the greatest prestige and recognition.

Overdone?

[A]
Lindsay, Urban Design Group

[L]
New York City

Manhattan's business districts changed noticeably after the new zoning ordinance of 1961 came into force. One after the other, New York's high-rises receded from the street edge, leaving behind broad surfaces decorated by a handful of plants in large tubs and perhaps an easily dirtied surface of water. None of these plaza-tower developers devoted much consideration to whether similar public spaces with similar bodies of water were being installed directly next door to theirs. Their highly focused gazes did not extend across the street—nor did they need to. The city's formerly spectacular street canyons suffered now from continuing erosion. In the early 1970s, under Mayor John V. Lindsay, New York's *Urban Design Group* attempted to counteract this erosion by means of regulative retaining walls: they sought a return to the traditional street corridor with continuous street walls [SWC] throughout the highly densified midtown and

Street Wall Continuity
[SWC] §4.11

downtown business districts. By way of thanks, buildings returning to the edge of the sidewalk were to be rewarded by a bulk bonus.

But how can we expect a building to look that stands along the edge of the street while *simultaneously* providing a public plaza, thereby taking advantage of the economic maxim of exploiting the maximum possible utilization? Above a certain parcel size, this model leads unavoidably to a building typology that had not been particularly prevalent in Manhattan previously: the "mega courtyard block type."

The *Urban Design Group* itself attempted to mediate between these apparently contradictory models by marking out a prototypical interpretation: a parcel on the South Street Seaport received a literal block perimeter development and extremely tall, stepped streetside façades, and a number of perforations toward an internal courtyard that was open on the waterside and which contained public facilities.

This project remains unrealized. In Manhattan, the underlying street-wall rule remained almost unnoticed until the late 1970s, only in order to visibly materialize again in the landfill of the World Trade Center, in Cooper and Ecksut's *Battery Park Master Plan* of 1979.

New York's self–critique and reflection was articulated explicitly six

Street Wall Continuity [SWC]

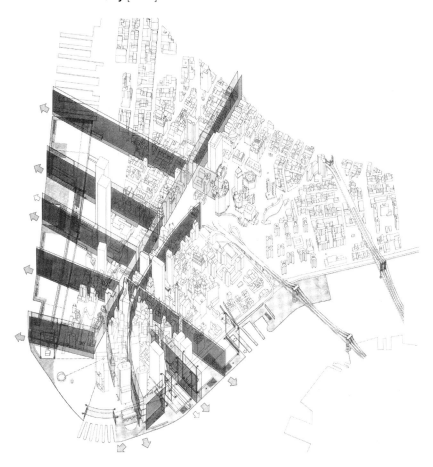

84 *Street Wall Continuity* along Manhattan's major streets.

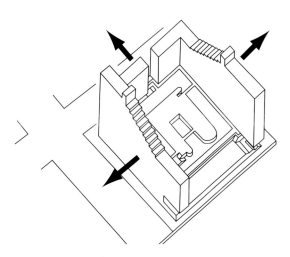

85 Superblock: Mayor Lindsay's Urban Design Group illustrating possible outcomes of their continuous street wall rules.

years after the rejuvenating cure of 1961 when Mayor Lindsay's Urban Task Force under the direction of William S. Paley published the report *The Threatened City*. It contained four chapters, entitled: "The Trouble—Opportunities—Toward a Method—Proposals."[39]

The report was introduced by a foreword by Mayor Lindsay in which he expressed himself explicitly regarding the scope of his urbanistic responsibilities: "Design is not a small enterprise in New York City today, nor should it be considered narrowly as merely a matter of aesthetics, a frail word. In our increasingly crowded man-shaped urban world, aesthetics must now include not only the marble statue in the garden but the house, the street, the neighborhood, and the city as a cumulative expression of its residents."[40] ... which is to say everything—which is much too much.

The *New York Times* replied promptly: "Unfortunately, the task force report fails in the definition of the meaning and urgency of urban design. It is overly preoccupied with traditional views and vistas, the esthetic smash or squalor of the grand visual approach; the individual elegant or ugly buildings. Its conventional brand of nineteenth-century urban esthetics has limited value for the dynamic disorders of the twentieth-century city."[41]

And according to the assessment of many experts, this report was based more or less on a "naive optimism," albeit endowed with extreme power and force: "(...) that pretty much under existing law the city could exert enormous municipal control over both public and private design."[42]

Self-consciously, the report underscored this advantage: "No one can build in this city without exposing himself to a bargaining position with the (municipal) government."[43]

Instead of setting a framework for future development, the city would henceforth negotiate with property owners. Discretionary leeway instead of as-of-right determinations. Still, private owners were not compelled to take part in such negotiations. The city simply made it clear that private developers would miss out on a profitable bonus if they remained within rigid basic standards (as-of-right) instead of entering into negotiations with the city, raising their personal profit by means of a few courtesies. The result was an extremely close connection between private enterprise and the municipal will to design. The bait on the hook had fulfilled its function!

---

[39] The Mayor's Task Force on Urban Design (1967), *The Threatened City*.
[40] Ibid., 3.
[41] The New York Times Editorial (1967), *The Design of the City*.
[42] Stephen Zoll (1973), *Superville: New York—Aspects of Very High Bulk*, 513–15.
[43] Mayor's Task Force (1967), 39.

7

Within or Without

Rules can on the one hand define specific zones, while on the other, their effect is limited to specific spheres of influence. Rules generally have a specific operating field. They can be roughly divided into three categories: The first category deals with the question of *who* or *what* is guided by a given rule. Rules are attributed to clearly defined agents. As a result of their operating effect causal relationships emerge that indirectly configure new conditions. These conditions are called "externalities."

The second category deals with *limit values* and the *tension* caused by the tolerance in development-potential, induced by the rules. Are the limit values absolute, or are they defined as a relation to other values?

The third category deals with *where* the rule is valid. In comprehensive zoning ordinances rules are complemented by plans, the rules of a building ordinance have a zoning-map, on which the zones where they apply are fixed.

The second category, amongst which includes the difficulty in defining thresholds, has already been treated in chapters 3 and 5. In this chapter, the first and the third category, concerning *who* and *where*, are dealt with.

86 Wooden laundry in San Francisco, ca. 1880.

7.1 Automatic Inclusion: Externalities

Plaza Bonus
[PB] §7.01–4

New York's *plaza bonus rules* [PB] couple private interests with collective ones, administered by the municipal administration. In the best cases, both sides benefit: the city sees the improvement of its public spaces, the private builder has higher profits. This arrangement is deliberate: each side is aware of the larger purpose of these negotiations, and of the desired outcome of these regulations.

In the past, however, official rules have been continually introduced whose true motivation does not lie in their immediate outcomes, but are instead related to less obvious outcomes, those that are guided now in an indirect fashion. Many rules, then, are introduced solely for their implicit potential.

Wrong for the Right Reason

[A]
Chinese Population

[L]
San Francisco

A legal fiction was concocted in the San Francisco of the 1880s: following the first large wave of Chinese immigration during the 19th century, California and its cities inaugurated laws designed to discourage the arriving Chinese from settling in California. They did not proceed directly—how can a country based on immigration explicitly bar people's entry? Had California introduced laws openly directed against Chinese immigration, they would have failed the test of the *Equal Protection Clause* of the *Fourteenth Amendment*, not to mention the *Civil Rights Act* of 1870. Given this circumstance, the new laws had to be formulated in such a way that they could withstand the accusation of racial discrimination.

Laundry Law
[LL] §7.03–6

In 1880, San Francisco did precisely that with the help of its *Laundry Laws* [LL], directed against the approximately 320 laundries in the city and in the county. In the form of a municipal order, the law stated that henceforth, no laundry could operate within easily flammable wooden buildings. The danger of fire was too great. At this time, 90% of the city was built of wood. Aside from a dozen or so, all of the laundries were of wood as well. And with a few exceptions, all were operated by Chinese immigrants. At that time, laundries were a public symbol of the business acumen of San Francisco's Chinese population. Over the next five years, more than 150 "subjects of China" were imprisoned for transgressing the laundry laws. At the same time, no Caucasian run laundry was adversely affected by the new rule.[1]

With the support of the *Laundrymen's Guild*, a test case involving laundryman Yick Wo, an exemplary and law-abiding businessman, went all the way to the Supreme Court. The court detected the evil intentions lurking behind the seemingly well-intended law, recognizing the charge of discrimination.[2] They put an end to all ongoing enforcement activities.

Of course, the case of the laundry laws involves a rather transparent pretext. But it also demonstrates the enormous potential for external inclusivity. Although neutrally formulated, and although entirely devoid of the attribute "Chinese," the rules were designed with unerring accuracy to have the desired impact on the Chinese population. On the surface, they are concerned solely with the public health, with minimizing the danger of fire in San Francisco. Only in the form of an externality do they have fatal consequences for the Chinese immigrants—and moreover with full awareness on the part of their drafters.

Urban steering is full of such deliberate deferred actions. And accusations of racial discrimination continue to be directed at certain zoning regulations in the USA.

Minimum lot size requirements [LS] and bans on apartment buildings in suburban areas are always under suspicion of being adroit attempts to prevent low-income housing from gaining a foothold in affluent neighborhoods.

Lot Size Requirements
[LS] §6.02

Claims that zoning laws were introduced to New York City solely in order to safeguard the public health can easily be exposed as pretexts designed to benefit the private interests of the city's wealthy business leaders. Zürich, meanwhile, reins in the construction of high-rises with its seemingly inoffensive shadow rule [2H].

2h Shadow
[2H] § 5.08

The pig is successfully kept out of the parlor—and without ever being mentioned by name. Whether the devisers of such rules can be said to be conscious of their actual effects depends on the degree to which the associated causal relationships can be identified. Such relationships vary enormously in degree of visibility and efficacy.

Right for the Wrong Reason

A retroactive inclusivity of rules is also found in situations where a specific causal relationship is established only years later—whether, for example, brought about by a "future twist of social or technological development"[3] or for some other reason.

[A]
Banham and the Garden City

[L]
Great Britain

Reyner Banham and other advocates of non-planning have identified such unpredicted externalities in the rules of the garden city of Patrick Geddes, Ebenezer Howard, and Raymond Unwin: "It's worth remembering that the garden in this theory was there specifically to grow food in: the acreage was carefully measured out with this *Fodder Ratio* [FOR] in mind. The houses in (say) Welwyn Garden City or Hampstead Garden Suburb were also scattered thinly because of the width of space allotted (for reasons of health) to the loop and sweep of roads.

Fodder Ratio
[FOR] §6.06

[1]   Garvin (1996), 432.
[2]   Yick Wo Vs. Hopkins (1886), 118 US 356.
[3]   Banham (2000), 9.

87 Typical downtown parking situation.

"Welwyn Garden City and Hampstead Garden Suburb were therefore built—and then duly mocked for dull doctrinairism. The layout made public transport almost impossible; the tin and the frozen pack rapidly outdated the vegetable patch.

"But then the spread of car ownership outdated the mockery: those roads lived to find a justification; the space around the house could absorb a garage without too much trouble; and the garden (as, even, in many inner-London conversions of Georgian houses) became an unexceptionable outdoor room and meeting space for children, away from the lethal pressed steel and rubber hurtling around the streets."[4]

Reyner Banham uncovered a procedural quality which had hitherto rarely stood in connection with the total planning of a garden city: "Now it's nice that a plan should turn out to have reasons for succeeding which the planner himself did not foresee."[5]

Here, the garden city loses its original purpose, becoming a "loft"—and long before this fate was suffered by any warehouse or industrial building.

128 Concerts

[A]
Shoup, Walt Disney
Concert Hall

[L]
Los Angeles

Where in New York City we encounter a plaza, we find a parking lot in Los Angeles. And the equivalent of the Manhattan high-rise in Los Angeles is the little parking lot guardhouse with a large "P" above it. This seems to be entirely in keeping with the anti-urban stereotype of Los Angeles.

With regard to criteria of density, however, the statistics do not support this stereotype. When the total surface area of Los Angeles is considered,[6]

4   Ibid.
5   Ibid.
6   Computed according to the definition of "urbanized areas" provided by the US Census Bureau, and not the political boundaries of cities. Michael Manville and Donald Shoup (2004), *People, Parking, and Cities*, 2–8.

it turns out to be the densest urban area in the USA. Denser than New York, denser than San Francisco. What is different is the distribution of this density: "New York and San Francisco look like Hong Kong surrounded by Phoenix, while Los Angeles looks like Los Angeles surrounded by … well, Los Angeles. In other words, Los Angeles is a dense area without an extremely dense core, while New York and San Francisco are less dense overall but enjoy the benefits of very dense core areas."[7]

An explanation is provided by the American traffic planner Donald Shoup and his colleagues. À la Reyner Banham before him, Shoup strikes an unusual (for the USA) pose: seated on a bicycle, a helmet strapped to his head. The Englishman Reyner Banham "learned to drive in order to read Los Angeles in the original."[8] The American traffic planner learns to ride a bicycle in order to better formulate a critique of his own city. This critique culminates in an incisive history of the differing parking regulations [PR] in the cities of Los Angeles, San Francisco, and New York. In the history of the 128 concerts of the *Walt Disney Concert Hall*:

Parking Requirements
[PR] §7.03–5

"New York and San Francisco have strict limits on how much parking they allow in their CBDs; Los Angeles, however, pursues a diametrically opposing path—where the other two cities limit off-street parking, LA requires it. This requirement not only discourages development in downtown Los Angeles relative to other parts of the region but also distorts how the downtown functions. Take, for example, the different treatment given by Los Angeles and San Francisco to their concert halls. For a downtown concert hall, Los Angeles requires, as a minimum, fifty times more parking than San Francisco allows as its maximum. Thus the San Francisco Symphony built its home, Louise Davies Hall, without a parking garage, while Disney Hall, the new home of the Los Angeles Philharmonic, did not open until seven years after its parking garage was built. Disney Hall's six-level, 2,188-space underground garage cost $110 million to build (about $50,000 per space). Financially troubled Los Angeles County, which built the garage, went into debt to finance it, expecting that parking revenues would repay the borrowed money. But the garage was completed in 1996, and Disney Hall—which suffered from a budget less grand than its vision—became knotted in delays and didn't open until late 2003. During the seven years in between, parking revenue fell far short of debt payments (few people park in an underground structure if there is nothing above it) and the county, by that point nearly bankrupt, had to subsidize the garage even as it laid off employees. The county owns the land beneath Disney Hall, and its lease for the site specifies that Disney Hall must schedule at least 128 concerts each winter season. Why 128? That's the minimum number of concerts that will generate the parking revenue necessary to pay the debt service on the garage. And in its first year, Disney Hall scheduled exactly 128 concerts. The parking garage, ostensibly designed to serve the Philharmonic, now has the Philharmonic serving it; the minimum parking requirements have led to a minimum concert requirement. The money spent on parking has altered the hall in other ways, too, shifting its design toward drivers and away

---

[7] Ibid.
[8] Reyner Banham (1971), *Los Angeles; the Architecture of Four Ecologies*, 5.

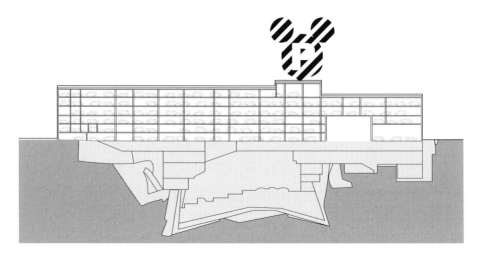

88 The Walt Disney Concert Hall by Frank Gehry in Los Angeles (idealized section).

Parking Requirements [PR]

89 More than 50% of(f) the blocks—Downtown Los Angeles parking.

from pedestrians. The presence of a six-story subterranean garage means most concert patrons arrive from underneath, rather than outside, the hall. The hall's designers clearly understood this, and so while the hall has a fairly impressive street entrance, its more magisterial gateway is a vertical one: an 'escalator cascade' that flows up from the parking structure and ends in the foyer. This has profound implications for street life. A concertgoer can now drive to Disney Hall, park beneath it, ride up into it, see a show, and then reverse the whole process—and never set foot on a sidewalk in downtown LA. The full experience of an iconic Los Angeles building begins and ends in its parking garage, not in the city itself."[9]

The ultimate question posed by this anecdote is: in this scenario, who conditions whom? Does the concert hall shape the parking garage, or is it the other way around? The structure subtending this scenario is determined by an inconspicuous parking ratio. The rest is distraction.

The lack of density in downtown Los Angeles is a consequence of its density of parking places. Downtown LA is fully occupied, if not necessarily by constructed mass! The maximum possible space is filled right to the borders—subdivided regulatively into offices and their parking places. This artificially created, perpetual demand for parking places also elevates the motivation for setting up small parking lots with low-wage employees on a given parcel rather than bothering to erect an expensive and troublesome office tower. The return on investment is much higher.

Assuming the parking ratio remains the same, then even raising the utilization coefficient would not effect a district's increased densification. The fixing of a FAR limit would be rendered redundant by the parallel action of the parking ratio. Except that the district would be zoned for mixed use (commercial and residential uses), and the obligatory number of parking places for residential uses is far smaller. All of a sudden, an inconspicuous approach to managing parking places becomes a "use mixer."

With this method of mixed-use, effected by means of a peripheral focus on apparently remote matters like parking (see also above re shadows), the city formulates—unnoticed, and so to speak as an ancillary product—a highly successful critique of the functionalist orientation of urban planning.

Houston: Same Results, Different Rules

Houston has no formally defined comprehensive zoning laws, that is to say no plan-based authority responsible for separating various types of land-use. But Houston is nonetheless a typically American city. All of the processes for which zoning is generally responsible occur here as well. Houston suffers from the same maladies as its zoned Sunbelt city counterparts.[10] Houston is less dense than most of North America's large

[A]
Land Use Laws

[L]
Houston

---

[9]   See Shoup (2004), 2–8.
[10] See Richard M. Bernard and Bradley Robert Rice (1983), *Sunbelt Cities: Politics and Growth since World War II*. According to their definition, a Sunbelt city was shaped by the impact of World War II and by federal funds for military, defense, and other programmes. A Sunbelt city also featured a "good business climate," a political structure dominated by the downtown business interests and devoted to a "growth ethic" and a high "quality of life."

cities. It sprawls in an exemplary fashion, and its residents are especially fond of traveling by car. The city is distinctly hostile to pedestrians. Houston's high-rise cluster is prototypical of the US-American central business district (CBD).

Does Houston illustrate the unavoidable results of an overly consumer-friendly city, one which strives to accommodate the freedom of choice of its residents in the absence of regulative intervention? Is Houston necessarily the result of removing all hands from the steering wheel?

Unfortunately, Houston exemplifies the laissez-faire city only to a limited extent. For operating here in place of conventional zoning codes is an apparatus consisting of land-use regulations:

Here, the artificial dispersal of the population is effected by the rule that, depending upon the district, a single-family house can only be built on a parcel of at least 5000 sqft (465 sqm). To be sure, this *Minimum Lot Size Requirement* [LS] is smaller than elsewhere but still prevents any significant densification from occurring; and bus lines have difficulty reaching sufficient numbers of residents to offer an alternative to auto traffic. In 1999, the city council acknowledged this reality, and suspended the regulations in places, especially in proximity to the city center.[11] Nonetheless, the lot parcels are still among the more robust urban elements [ROB]. Trapped between neighboring properties and interconnected via traffic infrastructure, they manifest a pronounced resistance to any form of change. And since the majority of Houston's residential development predates 1999, so that demand was for the most part satisfied, this deregulation effected no noticeable change.

Furthermore, Houston's building code prescribes that every structure must have a number of parking places [PR], and this figure may even surpass the number of residents. An apartment building, for example, must have 1.25 parking spaces per studio apartment and 1.33 parking spaces per bedroom.[12] Similar codes apply to supermarkets and department stores. This makes walking through the city doubly unattractive. In the first place, no one enjoys strolling through a sea of cars, and in the second, the distances between destinations is distended significantly by the presence of parking lots set between them. Urban density thus falls even further.

Nor do prescribed *Street Widths* [SW] of more than 30 m for main streets and 18 m for residential streets contribute to making the streetscape more attractive to pedestrians.

In addition, Houston planners stipulated that main street crossings must lie 600 ft (180 m) from one another. Jane Jacobs,[13] among others, has already pointed out that for a lively urban corner to emerge, the length of blocks must be kept as short as possible [SHB].

Finally, Houston has laid down more freeways for residents along its margins than any other city. With double the population, for example, Chicago has only 10% additional kilometers of freeway length than Houston [PSL].[14] Independently of the normative character of these rules, they are highly effective as descriptions. For those unfamiliar with Houston, this set of

Lot Size Requirements
[LS] §6.02

Robustness
[ROB] §4.15

Parking Requirements
[PR] §7.03–5

Street Width
[SW] §4.14

Short Blocks
[SHB] §4.02

Population to Overall Street Length
[PSL] §2.05

[11] Michael Lewyn (2003), *Zoning without Zoning.*
[12] Ibid.
[13] Jacobs (1961).
[14] Lewyn (2003).

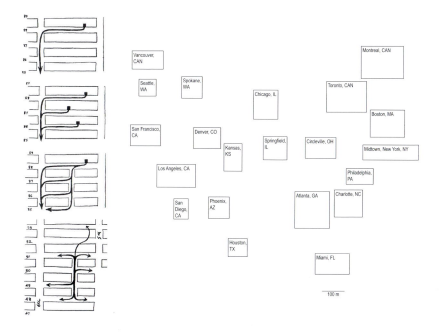

90a The blocks must be short. Actually, these are the only illustrations among the 450 pages of Jane Jacobs' *Death and Life of Great American Cities*.
90b Typical *Block Sizes* across North America.

four rules constitutes a rough but nonetheless accurate sketch of the city. Let us continue to fill in the details:

Houston's Simplicity

With regard to its standards, Houston's ordinances know only two zones, the urban and the suburban. The demarcation line between this black-and-white division is marked out by the highway loop 610 [SUL]. Everything found inside of this ring resembles miniature editions of suburban standards, a sort of "lite" version with smaller minimum building lot sizes and setbacks. This is the case too with the locally typical specialty of *Compensating Open Space* [COS]: if a developer further subdivides his building lot into smaller parcels, each of which is smaller than the prescribed minimum lot size, he must compensate by leaving a specified area of his "private" space undeveloped on the property. Inside of the loop, this ratio between lot size and undeveloped area is smaller than outside of it. Nonetheless, the Texans seem to exhibit a bizarre public-minded interest in open, undeveloped space, both within and outside of the loop—even though such surfaces are by no means publicly usable, or even physically accessible. In the best cases, they do perhaps provide a feeling of landscape, of views into the distance. And such perspectives, moreover, may not be blocked by carports, garden houses, or other smaller structures. By means of this rule, the third, the spatial and aesthetic dimension of public space is acknowledged, but at the same time, the dimension of its physically available usability is marginalized. Public space must neither

Sub Urban Loop
[SUL] §2.13

Compensating Open Space
[COS] §6.03

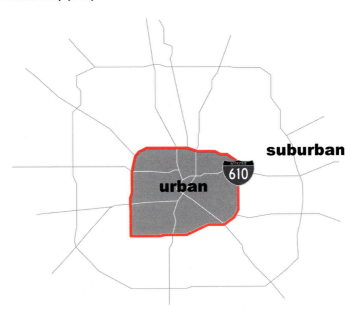

91 Houston's simplicity.

be physically accessible, nor even public—that is to say, there is no need for it to be owned by the city at all. In its capacity for the schizophrenic nullification of space lies the fundamental potential of this urban rule. It even has a certain tradition, a prominent forerunner:

Sugarcoated Private Space—From Rome to the US

[A]
Nolli

[L]
Rome

Sketched in 1748 by Giovanni Batista Nolli, the "Nolli Map" represents the Roman network of medieval and baroque streets, supplemented by perspectives of major monuments drawn by Piranesi. Originally prepared in order to determine basic taxes, the plan is well-suited to the study of the relationships between private and public spaces—as registered in Rome's urban space: the certification of the presence of public space on a private lot reduces the surface area of the property that is subject to taxation. This circumstance promotes a tendency toward slight exaggeration in order to lower one's tax burden. Public space as clearly defined in terms of streets and plazas is now supplemented by a finely woven network of quasi-public surfaces, all held in private hands, and most of them even roofed over. By means of this sugarcoated image, Nolli's map overcame the division between public and private spaces that was necessitated by ownership relations, instead coupling public space via tax law to private economic and profit-oriented interests.

Together with New York City's plaza bonus regulations and Houston's compensatory measures, Nolli's map represents a third case in which public space sacrifices its territorial distinctness. It becomes a commodity, is marginalized as a resource in the search for loopholes or serves as a compensatory performance for falling below an artificially determined threshold. Public space is not regarded as an originary object or quality,

198

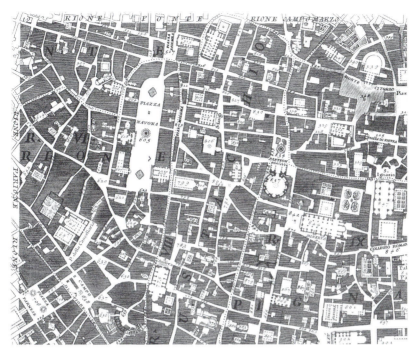

92 **Nolli.**

but instead as something abstract, as a quantity or method of payment capable of circulating.

7.2 Artificial Conclusion: Plans and Special Districts

A structural, plan-based definition of inclusivity gives us the concept of a specialized zone within an area governed by uniform regulations. Around the world, municipal administrations exploit this option for better accommodating local specialties—exceptions within the larger order of uniform, citywide land-use control.

Significant portions of North American cities and rural areas have been stamped by *special purpose districts* and *preservation districts* of various kinds [SD]. "The basic tripartite classification of land as residential, commercial, or industrial has shifted towards the concept of 'special districting.'"[15] Valid here are special rules, while some of the rules *normally* in effect are suspended in these areas. In many cases, such special districts are characterized by special plans whose regulations supplement the generally applicable municipal code. In this sense, and on a larger scale, every city, of course, positions itself as a single, expanded special zone. The city of London has its *Canary Wharf*, Great Britain's tax-free oasis for many years. New York and Chicago have their *special theater districts*, where the incorporation of a theater into a construction project involves a utilization bonus for the development that rises above it. The Swiss city of Zürich has its *Gestaltungspläne* (comprehensive design plans), which insulate certain special zones by means of specific rules from the gener-

Special Districts [SD] §3.01

[15] Allan Fonorof (1970), *Special Districts: A Departure from the Concept of Uniform Control*, 82.

BPC Battery Park City
CL Clinton
GC Garment Center
HY Hudson Yards
L Lincoln Square
LC Limited Commercial
LI Little Italy
LM Lower Manhattan
MiD Midtown
MP Madison Avenue Preservation
PI Park Improvement
TA Transit Land Use
TMU Tribeca Mixed Use
U United Nations Development
US Union Square
WCh West Chelsea

93 Islands within the island of unified control: Manhattan's *Special Districts*.

ally applicable building and zoning ordinances. In this way, a city can complement and complete itself on the basis of special measures, however these are fashioned. The motivation for such special cases is the desire for the freedom to formulate new rules for a specified portion of the city and to design an independent and quasi-exterritorial plan. By their very nature, such districts are a combination of plans and policies (rules)—and artificial (and artistic) connections between urban visions and instrumental considerations.

Urban Village Envelope

[A]
Downtown Urban Center
Planning Group

[L]
Seattle

Seattle's downtown urban village is composed of Belltown, Denny Triangle, the commercial core, and parts of Pioneer Square and Chinatown. In 1999, the *Downtown Urban Center Group* published its *Downtown Urban Center Neighborhood Plan*[16] for this area. Designed to supplement the *Seattle Municipal Code*, this plan was meant to guide future growth, to preserve existing qualities, and to generate new public amenities. Alongside the

---

[16] The City of Seattle (1999), *Downtown Urban Center Neighborhood Plan*.

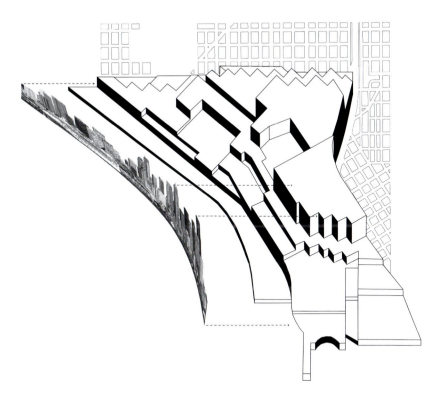

94 Sculpting the Urban Village in Seattle.

usual statement of intention, the plan also contained a series of rule-based instruments which form a structure of hierarchical interdependency which almost amounts to a comprehensive plan. Not unlike nesting Russian matroshka dolls, a virtual *Urban Envelope* [UE] formed the outer shell. Encompassing individual blocks and districts, it delineated a "sculpture" of the overall development in height of downtown Seattle. This configuration was terraced all the way down to the water in the form of a cascade, thereby reflecting the underlying topography. Within this three-dimensional boundary was found the second set of rules: provided that their originally projected floor area was not increased, and following a special review process, individual buildings were permitted to surpass the maximum height of the urban envelope by 20%. This helped to reduce the tendency towards low, compacted building volumes, which made every effort to squash themselves down below the legal height limits (apparently, Seattle had learned from the case of San Francisco's Fontana Towers[17]).

Urban Envelope
[UE] §2.12

---

17 See p.133.

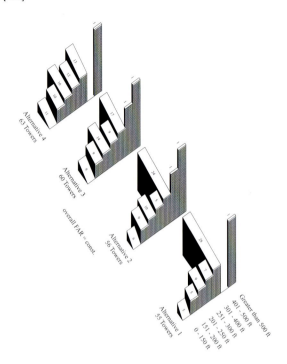

95 Numbers of projected new buildings by height range in Seattle.

Height Range
[HR] §3.07

The city also studied the option of introducing a *Height Range* [18] [HR] within the legal envelope. This would have meant that a maximum total number of new buildings would have been determined for the further densification of the downtown area. This absolute number of allowable new towers, furthermore, would have been subdivided into groups graded by height. In this way, the city would have gained absolute control over the total quantity of urban growth, and simultaneously over the height variances for future development.

Additionally, this measure would have safeguarded existing view corridors from the streets which offered views of Elliott Bay, West Seattle, Mount Rainier, and the Olympic Mountains [BP]. These axes would have additionally sliced into the urban envelope in the third dimension.

Backdrop Preservation
[BP] §2.08

Seattle's Urban Village, as elsewhere, is subject to territorial subdivision into zones with an eye toward utilization programming and desirable functions. Coming into play at street level, meanwhile, are additional sets of rules. Besides being precisely defined open spaces, streets are also classified with regard to their value to pedestrians [PS]. Various classes of streets are distinguished in terms of permissible automobile traffic, and there are also so-called *green streets*. For these, special emphasis is accorded to the adjacent landscaping. Depending on the street classification, there are rules governing the provision of public amenities, and utilization

Pedestrian Streets
[PS] §4.07

---

[18] The City of Seattle (2002), *Downtown Seattle Height and Density Changes—Numbers of Projected New Buildings by Height Range*, 3–76.

Required Street Level Use

Freeway
Park

Elliott Bay

——— Class I Pedestrian Street   60% Transp. 🚳

·········· Class II Pedestrian Street   30% Transp. 🚗

······ Green Street   60% Transp. 🚗🌳

500 m

96 *Pedestrian Street Classification* and its network, Seattle.

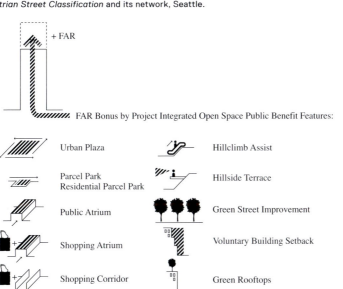

+ FAR

FAR Bonus by Project Integrated Open Space Public Benefit Features:

Urban Plaza   Hillclimb Assist

Parcel Park
Residential Parcel Park   Hillside Terrace

Public Atrium   Green Street Improvement

Shopping Atrium   Voluntary Building Setback

Shopping Corridor   Green Rooftops

97 Seattle's FAR bonuses on *Pedestrian* and *Green Streets* for special public amenities.

bonuses may be awarded to property owners who make contributions in
or around their building.

On the whole, Seattle is the US-American city having the most ingenious
incentive zoning [PB]. Introduced already in 1963, bonus-bestowing elements were raised in 1986 by zoning reforms from 5 to 28.

In Seattle's downtown, the basic utilization was able to be doubled from
a FAR of 10 to a legal maximum of 20. The *Washington Mutual Savings Bank
Building* with its 27 stories plus an additional 28 is probably the most
prominent instance of this allowable doubling. The applicable amenities resemble those in New York, and can be divided into four categories:

Plaza Bonus
[PB] §7.01–4

(1) *pedestrian amenities* such as public plazas, small parks, public interior spaces, wider sidewalks, as well as elements specific to Seattle, such as hillclimb assists, that is, public escalators, and roofed arcades designed to shield pedestrians from frequent rainfall; (2) *land use preferences* such as performing arts theaters, cinemas, shopping facilities and museums; (3) *social services* like affordable housing, day care, etc.; and (4) *design features* like sculptured building tops, atria, or public rooftop gardens designed to beautify the roofscape and to safeguard public views of the city and its spectacular surroundings.[19]

Finally, regulations also determine which ground floors must have continuous shop frontage, and what percentage of transparency ground floor façades must have according to the pedestrian street class [FT].

Façade Transparency
[FT] §4.08

But the doubled size of the 55-story Washington Mutual Savings Bank Building and other "out-of-scale" skyscrapers provoked strong resistance in Seattle. Opponents developed the *Citizens Alternative Plan* (CAP), which was met with acclaim. Endowed with the force of law, it specified that up until 1995, a maximum of 0.5 million square feet per year could be constructed in downtown Seattle, and from then until 1999, an overall maximum of 1,000,000 square feet.[20] This quota resembled the *Proposition M*,[21] introduced by San Francisco in 1986, which equally reduced the maximum constructive volume of new office towers per year.

Peek-a-boo at Mulholland

[A]
Mulholland Drive

[L]
Los Angeles

The Mulholland Scenic Parkway was opened in 1924, and ever since, it has afforded residents and visitors to Los Angeles spectacular views of the mountains and the Pacific Ocean, and of the city set below them. It meanders through the Hollywood Hills and the Santa Monica Mountains, from Hollywood Freeway all the way to the western Los Angeles City-County boundary line. For long stretches, one drives through seemingly undisturbed nature—only oak trees and a few coyotes are visible along the sides of the road. A couple of sections are not even paved. The district is astonishingly empty and undeveloped—yet the city seems to be besieging this altitude from all sides. Hollywood presses in from one side, the San Fernando Valley from the other. For a long time now, more than a few Angelenos have been quite prepared to pay handsomely for a mailing address on *Mulholland Drive*.

Except that Mulholland's constructive emptiness is faced by enormous regulatory density: distilled as the *Scenic Highway* from the *Los Angeles General Plan* and its *Scenic Highways Plan*, the *Mulholland Scenic Parkway—Specific Plan*[22] came into force in 1992.

The plan was created "in response to public concerns that the majestic views and natural character of the Mulholland Drive setting were threatened by unrestricted development."[23]

This plan complemented the also valid *Los Angeles Municipal Code* (LAMC),[24]

---

[19] See Garvin (1996), 446.
[20] Ibid.
[21] See *Little Big Plan* p.126.
[22] The City of Los Angeles (1992), *Mulholland Scenic Parkway—Specific Plan*.
[23] The City of Los Angeles (2003), *Mulholland Scenic Parkway Specific Plan—Design and Preservation Guidelines*.
[24] The City of Los Angeles (2007), *City of Los Angeles Municipal Code*.

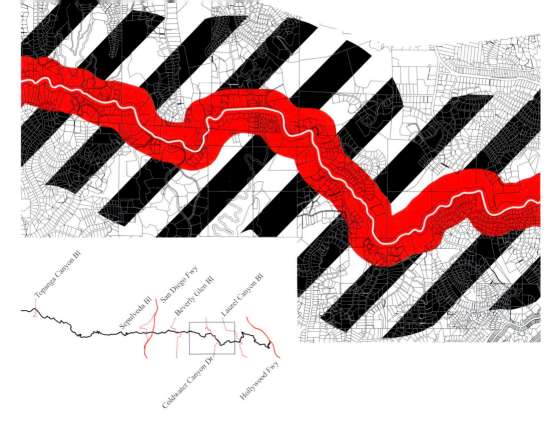

Topanga Canyon Bl
Sepulveda Bl
San Diego Fwy
Beverly Glen Bl
Laurel Canyon Bl
Coldwater Canyon Dr
Hollywood Fwy

98 Mulholland Drive's inner and outer protection corridors, Los Angeles.

and stipulated the involvement of a special review board, to which every project planned for the Drive had to be submitted. In order to prevent the board's decisions being left to the whims of their discretionary authority, and to make them sufficiently transparent, the review process operated on the basis of a specially prepared set of *Design and Preservation Guidelines*.[25]

"The ordinance created the Mulholland Scenic Parkway, including both the Inner and Outer Corridors, which established land use controls and a design review process tailored to ensure that development within the Parkway is compatible with the unique character of the Santa Monica Mountains."[26] Alongside these regulations, there are also those enacted under the *Subdivision Map Act*, the *Hillside Ordinance*, ...

Of course, this does not mean that building is to all intents and purposes forbidden. Ambitious owners must simply ensure that their homes comply with a variety of regulations which condition one another reciprocally in a vertical hierarchy.

The greatest advantage is enjoyed by projects not immediately visible from the street. In fact, the *Mulholland Specific Plan* and its "Guidelines" should be read as what they actually are: instructions for a game of hide-and-seek.

According to the guidelines, a suitable hiding place is composed of three critical ingredients: site planning, architecture, and landscaping.

Here are some of the rules that guide builders on their way to the successful concealment of homes—remote from privately owned public views:

[25] Los Angeles (2003).
[26] Ibid., 3.

99 Mulholland Drive—where do all the buildings hide?

No Site Grading
[NSG] §2.14

No Skylighting
[NSL] §7.02–9

Stepped Profile
[SP] §7.02–12

Visibility Study
[VIS] §5.15

Scenic Drive
Protection
[SDP] §2.07

Dirt Mulholland
[DM] §4.06

No Site Grading [NSG]: The natural topography should be preserved. Changes to it should under no circumstances extend up to the street.[27]

No Skylighting [NSL]: as seen from the street, no building is to be seen set against the skyline: no silhouetting![28]

Stepped Profile [SP]: If more than 25% of the given building is sited on a sloping site, then its volume should be stepped to follow the shape of the incline, with no wall taller than 25 ft (7.6 m).[29]

Visibility Study [VIS]: Of critical importance are all views of a building project from Mulholland Drive, and within a radius of 3/4 of a mile around it. This restriction is vital, since if all views from the street were forbidden, this would amount to an implicit ban on building altogether (due to the curved contour of the road almost any house is bound to be visible from one point or another).[30]

Scenic Drive Protection [SDP]: Measurements (views) are taken from the edge of the road at a height of 4 ft (1.2 m). The height corresponds to the view from the side window of a traveling automobile. If the edge of the road cannot be precisely determined (i.e., in the absence of surface paving), measurements are taken from a position past which a vehicle can definitely drive![31]

Dirt Mulholland [DM]: Even the dirt found on the road surface has been placed under protection: "It is recognized that the unpaved portion of Mulholland Drive is considered to be an outstanding and unique feature

[27] Ibid., *Guideline 17*, 12.
[28] Ibid., *Guideline 17*, 6.
[29] Ibid., *Guideline 02*, 5.
[30] Ibid., *Guideline 17*, 12.
[31] Ibid., *Guideline 19*, 13.

Stepped Profile [SP]

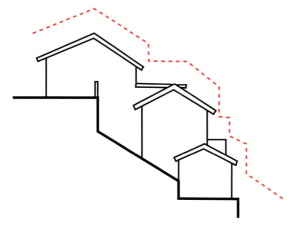

100a The roof mimics the slope (guideline 2, 5).

Visibility Study [VIS]

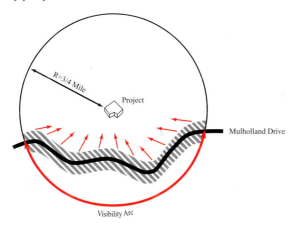

100b What may be visible from which point (guideline 17, 12).

Scenic Drive Protection [SDP]

100c What cannot be seen from the drivers's seat (guideline 19, 14).

Color Wheel [CW]

Spring   Winter

Artemesia   Water

Sky   Dark Greens

Greys: Stachys   Cool Gray

Bottle Tree   Red Berries (Toyon)

Streams   Shade

Dark Greens   Bark

Lush Vegetation   Rocks

Greens: Lush Vegetation   Soil

Oak   Sand

Toyon   Yellow Sun

Golds: Liquid Amber   Dry Grasses

Rust   Greens: African Sumac, Rhus

Purples: Vinca   Blues: Sky, Caenothus

Pinks: Vinca, Periwinkle

Fall   Summer

100d The Santa Monica Mountains Color Wheel stipulates a building's color according to the surrounding vegetation and season.

Landscape Screening [LSS]

100e Buildings are screened off by vegetation (guideline 63, 29).

Height Difference Max [HDM]

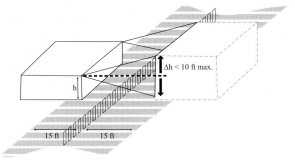

Δh < 10 ft max.

h

15 ft   15 ft

100f Neighboring home height: max. difference = 10 ft (3 m) (guideline 51, 25).

Neighborhood Compatibility [NC]

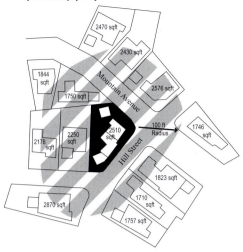

Codified average—*Neighborhood Compatibility* radius map (guideline 50, 25)

of the Mulholland Scenic Parkway."[32]

Exterior Colors [CW]: "Colors for residences, walls, fences, and all other exterior structures should complement or be consistent with the naturally-occurring colors of the Santa Monica Mountains, as shown on the Color Wheel. Visible roof coverings and deck surfaces should consist of non-reflective, earth tone colors."[33]

Color Wheel
[CW] §7.04–4

A specialty of these guidelines is the *Color Wheel*—the Pantone color chart for the mountains of Los Angeles: found in Appendix A are the 34 colors arranged in a circle, each quadrant oriented to one of the four seasons. The wheel is concerned with the bureaucratic determination of all natural coloration visible in the Santa Monica Mountains, as observed throughout the year: from the late summer pink of the periwinkle to wintertime ocean blue! According to the guidelines, this color palette facilitates the decreed mimicry to be undertaken by local buildings.

Neighborhood Compatibility [NC] [HDM]: in order to blend in perfectly, each project must be compared directly in terms of form, use, height, setback, and landscaping with all architectural development within a range of 100 feet (30 m). Each home must be built in accordance with the existing average, with only minor deviations...[34]

Neighborhood Compatibility
[NC] §5.09
Height Difference Max
[HDM] §5.07

Landscape Screening [LSS]: Should a portion of a building project too far and "penetrates the viewshed," then there always remains the fallback solution of planting a tree or bush. "Informal/natural groupings of plant material should be used as screening whenever possible instead of walls or fences. A minimum of 50% of all screening plant material should be evergreen. Landscaping should be used to screen structures, while permitting views out in a 'peek-a-boo' fashion."[35]

Landscape Screening
[LSS] §6.14

The guidelines continue with a number of detailed specifications con-

[32] Ibid., *Guideline 27*, 17.
[33] Ibid., *Guideline 38*, 21.
[34] Ibid., *Guideline 50*, 24.
[35] Ibid., *Guideline 63*, 29.

cerning how buildings should be arranged and which plants should be given preference. Also valid along the inner and outer corridors in an off-set from Mulholland Drive are extreme and as a rule non-negotiable zoning regulations: nearly everywhere there are RE-40 zones with a minimum lot size requirement [LS] of 40,000 sqft (3700 sqm) and minimum lot widths of 100 ft (30 m) per unit and per lot.

Lot Size Requirements
·[LS] §6.02

This wealth of details, contained in the 90 guidelines, combined with all of the additional rules and related ordinances, serves to preserve the character of Mulholland Drive as "a low-density, low-volume, (s)low-speed roadway in a hillside parkway-type"[36] on a terrain that is already difficult of access. The result is a gravely threatened landscape, but at the same time one of the best protected worldwide.

Freedom at the Edge

Special Districts
[SD] §3.01

The designation "*special district*" [SD] is a pleonasm. Every district and every geographical region is in some sense special, otherwise there would be nothing to distinguish it, and no reason to delimit it from the surrounding context. In any event, different rules are operative within such an unambiguously defined territory than those outside of it. If such special rules are codified, then special district status can constitute an instrument of municipal administration.

Such special cases are of special interest for the way in which their boundaries are defined. Occurring here in particular, along these artificially determined lines, are those "hygienic violations" which zoning has always sought to avoid ever since its introduction. For the sake of clarity, the demarcation line separating two districts is usually located along the central line of a street. Vis-à-vis development, this means that entirely different rules may apply to the left side of the street than those that are valid for the right side. Height limits can vary, certain forms of utilization may be banned on one side of the street but allowed on the other. In this regard, a zoning map knows no indistinctness—a circumstance that is recognizable already in the use of richly contrasting and intense colors for the indexing of the various zones. The legend of the zoning map is limited in scope, and as a planning key, it has an almost pacifying effect on the eyes of the urban planner, so plagued by urban unclarity. An explicit territorial order appears to stand behind urban reality, a plan that is subdivided into residential, industrial, commercial, and special!

But what happens along the borderline, where saturated red converges directly with pale yellow?

Wilshire Boulevard

[A]
Wilshire Boulevard

[L]
Los Angeles

Wilshire Boulevard is a typical American avenue. Like many large American boulevards, it is flanked by zones of heightened utilization. This linear zone—which is often only as deep as a single building lot to the left and right of the street—has extremely long edge lengths in relation to the total surface of the zone. On its path through Los Angeles, traveling from the Pacific in an easterly direction, the Boulevard with its tall flanks

---

[36] Ibid., 3.

traverses a zone of quite tall residential towers as well as passing through the residential zone of Westwood—the latter having almost as many front doors as residents.

The contrast could hardly be greater: R1–1 comes into immediate contact with R5–3. A zone of single-family homes touches without transition one that contains multiple dwellings without height limits and an allowable utilization of 10 times the plot area (FAR = 10). Buildings whose apexes accommodate helicopter landing pads instead of tiled saddleback roofs.

The situation is dramatic: the tower sitting in the backyard of a charming, one-story single-family dwelling seems to spectacularly flout zoning ordinances. The prefix [Q][37] in the zoning code is intended to oblige developers to be considerate of neighbors. On a given day of the year, for example, the shadows of the tall tower may fall onto flat land only up to a length of 200 ft (60 m), and the tower may not exceed 75 ft (23 m) in width in the east-west direction—this is in order to allow sufficient natural light to fall on the building lot to the north.

But no matter how many prefixes the zone has, the first row of single-family homes along the zone's frontline will unavoidably be sacrificed—if not without enjoying a certain special charm—after all, how many ordinary houses have high-rises in their backyards?

On the other hand, as soon as the apartments contained in these residential towers rise above the tree line of the neighboring gardens, they enjoy incomparable and priceless views into the distance—an enhancement of value and quality that arises inadvertently, as a side effect of this abrupt change of zone.

Furthermore, the city of Los Angeles has not neglected to place this morphologically unique feature under special protection. Whereby the *Wilshire—Westwood Scenic Corridor Specific Plan*[38] is concerned with the interior portion of the regulated area, with the streetscape of Wilshire Boulevard from the perspective of the driver. The city writes:

"It is the purpose of the development standards established in this Plan to minimize traffic and parking problems along Wilshire Boulevard, enhance the aesthetic qualities of the Specific Plan area, encourage more open space, reduce the impact of high-density residential development and reduce the impact of shadows caused by high-rise buildings within and adjacent to the Specific Plan Area."[39]

Codified Icons

The consistently highly contrasting boundary situation in the zoning plan has endowed Wilshire with an iconic status. The Boulevard extending from the sea to LA's actual downtown has itself developed into a linear downtown. The former infrastructure has become a three-dimensional object visible from afar, a notable address with a prominent sky-lit silhouette. This is what distinguishes Wilshire Blvd. from its counter-

---

[37]   [Q] means "Qualified Classification: Restrictions on property as a result of a zone change, to ensure compatibility with surrounding property," according to Section 12. 32 of the *Los Angeles Zoning Code*.

[38]   The City of Los Angeles (1981), *Wilshire—Westwood Scenic Corridor—Specific Plan*.

[39]   Ibid., 3.

101a Wilshire Boulevard: Westwood Scenic Corridor Specific Plan—aerial taken from the southwest.

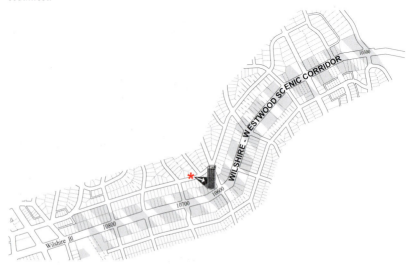

101b Westwood Scenic Corridor Specific Plan (plan view).

101c Lindbrook Drive: picture taken from the corridor's back alley—right at the edge (*).

part, Mulholland Drive. William Mulholland (1855-1935) was the worthy, self-effacing engineer who facilitated the growth of Los Angeles through his Southern California water infrastructure. In contrast, H. Gaylord Wilshire (1861-1927) was an offensive braggart from a rich Ohio family who made and lost his fortune in real estate, farming und gold mining.

Transition and Overlay: Gradients

Rarely is the coloristic contrast of a zoning plan so distinct and three-dimensionally legible as in the case of Wilshire Boulevard. More frequently, a third zone is formed by the convergence of two neighboring and strongly contrasted ones: the boundary line between them is thickened to form a mediating overlay or transition zone [TS]. A boundary line running through the center of a street amounts to the provision of certain freedoms on one side of the street, while the same possibilities for development are withheld from the other. Such regulatory discrepancies on one and the same street often make an impression of arbitrariness and unfairness, and are strongly resented by the affected property owners. As a rule, the city government approaches such a potential conflict situation in two different ways. Either exceptional rules which apply to specific affected sections of the street are anchored in the zoning ordinance, or else each problem is dealt with individually as it emerges as a special hardship case by the responsible board of appeals.[40]

All the same, such boundary areas are probably the most interesting elements in the zoning plan and for the city it regulates. These putatively marginal surfaces have the potential to become genuine mixed-use strips. They contain not just separated residential and business uses, but often involve a healthy coexistence of these normally hygienically isolated functions. Such utilizations—usually declassed to the status of "LULUs" (locally undesirable land uses) from the perspective of property ownership—suddenly find themselves in direct proximity to residential buildings.

For areas of sufficient dimensions, this indistinctness means an opportunity to generate genuine mixed-use development, so that an area is suddenly more than a boundary line joining two zones, and instead becomes their common center.

Designated by New York's zoning ordinance are special overlays [OZ] within which certain types of mixed use are specified. It can be stipulated, for example, that even where residential, work, and retail functions are permitted to coexist in a single building, residential uses must always be stacked on top of commercial ones.[41]

[A]
Zones

[L]
North America

Transition Zoning
[TS] §3.09

Overlay Zones
[OZ] §7.03–4

---

[40] On this topic, see also Arthur C. Comey (1933), *Transition Zoning*, 8.
[41] See C1 & C2 overlays in New York (2006), *Zoning Handbook*, 53.

Overlay Zones [OZ]

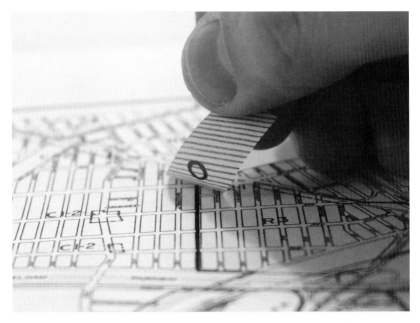

102 *Overlay Zones.*

8

Difference and Consistency

Protecting the public interest and, by doing so, going beyond fostering the pursuit of individual interests, also means to mediate, on a variety of levels, between a desired degree of coherence and continuity and an inevitable and potentially desired diversity of urban form. The following cases demonstrate how urban elements as such are formed by mutual consistency, while at the same time they possess the capacity to facilitate differences to emerge from their context.

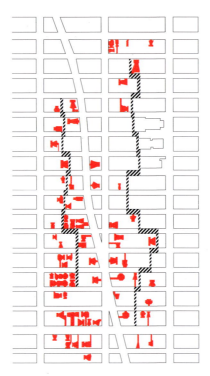

103 Thwarting the grid #1: New York Theater District (map with arcades, old and new theaters, 1969).

Contrast by Forced Consistency: New York's Special Theater District

[A]
Mayor Lindsay, Weinstein

New York's theater district exhibits a strong contrast with its surroundings—and this precisely by virtue of a heightened level of inner consistency and continuity.

[L]
New York City

After New York City had successfully updated its zoning ordinance in the 1960s, introducing innovations like incentive zoning, the formerly so celebrated Midtown, with its theater district, was aging drastically. Worse yet, the theaters were threatened with extinction. Historic institutions like the Empire and Paramount theaters and the Metropolitan Opera House testify to the silent death of more than 45 theaters[1] since the flowering of this branch of urban entertainment in the 1920s.

"The expansion of midtown office building concentration had begun to threaten the continued existence of the legitimate theaters, which were only an economic land use because they were old and had been paid for long ago. No one would build a legitimate theater as an investment today, and there was no way for the city to insure the preservation of the old theaters—unless the City could buy them all, which would clearly be impractical."[2]

Something had to be done, private business had to learn to love the theater again.

The solution was the setting up of a *Special Theater District*, one that would be territorially delimited from the Times Square area of Midtown Manhattan [SD]. The city combined this theater protection zone with its pre-

Special Districts
[SD] §3.01

[1]   Stern (1995), 444.
[2]   Jonathan Barnett (1970), *Introduction to Part III: Case Studies in Creative Urban Zoning*, 127.

viously instituted system of bonuses. In this, a building would receive a utilization bonus not for the provision of just *any* public amenity, but specifically for the establishment of a theater and its obligatory infrastructure.

Not unlike that which Robert Moses achieved with his expressways, the city's normally delimiting street grid was pierced, overlaid, and counteracted—not by new streets, however, but instead in the form of midblock walkways and arcades. Pure geographical proximity was no longer the sole binding criterion for the block. Instead, "certain points of continuity between adjacent developments are made mandatory."

The cultural *Lincoln Square District*, for example: "Developers are encouraged to provide a continuous arcade along the east side of Broadway, creating a uniform backdrop for Lincoln Center, as well as a sheltered pedestrian promenade."[3] Individual plazas, hitherto distributed thoughtlessly through a city, began (if tentatively) to be coordinated with one another, forming a continuous public space in conjunction with the new pedestrian infrastructure.

In a heroically tinged anecdote, one reminiscent of a crime novel by Raymond Chandler, Richard Weinstein—a member of New York's Urban Design Group, established in 1967—describes how he and Mayor John Lindsay negotiated late into the night with the developers of the Astor Hotel site in order to build a new theater there.[4] They sat together on massive leather sofas in the offices of Sam Minskoff & Sons, drinking expensive whiskey and enjoying the fabulous view of the Manhattan skyline from the posh penthouse of the wealthy developer. But none of that succeeded in distracting the mayor from the actual motive for his visit. Weinstein quoted Lindsay as follows: "Every day in my life I ask people to do something which is in the interest of the City. Sometimes it makes them richer, sometimes it makes them poorer. I don't know how this will affect you, but I do know that a theater on this site is in the interest of the City, and today, the finger is on your shoulder."[5] Thus were the battle lines drawn. The city wanted a theater, the developer wanted adequate compensation for building it—or more precisely, wanted to be paid for building it. A series of such meetings ensued, each involving office, theater, and building organizations assembled by both the Urban Design Group and the developer. In the end, the ad hoc connection to the developer set up by the mayor led to the suspension of numerous general provisions: "The city offered the developer a floor-area bonus up to 20% more space above the current zoning ceiling, the waiving of height and setback regulations, and the use of full bonus provisions for a plaza without the provision of a plaza as defined in the zoning resolution."[6]

Standing on Times Square by the year 1972 was a 227 m high structure referred to as the *One Astor Plaza Building* (formerly the *W. T. Grant Building*)—precursor to the *Special Theater District Zoning Amendment* of the following year.

3   Ibid., 128.
4   Richard Weinstein (1970), *How New York's Zoning Was Changed to Induce the Construction of Legitimate Theaters*, 131–36.
5   Ibid.
6   Ibid.

The new regulations also manifested the two future lives that lay in store for Times Square—a schizophrenia neatly demarcated by the arrival of nighttime: a glamorous entertainment district by night, a respectable business district by day.

Conceived by planners who assumed that the presence of new office buildings within the theater district was both unavoidable and desirable, the new rules dealing with offices and theaters were far too little concerned with preserving the older theaters still in existence. For these historic structures, the option (for example) of exploiting their underused air rights by selling them at enormous profits to adjacent properties came far too late.[7]

Perpetual Inconsistency—Space

But rules reputedly suffer from a disadvantage in planning terms. Of critical importance in this context is the rule's reference element. If rules pertain to truly local elements, to individual building lots, for example, then their orientation toward an individual object automatically endows them with a certain ignorance in relation to its surroundings and immediate context. In this case, they work exclusively with the prevailing characteristics and parameters of the relevant building lot or special element to which they refer. A process of individualization takes place, one which in the best cases can lead to heightened urban diversity within an area, but often instead involves a certain redundancy.

If the reference element is general in nature, for example the streetscape, superordinate infrastructure, or the vicinity of the object to be regulated, then the structural continuity of the reference magnitude is also transferred onto the object that is to be regulated. A district-wide continuum is then formed.

When it comes to urban rules, the distinction between a general (public) and an individualized orientation can be exemplified through another comparison between the 1916 zoning resolution and its 1961 successor. The 1916 ordinance contained a series of rules which addressed infrastructural units that went beyond individual pieces of property. Just think of the setback regulations and the height districts, which were based on

Setback Street Ratio
[SSR] §4.13

street widths [SSR]. In this instance, the continuity of New York's street space was transferred to the individual building in the form of a consistent setback line which went beyond the boundary of the parcel.

Beginning in 1961, and at the latest with the introduction of the Floor

Floor Area Ratio
[FAR] §7.01–1

Area Ratio [FAR], many of these continuities were sacrificed. The FAR, for example, determines the gross surface area of a building via direct reference to the lot size and its surface area—an absolutely local reference. And accordingly, all of the regulations based on this premise, such as the FAR bonus for the provision of public amenities, took no account of the surrounding urban context. As a result, New York wound up with "towers that stand in their individual pools of plaza space. Shopping frontages are interrupted and open spaces appear at random, unrelated to topography, sunlight, or the design of the plaza across the way."[8]

---

[7] Initially introduced through the 1998 *Theater Subdistrict Zoning Regulations*.
[8] Clifford L. Weaver and Richard F. Babcock (1979), *City Zoning, the Once and Future Frontier*, 62.

Retail Frontage Continuity [RFC]

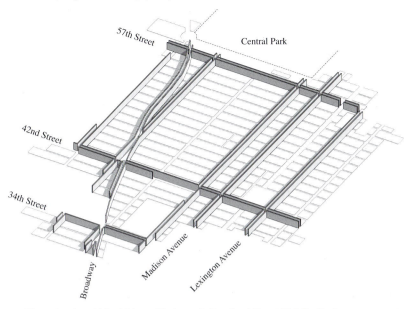

104a Thwarting the grid #2: Midtown Manhattan's *Retail* and *Street Wall Continuity*.

Shop Front Diversity [SFD]

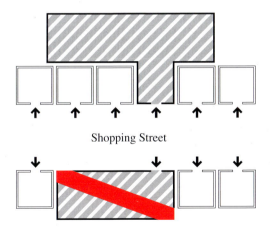

Shopping Street

104b No large-scale commercial facilities to take over frontages larger than 1 ½ of their neighbors in Seattle's shopping streets.

Subsequent decades saw the arrival of numerous critiques of this modernist concept, and a series of countervailing measures were adopted—and this meant again decreeing that consideration would be accorded to neighboring properties. As the preeminent planning tool, the FAR had not relinquished its adequacy, and the accompanying bonus system continued to be a much-favored instrument for inducing owners of private property to provide public amenities. But working now in a way that

[A]
Jacobs, SoHo Artists Association

[L]
New York City

complemented the FAR was a set of continuity-generating rules—not seldom in the form of a drawn plan: for example the in the meantime prescribed *Retail Frontage Continuity* [RFC] in Midtown Manhattan (see also San Francisco, Seattle, Vancouver) and the networking of individual theaters in New York's Theater District via continuous arcades and walkways, but also *Neighborhood Compatibility* [NC] on Mulholland Drive, Los Angeles, *Contextual Base* [CB] and *Street-Wall Continuity* [SWC] in New York, all the way to the *Pedestrian Street Classification* [PS] in Seattle, and so forth. Many cities, moreover, prepared explicit plans effecting the consistent subdivision of green zones and other public spaces.

Killing with Kindness

In the eyes of many critics, New York's flood of plazas, its wave of theaters, all ostensibly conjured by well-meaning urban planning instruments, had led to monotony and decay. The problem, however, did not necessarily lie with the rules themselves or with their aims, but far more with their unrestricted success [GT]. And the only thing the city can be reproached for is having underestimated its own achievement.

But such urban natural catastrophes are not always administered by municipalities. The tendency toward such flooding, driven by particularly (economically) successful utilizations is described in detail by Jane Jacobs in her apocalyptic but optimistic book *The Death and Life of Great American Cities*. Alongside the above-named functions, she lists the flood of art galleries, restaurants, nightclubs, apartments, clothing stores, and tourists attractions. In principle, none of these functions are undesirable. On the contrary, it is precisely their widespread acceptance that allows them to multiply so quickly that they force out other programmes that remain important for maintaining balanced and diverse urban quarters—thereby undermining the very basis for their own success, namely, a complex urban environment.

The urban district "de-diversifies" and stagnates. And this ushers in the "self-destruction of diversity,"[9] or even the production of "has-been" districts. And it is all the same whether we are talking about restaurants, office towers, or theaters.

In 1974, three years after SoHo became a legal entity as the district for New York's artistic community [AC], an article entitled "SoHo a Victim of Its Own Success" appeared in the *New York Times*.[10]

In 1971, the city rezoned the district's manufacturing lofts as apartments for artists, thereby legalizing the residencies of approximately 600 families. Now that it had become a "residential district," the pressure was on to allow all social groups—at least those who could afford it—to live in SoHo. Landlords and real estate brokers in particular argued that the zoning laws then in effect were too strict.

SoHo's official classification in the zoning plan as an artist's oasis exacerbated the situation noticeably. Of course, residents no longer had to worry about being evicted by the police. But the district was attracting throngs of tourists and other passers-by who wanted to see for them-

---

9   Jacobs (1961), 241–56.
10 Wendy Schuman (1974), *Soho a 'Victim of Its Own Success'*.

selves just how artists lived in SoHo. Such people supplied a customer base for cafés, restaurants, bookshops, and art galleries, with growing numbers of such establishments following in their wake. A former refuge that offered artists abundant living space for little money had now become a high-priced commercial display window. "Not another Eighth Street" was the battle cry of residents—the reference being to Greenwich Village commercialism.[11] The saying: "SoHo is a victim of its own success" comes from Marilyn Mammano, an urban planner for SoHo.

Although entitled to do so, relatively few artists have had themselves certified in SoHo at the *Cultural Affairs Department*. The reason for this avoidance is the fact that all of them live in lofts that are too large for the zoning, and none of them wishes to call attention to their own personal misdemeanors. The *SoHo Artists Association*, on the other hand, is not necessarily in favor of an exclusive artists' district, and has nothing against related professional groups living in SoHo, gallery owners, for example, or art critics, etc.

The Association had promised the city it would assume responsibility, as a kind of self-administration, for maintaining compliance with zoning ordinances. Once these "independent civil servants" have been accused by residents of resorting to "Gestapo tactics," they restricted their activities to encouraging residents to at least become certified.

The city, meanwhile, was facing more challenging tasks than that of unmasking SoHo residents as non-artists. The neighborhood was opened up to the real estate market, and rising prices soon chased most of the impoverished artists out of the area.

According to the *New York Times*, however, it was not necessarily the illegal residents that presented a problem for the municipal administration, but instead the illegal residences. Many buildings inhabited by communes were not zoned for residence. They were either in too poor a condition, or were too large. Determined to protect existing industries and handicraft enterprises from the danger of heightened pressures on SoHo's apartment market, the *Department of Buildings* had to date permitted only smaller units to be used as residences. Since it was in all likelihood the overall economic situation that was responsible for the out-migration of the textile manufacturing industries, real estate people and planners hardly knew what was to be done with such buildings. Perhaps they could be used as discos, or for functions regarded as undesirable by locals? In the face of such programmatic threats to their tranquility, SoHo residents even attempted to exert pressure on the City Planning Commission; the utilizations permitted in SoHo must be restricted accordingly.

Who would have believed that a group of individualistic artists, plagued by extreme anxiety in the face of any form of official classification, would come together to form a genuine neighborhood, in the process invoking exclusive, segregationist planning instruments!

---

[11] Ibid.

Revision Cycles [RC]

(. . .)

(b) Nighttime closing of existing public open areas

In all *Residence Districts*, the City Planning Commission may, upon application, authorize the closing during certain nighttime hours of an existing ~~plaza, plaza connected open area or residential plaza~~ *publicly accessible open area* for which a *floor area* bonus has been received, pursuant to Section ~~37-06~~ 37-727 (~~Nighttime Closing of Existing Public Open Areas~~ Hours of Access).

105 Constant code amendments.

Perpetual Inconsistency—Time

[A] Greenwich Village Civic Groups

[L] New York City

The problem of the unavoidable destruction of vital diversity is closely associated with regulatory measures—and moreover precisely at the point where positive developments go awry. The greatest defect of such an excessive development is that it is not self-modifying. The quantum of a certain utilization continues to grow to the point of saturation and the displacement of other functions.

Required here is a temporally calibrated countermeasure. In this regard, the zoning changes of 1961 introduced an error while at the same time effecting something positive [RC].

Revision Cycles [RC] §1.05

First, the positive aspects: the rules have changed fundamentally, that is to say, this regulatory break contributed greatly to the diversification of the city, simply by modifying or interfering with the routine development process. But in principle, the "how" played no great role; the main thing was that tried-and-true rules and their associated conventions were compelled to change. Halted in Midtown, and prevented from flooding throughout the city, for example, was the further growth of the *Bulky Block Type* [BBT], which had hitherto proliferated, propelled by its own economic success. This rupture was long overdue.

Bulky Block Type [BBT] §7.02–16

And now for the downside: the altered rules tended to amplify a trend that had enjoyed much success during this period. A refreshing rarity prior to 1961, the plaza-type office tower multiplied without cease, in the process receiving the support of the city. The avalanche was perfect.

Beginning much earlier, in the 1930s, precisely when New York's tallest prewar buildings were being erected, there had been the Great Depression. This phased displacement, mentioned earlier, between elevated levels of speculative building activity and economic boom and bust cycles came to regulate the tall office tower. This thermostat had prevented the construction of many even taller buildings in Midtown, thereby also rescuing a number of older buildings and hence preserving a certain level of architectural diversity.

In 1959, Greenwich Village civic groups succeeded in implementing a drastic maximum development height for certain streets. Many of the streets, however, were already occupied by numerous buildings that were considerably taller than the limit.

Did the rule come too late?

Not at all, for it was not concerned with preventing tall buildings in gen-

106 The gentlemen with one exception at the UN Secretariat, New York.

eral, but instead with halting their rampant multiplication. "Again, sameness was being zoned out—or in effect, differences zoned in…"[12] The most important aspect of rules, then, is their potential for being inscribed with a definitive, temporally-delimited durability.

New York's zoning ordinance was endowed with an extraordinary design quality only through thousands of alterations, and through the general revisions introduced on an average of 40–50 years. Which is very probably too long! That rules are modified is no evidence of their failure, but is instead the necessary result of a dynamically behaving regulatory mechanism with a thermostat character. One that is perhaps too inert at times, and which has a sluggish reaction time.

This calculable inconsistency is further supported by the direct private pressure in revolt against excessive orderliness.

Gentlemen's Agreements

New York City prior to the turn of the millennium: standing on the banks of the East River is the UN *Secretariat Building*, erected by Wallace K. Harrison between 1947 and 1952. At a height of 152 m, the UN slab dominates the scene. Taller towers maintain a respectful distance, and there is no structure in the direct vicinity which surpasses the Secretariat Building in height. The tower at *One United Nation Plaza*, built by Kevin Roche John Dinkeloo & Associates in 1975, has exactly the same height as the UN building. This maximum building height was determined by a kind of gentlemen's agreement [GA], and everyone has adhered to it. Or nearly everyone!

[A]
Trump and the UN

[L]
New York City

Gentlemen's Agreement [GA] §3.03

[12] Jacobs (1961), 253.

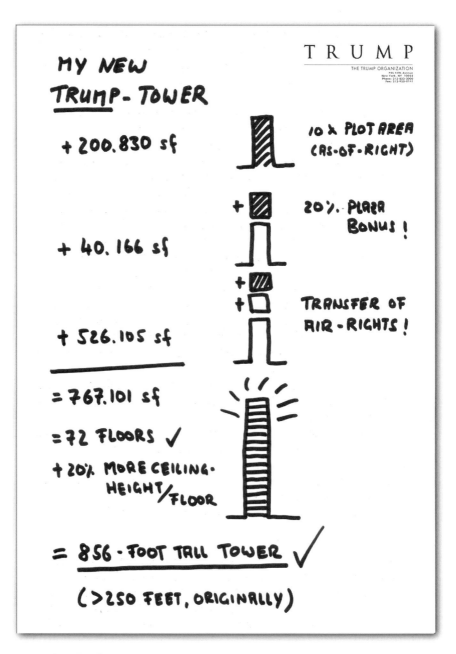

MY NEW
TRUMP-TOWER

+ 200.830 sf

10 x PLOT AREA
(AS·OF·RIGHT)

+ 40.166 sf

20% PLAZA
BONUS !

+ 526.105 sf

TRANSFER OF
AIR-RIGHTS !

= 767.101 sf

= 72 FLOORS ✓

+ 20% MORE CEILING·HEIGHT/FLOOR

= 856·FOOT TALL TOWER ✓

(>250 FEET, ORIGINALLY)

TRUMP
THE TRUMP ORGANIZATION

107 Possible calculation of tower height.

Rising in the year 2000 was a building that would remain during the subsequent two years the tallest residential tower worldwide. This was the slender *Trump World Tower*, built by Costas Kondylis & Partners LLP Architects. With its height of 261 m, it was sited not just anywhere, but on 47th St at the corner of 1st Ave—in the direct vicinity of the UN Secretariat Building.

As an expert in challenging and playing with the city and its rules, Donald Trump managed to exceed the determined height limit for his World Plaza Tower next to the UN Secretariat Building to an extent that it was almost as though there were no restrictions at all. On the purchased lot, which measured 20,083 sqft (1,865 sqm), Donald Trump was able to build by law a tower ten times the size of the plot's floor area—200,830 sqft (18,650 sqm) *as-of-right*.

By not covering the entire plot, the tower's slenderness adds to its height and creates an empty space around the base of the building. In zoning terms, this space is considered a "plaza." This area, then, earned Trump the above-mentioned plaza bonus [PB], which allowed him to build 20% larger. Trump was able, then, to add 40,166 sqft (3,731 sqm) to his tower. Meanwhile, Trump took a close look at the surrounding buildings and their plots. Indeed, the plots are all covered by buildings, but do not rise all the way to the heights stipulated by zoning limits. After being offered substantial incentives, the owners of seven plots willingly sold their theoretical option of building higher. These air rights [TDR] were transferred to Mr. Trump, and henceforth belonged to him as development rights. Piled up on his own plot, they allowed him to exceed the original zoning by an additional 526,105 sqft (48,875 sqm) of floor area. Now, the resultant 767,101 sqft (71,263 sqm) could be piled up. But none of these machinations drew public attention—at this point, not even later opponents of the project were aware that anything was amiss. Not without a dose of *Schadenfreude*, Trump later commented on this belated awareness: "You could say they were asleep at the wheel."[13]

Since the zoning resolution does not stipulate ceiling heights, Trump simply extended them 20% above average, thereby increasing the height of his tower even further.

Starting with merely ten times the size of the lot, Trump's tower now has more than 38 times that size. With its height of 856 ft (261 m), the tower clearly transgresses the gentlemen's agreement that prevented any building from surpassing the flanking UN Secretariat in height. And not by just a little, but instead by more than 90 m![14]

It's easy to be great, when everyone else must remain small!

The Public View onto the Private

As a consequence of an artificially low development height, one maintained for decades, Trump's tower stands out against the heavens like an obelisk, a prominent eye catcher that provides residents with perhaps the most spectacular views in all of New York City. The penthouse level has qualities comparable to those of the observation deck of the Empire State Building.

The project's opponents—primarily residents, but also celebrities, architectural societies, community groups, lawyers and much money—never tired of pointing out the injustices brought about by this building. According to Mr. Vilar, who could see the Empire State Building now only from the bedroom of his 30 room apartment, as much as $400,000 went into the war chest of the anti-Trump campaign. Mayor Giuliani, among others, was reproached for remaining deaf to the complaints of residents;

Plaza Bonus
[PB] §7.01–4

Transfer of Development Rights
[TDR] § 5.14

---

[13] Donald Trump, quoted in Blaine Harden (1999), *A Bankroll to Fight a Behemoth; Rich Neighbors Open Wallets to Battle Trump's Project for Residential Skyscraper.*
[14] Park Chapman (2000), *Built with a Merger Here, a Bonus There—Trump Plaza.*

108 Views are not perpetual—not even bad ones. Tudor City, Manhattan.

there were even attempts to exert pressure on participating investors (a letter went out to Kim Dae Jung, former South Korean head of state, seeking to prevent the Korean Daewoo Concern from investing in the Trump Tower). Ultimately unsuccessful as well was an attempt to certify that the tower was going to interfere with flight patterns above New York City.

The tower's most prominent opponent was probably Walter Cronkite, former anchorman at CBS News. Small wonder, since the building was going to completely block views of the Chrysler Building from his apartment. On September 8, 1999 a *New York Times* article by Blaine Harden cited him as follows: "Most of us recognize that in the vibrant, constantly changing metropolis that is New York, only those fortunate and wealthy enough to live on Fifth Avenue and Central Park West or facing one of the rivers have any sort of guarantee of a perpetual view!"[15]

The majority of the project's opponents were no less affluent than the average Fifth Avenue New Yorker.

In his complaint against inaction on the part of the city, which apparently failed to recognize its responsibilities toward the protection of existing views, Cronkite linked the "vibrant, constantly changing metropolis" indirectly with rules that lacked permanent status, but were subject to alterability.

The conversion of Cronkite's recriminations into an inherent quality of New York City makes good sense: New York's vibrancy consists precisely in its absence of guarantees. Here, contexts reserve the right to evolve.

[15] Harden (1999).

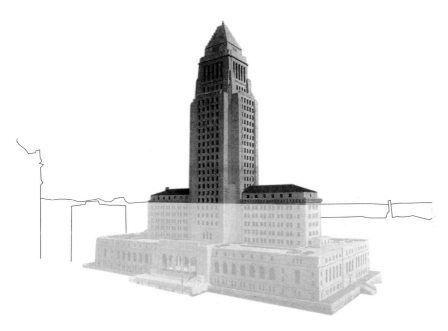

109 Los Angeles City Hall.

And rights to good views are not "perpetual"—nor are rights to bad ones: the residents of *Tudor City*, directly across from UN Headquarters, are reminded daily of this fateful fact. "Situated above First Avenue, Tudor City isn't lacking in spectacular views: the sun rising over the East River, the retro Pepsi-Cola sign in Queens, the UN. Take a closer look at this building's eastern facade and you'll discover it's the windows that are lacking. Back in the 1880s this was a good thing. The waterfront reeked from the smells of slaughterhouses, tanneries, breweries, and overcrowded tenements. A gang of criminals, Corcoran's Roosters, even occupied a brownstone on 40th Street. Hoping to introduce respectability to the area, architect Fred French began work on the Tudor City residences in 1925. He envisioned the community as a 'city within a city' and oriented the buildings inwards without windows on the east side. The slaughterhouses may have been cleared out in the '40s, but there's no looking back."[16]

Official Break-Outs and Break-Ins
Donald Trump, then, provides us with a lesson on how to erect urban icons: playing a decisive role is not just the building itself, but also its contrast with its immediate context, with neighboring buildings.
By slipping a building through the vicinity's last remaining loophole, Trump succeeded in constructing a private landmark or reference point —an almost textbook instance of something described by Kevin Lynch: "Landmarks become more easily identifiable, more likely to be chosen

[A]
US municipalities

[L]
Boston, Chicago, Los Angeles, Philadelphia and Washington D.C.

[16] Stern (1995), 279.

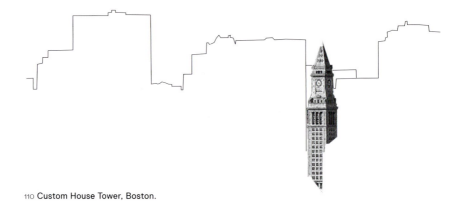

110 Custom House Tower, Boston.

Where is William? [WIW]

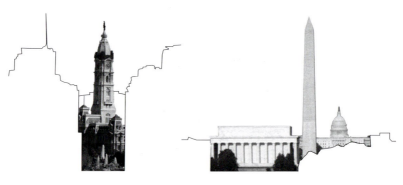

111 William Penn in Philadelphia.

112 Skyline of Washington, DC.

as significant, if they have a clear form; if they contrast with their background; and if there is some prominence of spatial location. Figure-background contrast seems to be the principal factor [LMI]."[17]

Landmarks and Icons
[LMI] §5.04

Municipal administrations had already turned to such methods much earlier: until the late 1950s, Los Angeles limited the heights of office buildings to 45 m. The reason for this was the danger of collapsing buildings in the event of an earthquake. Back in 1928, nonetheless, Los Angeles had built a *City Hall* 139 m high within the boundaries of the 45 m limit. In Los Angeles, the earthquake hazard seems not to have affected public buildings. In Boston in 1915, the US federal government built its *Custom House Tower* despite a citywide height limit of 38 m, one originally designed to avoid traffic congestion. Only in 1964 would the *Prudential Tower*, with its impressive height of 229 m, displace the Custom Tower as the city's tallest building.

Both Los Angeles and Boston were prepared to transgress their own rules, degrading all of the surroundings to mere context—just like Donald Trump (so compliant!) in New York.

Where Is William?
[WIW] §2.09

William Penn was not so steadfast: Philadelphia had a height limit of 150 meters, allowing William Penn to gaze downward onto the city from the 167 m tall tower of City Hall for all eternity [WIW]. But in Philadelphia, "eternity" lasted only into the 1980s. By then, William Penn had sunk

---

[17] Lynch (1960), 78.

228

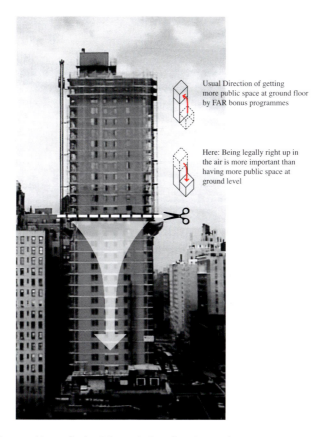

Usual Direction of getting more public space at ground floor by FAR bonus programmes

Here: Being legally right up in the air is more important than having more public space at ground level

113 The 12 illegal floors could move horizontally—onto the adjacent open plaza.

forever. Helmut Jahn's *One Liberty Place*, which takes the form of a 1980s version of New York's Chrysler Building, soared above William, almost doubling his height, reducing him to a pedestrian in his own city. Washington DC today bans all tall buildings from the capital, allowing its national monuments to dominate the cityscape from afar.

Law and Order—Consistent Legislation Versus Free Interpretation
The enemies of the Trump World Tower near the UN nourished their hopes on a (subsequent) preventive obstacle to the building based on a quite different but not exactly ancient incident.

The scene of the crime was 108 East 96th Street in New York's Upper East Side, just off Park Avenue, where in 1988, Albert and Laurence Ginsberg completed their apartment tower. Of the building's altogether 31 stories, 12 were in violation of code according to the applicable zoning regulations. The original construction permit issued by the Department of Buildings had been based on an erroneous municipal zoning map which allowed the 31 stories. In this obvious error, one whose existence had been sufficiently apparent even prior to the commencement of construction (a district with elevated allowable utilization had been drawn too big by mistake), the developers espied their opportunity and continued building.

Now, the Building Department has determined that the 12 illegal stories would have to be removed.

[A]
Ginsberg, Eichner and Macklowe

[L]
New York City

The first appeal, filed in the hope of receiving a zoning variance,[18] was dismissed by the court. The Court of Appeals assumed that any "prudent investigation" by the development, their architects, and their lawyers, would certainly have uncovered the mistake contained in this *single* zoning map in time to have halted construction.

The second appeal filed by the Ginsberg brothers was also rejected. This time, the developers argued that the decision presented them with unreasonable hardship. They reckoned that the tower's massive shrinkage would cost them up to 20 million dollars, including the loss of 24 apartments. This figure was attenuated and reduced in studies carried out by *Civitas*, the same public interest group that had identified the building's illegal height publicly for the first time.

Once the 12 stories had been removed from the tower's apex, according to their investigations, a 13-story infill structure could be constructed directly adjacent, on an area originally envisioned as a plaza. This building would produce enough profit to offset at least some of the loss incurred by the necessary demolition.[19]

Plaza Bonus
[PB] §7.01–4

The ironic aspect of this case is the way in which it totally reverses the logic of the still commonplace *Plaza Bonus* [PB] procedure. Now, architectural volume is not to be transferred from the ground into the heights, but instead the other way around: potentially valuable public space is eliminated by the building's horizontal spreading out into space.

Instead of destroying such a massive quantum of value (so argued the developer), the case could instead be decided in a way that benefited both sides. Their offer was as follows: in exchange for allowing the critical 12 stories to remain, they would remodel a pair of abandoned five-story apartment buildings located at 113 and 115 East 102nd Street as apartments for the elderly. Albert Ginsberg concluded a press release containing the proposal with the following emphatic words: "Sometimes you have to bite the bullet."[20]

The developer found spiritual encouragement in the pastor of the Roman Catholic church of St. Francis de Sales, Father Robert V. Lott: "Rather than going through the route of ripping down, you should look at it from as many points of view as possible. There are housing needs. Perhaps something can be done for housing while at the same time saying to developers that zoning laws are important."[21]

To date, buildings had been demolished in New York only in order to multiply the built volume resting on the same parcel. Not in this case. The developers went to extraordinary lengths to avert a financial disaster. Without success.

The building's enforced decapitation presented the greatest challenge involved in the decision. To begin with, a second scaffolding tower had to be constructed around the building. New York law forbids anyone allowing demolition debris to fall downward unprotected. In cases of total

---

[18] With a variance, existing zoning limits can be surpassed. There must be strong arguments for doing so. Moreover, public hearings are required, to be held by the community boards and the NY Board of Standards and Appeals or the New York City Planning Commission.

[19] After Richard D. Lyons (1988), *Beheading a Tower to Make It Legal*.

[20] David W. Dunlap (1988), *Owners of Too-Tall Tower Offer to Renovate 102d St. Tenements*.

[21] Ibid.

230

razings, New York's demolition firms normally allow the debris to fall down through the now empty elevator shafts. In this way, buildings travel downward through their own elevators. An impossibility in this case.

In 1993, once the remaining amnesty had elapsed, the tower lost its extra 12 stories.

But this denouement was preceded by a public debate, one instigated among other things by Paul Goldberger's article "When Developers Change the Rules During the Game," which appeared in the *New York Times* on 19 May 1989.

At that point, the decapitation of the Ginsberg Tower was not yet a fait accompli, so Goldberger was able to relate the case to a series of others in which "private developers can make their own rules, or at least negotiate with the city to revise the rules if they are not happy with them."[22]

Planning had become deal-making, and zoning had sacrificed its moral authority as an institution.

The height of the *CitySpire Center* of 1987, which surpasses the height originally agreed upon with the city by 11 feet, also serves to underscore this point. Less as a token of regret and instead in response to pressure exerted by the city, the building's developer, Mr. Eichner, installed a rehearsal studio for nonprofit dance companies. But what is the relationship between a dance practice space and the height of the tower? And what is to prevent the next developer from building 22 feet higher than permitted, and installing two dance studios by way of compensation?

And then there is the case of Mr. Macklowe. Under cover of darkness, his contractor illegally demolished an old single room occupancy hotel in a hush-hush operation. Stigmatized thereafter by his colleagues as "Rambo," he donated 2 million dollars to the city for housing to be located elsewhere, and began building his luxurious *Hotel Macklowe* on the site at West 44th Street, east of Times Square.

Thicken the Threshold

By compelling the demolition of 12 stories of the Ginsberg building, the city had made its point. And this despite the fact that Ed Koch, who was mayor at the time, was initially in favor of making a deal with the Ginsberg brothers. Time to put a stop to such criminal goings-on!

[A] Parker

[L] New York City

For the municipal administration, such open legal confrontations or code violations, pursued in search of refreshing variations in urban regulations and the concomitant differentiation of urban architectural structure, have little to do with "creative" approaches to rules and their interpretations. In the eyes of the city, they are simply against the law.

How close may two buildings stand alongside one another: for the most part, a brief glance at the ground story plan, or an examination of parcel boundaries make it possible to determine with relative certainty whether one is dealing with one building or two.

Zoning regulations always pertain to the individual building or unit of property. Accordingly, practically no owner or developer would hit upon the idea of claiming that an especially long or wide building is—contrary to the general perception—not one, but instead two or more buildings.

---

[22] Paul Goldberger (1989), *When Developers Change the Rules During the Game.*

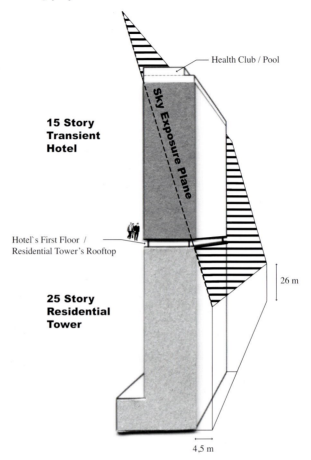

Health Club / Pool

15 Story Transient Hotel

Sky Exposure Plane

Hotel`s First Floor / Residential Tower's Rooftop

26 m

25 Story Residential Tower

4,5 m

114 The Parker Meridian: is it one building or two?

Why would they do that? The necessary surface for the entire building is assembled beforehand through the combination of numerous smaller parcels.

In the case of an especially tall construction project in New York, such reasoning can be worth one's while. Particularly if its various utilizations classify the building as "mixed-use." In New York, such "exceptional mixed cases" fall under a special review process, and are subject to additional restrictions.

In the case of his projected hotel and apartment tower on the former site of the *Great Northern Hotel* on 56th Street (West 56th Street & 7th Avenue), developer Jack Parker claimed to be erecting not a single building, but instead a pair of them, the one stacked on top of the other. That is to say, a 25-story apartment tower and a 15-story hotel tower [VA].

Vertical Assembly [VA] §7.03–3

This interpretation was intended to avoid an uncertain and wearying public review process.

Valid at the site when planning began in 1979 was a FAR of 12 for apartment buildings and one of 18 for commercial uses. Parker's apartment/hotel project had a permissible FAR of 16.

Alongside its bulk rules, however, New York also has the already familiar Sky Exposure Plane [SEP], designed to allow light and air to reach the street. They would have compelled the building to undergo a setback at a height of 26 m. But not according to Parker's lawyer, with approval from the Building Department. According to the zoning ordinances, a tower used for commercial purposes which occupies only 40% of its site does not have to comply with all Sky Exposure Plane and setback regulations. Given the small parcel size, building 40% of it proved impossible, so Jack Parker's lawyer pointed out that the regulations for residential buildings are far more liberal than those for commercial or mixed-use buildings.

Sky Exposure Plane
[SEP] §7.02–6

Parker and his architect Philip Birnbaum took advantage of this state of affairs, characterizing their tower not as a mixed-use building, but instead as two separate buildings—an apartment building and a hotel—the one set on top of the other.

In the end, Parker's stacked tower project rose to a majestic height of 115 meters—but without a setback; only a continuous, single storied incision was to have marked out the lobby of the apartment tower, set above the residential tower at a height of 43 m (although in the end, this accentuation would remain unexecuted). As with any two ordinary buildings, these twinned buildings have two separate construction permits, two different corporate owners, and two distinct tax lots.[23]

Accommodated in the topmost story is a health club with extraordinary views of the city and Central Park—an absurd culmination of these "buildings," which measure respectively only 43 and 73 m. On the whole, a worthy 1980s successor of New York's celebrated *Downtown Athletic Club*—and an expression of a persistent instability between structural definition and bizarre interpretation.

[23] Carter B. Horsley (1979), *Is It One Building or Two? New Project Halted by Dispute.*

9

Designed Variation

Rules ought to observe, not only in their function as administrative instruments, but especially as tools for urban design, three important principal tasks: firstly they should serve to generate diversity by facilitating development potential within clearly defined limitations. The resulting diversity should allow different development strategies. Second, they exert a certain automatic guidance on design processes and the resulting urban development, in other words, they act as a regulatory mechanism. Third, they function as an evaluation instrument: does the resulting urban ensemble comply with every underlying rule and is this according to the original intentions? Where does the regulatory mechanism fail? What adaptations are conceivable?

115 Raymond Unwin juxtaposes "two systems of development" of the same area.

Constants and Variables, Variation on Density

[A]
Holl, Clark & Kingston,
March & Martin and Unwin

[L]
Great Britain, New York
City

In 1912, Britain's *Garden Cities and Town Planning Association* published the article entitled "Nothing Gained by Overcrowding,"[1] authored by British town–planner Raymond Unwin.

Like his comrade-in-arms and predecessor Ebenezer Howard, Unwin promoted the idea of the *Garden City*. The focus of the article, however, was not the social reformist approach, but instead the measurable economic advantages of parceling districts according to the principles of the Garden City. Unwin wanted to dispose of the prejudice according to which the Garden City suffered from economic deficits by virtue of its lower density, that in contrast to the then modern row developments, it represented an excessive financial burden on individual homeowners.

Of interest is his method. One of the first city planners, he works with variants, juxtaposing them. In a first phase, he subdivides a hypothetical building lot measuring 4 ha according to the guidelines and laws in force, which prescribed efficient row development. There are 340 houses which are configured as 20 rows, oriented toward the street, and provided with additional, obligatory access routes via a back road.

The second variant positions clusters of 2, 4, or 6 houses with front and back yards inside a public perimeter, separated by additional accesses and supplemented by publicly accessible surfaces (play areas and tennis courts). Altogether, the second variant accommodates 152 houses. Apparently, the first variant—with more intensive utilization and hence more effective exploitation of surface area—is the more economical of the two. In an appended table, however, Unwin demonstrates the reverse. He juxtaposes the cost of the land purchase with that of the development. Because the conventional variant entails a far greater proportion

---

[1]   Raymond Unwin (1912), *Nothing Gained by Overcrowding! Or How the Garden City Type of Development May Benefit Both Owner and Occupier.*

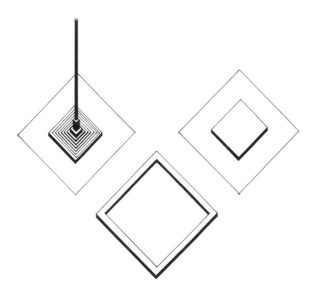

116 Housing density in relation to its distribution.

of street space per housing unit than the Garden City variant, the latter is in fact more cost-effective—not to mention its other advantages, including more green space and recreational areas.

Decisive here is the relationship between building lot price and the cost of street construction. Unwin explicates the impact of the variables involved as follows: "Where the land is comparatively expensive, and road making comparatively cheap, the advantage in the price per lot to be gained by overcrowding will be greater than where land is relatively inexpensive and road making relatively dear."[2] This relational interaction between constant and variable factors and variants, between quantities and their qualitative effects, marks a decisive step toward a "modern" (i.e. rational) approach to urban planning.

The impact of Unwin's methodology is detectable in instances of 20th-century urban planning practice at many different locations—and regardless of the respective ideologies involved.

1: Clad in the garb of economic considerations, such variant formation can be found, for example, in the above-described work *A Study in the Economic Height of Modern Office Buildings*,[3] published in 1930 by Clark and Kingston [EH]. The most effective height for a New York high-rise is conveyed via a series of height variants and constants, of the framing conditions valid at the time.

Economic Height [EH] §7.01–6

2: In the 1960s, Leslie Martin and Lionel March took Unwin's variant subdivisions of architectural volume further.[4] The *Fresnel diagram* is the point of departure for this in principle geometric approach: each of the

2   Ibid., 7.
3   William Clifford Clark and John Lyndhurst Kingston (1930), *The Skyscraper; a Study in the Economic Height of Modern Office Buildings*. See also p.184.
4   See Leslie Martin (1972), *The Grid as Generator*.

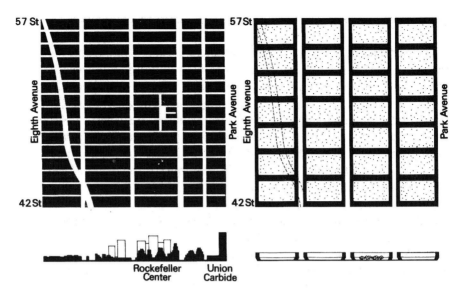

117 "We don't need them, we will them!"
Two variations on the same building mass in Midtown Manhattan.

diagram's annular rings is reduced in thickness, but all have the same volume as the one in the center. This simple diagram thereby represents nine subdivision variants of the same (constant) volume.

As soon as one imagines these volumes represent buildings, entirely different questions emerge concerning the relevant criteria, for example concerning access and the treatments of open areas.

On the basis of this geometric principle, March and Martin carry out an experiment in their article "The Grid as Generator": they take a square section of Manhattan's densely filled-in Midtown and reconfigure the entire built volume as courtyard blocks occupying the same surface area. This translation effects an enormous increase in the proportion of open surface area while at the same time reducing the maximum height of the perimeter block development down to seven stories from the actually present average of 21—at the same time maintaining the total gross floor area constant.

This experiment transforms the appearance of Midtown Manhattan. No longer do we find a highly efficient, maximally profitable and highly densified urban space, but instead a spatial spectacle, one whose rules are no longer based on an optimized, rational exploitation of land. Years before, Philip Johnson had underscored this point, saying: "There is no reason, why we should have tall buildings at all. We don't need them; we will them. We build them only because we want them. With proper planning and distribution of the city's functions smaller buildings could do the job. Tokyo has little over seven stories; Paris has one skyscraper [1960! Obviously long before any La Défense] The high building is just American arrogance."[5]

Indirectly, Philip Johnson here describes a potential space of play for variation within urban morphology, one in which performance capacity remains the same according to measurable criteria, for example that of profit.

---

5   Quoted in Ada Louise Huxtable (1960), *Towering Question: The Skyscraper*.

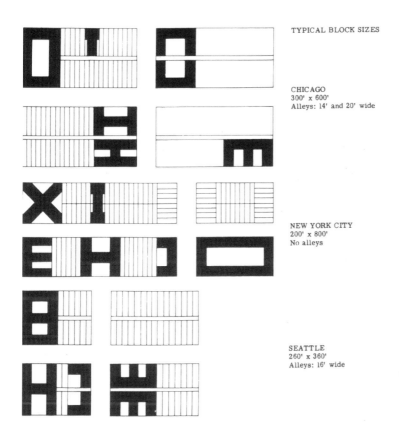

TYPICAL BLOCK SIZES

CHICAGO
300' x 600'
Alleys: 14' and 20' wide

NEW YORK CITY
200' x 800'
No alleys

SEATTLE
260' x 360'
Alleys: 16' wide

118 Steven Holl's Alphabetical City.

3: Apparent is the tendency of cities and their buildings to subject sets of applicable rules to interpretation. Steven Holl demonstrated this in his *Alphabetical City*[6] of 1980. In his book, Holl offers a typology of North America's early high-rises and of the ways in which they were able to develop up until 1930 under the regime of rules then in force. These underlying sets of rules encompassed on the one hand (1) the regulations contained in official zoning ordinances, but also (2) the natural necessity for light and air depending upon utilization, (3) the regulating factor of the grid, and (4) the size of the building lot. The spectrum of possible, built manifestations of these rules is large. On the basis of the resemblance of their ground plans to the shapes of the letters of the alphabet, Holl catalogs buildings as T, I, U, O, H, E, B, L, and X types, also appending a couple of additional combinations of these shapes.

In fact, the formal leeway of possible volumetric configurations was far higher than the polemical pencil-drawn warnings proffered earlier by Hugh Ferriss[7].

[6] Steven Holl (1980), *The Alphabetical City*.
[7] Hugh Ferriss, 1929: "Certainly there are conscientious city-planners who perceive, in the present trend towards closely juxtaposed towers, a serious menace. The trend indubitably exists; and it is therefore proper, perhaps, for the draughtsman to indicate where it will lead if it is unchecked. Such drawings, however, far from being intended as an inspiration, may rather serve as a warning. 'It may look like this—if nothing is done about it.'" In Ferriss (1929), 62.

119 The production of choice. Exploratory testing at Neutelings & Riedijk.

Still, Holl's study only goes up to 1930; in subsequent years and following the introduction of some of the innovations discussed above, including efficient elevators, climate control, and artificial office illumination, a series of quasi-natural restrictions fell away, and the rigid envelope of the zoning ordinance would be filled in increasingly to approach maximum boundaries. The maximum volume of the zoning envelopes was neither the most profitable option, nor was it an attainable ideal, nor a jaded bogeyman, but instead a stealthily approaching reality. The disappearance of natural light-air rules also led to a loss of the formal abundance of high-rise shapes and the emergence of a minimal number of contrasting types, to the advantage of the *bulky block type* [BBT]. Only this type corresponded fully to the stereotype of Hugh Ferriss' envelopes, now materialized as buildings; "a shape that the Law puts into the architect's hands"[8] became the standard—and an undisturbed, economically conditioned automatism led the way; not through more, but instead through fewer apparently determinant rules and restrictions.

Bulky Block Type [BBT] §7.02–16

Methodology: Design Rules—or the Importance of Being Unspecific
Rules have the capacity to generate variety. The results can take the form of diversity with regard to social or spatial configurations. Precise outcomes are materialized as the effects of loose rules.

According to Horst Rittel's work on design methodology, the formation of variety is consistently helpful in solving *complex* problems. Architects too have looked to this working approach for design. Not necessarily in order to generate diversity, but primarily to approach the best solution progressively via a multiplicity of variants.

Quite helpful in this context is a studio atmosphere with adequate manpower. A necessary division of labor obtains between those who formulate specific criteria in the form of loosely defined rules or constraints and a maximally large group of individuals who are capable of interpreting these freely. Only in this way can a sufficiently large number of vari-

[8] Ibid., 74. See also *Two Uneven Twins*, p.167.

ants be produced. In the process, however, the rules themselves are not necessarily interpreted, but instead the degree of freedom that arises from them and from their underspecification.[9]

This principle corresponds to Rittel's main strategies concerning the process of variety formation: the formation of multistage alternatives.[10] Rittel defined altogether four possible design strategies:

The first and linear way of arriving at solutions is that of the veteran designer, who proceeds on the basis of experience and recognizes no problems. Each variant represents only a distraction from an already firmly defined objective.

The second strategy is that of exploratory testing. The designer begins with a solution. If this fails to lead to results in the course of the design process, he returns to his point of departure.

The third strategy is the formation of alternatives. A number of alternatives are developed and evaluated for their capacity to solve the problem. The best solution is determined via performance standards which serve as an evaluative framework, and the solution supplies the basis for the subsequent design process.

The fourth strategy is the multistage formation of alternatives. A number of alternatives are developed in order to solve the problem; then, a series of successive alternatives is developed through a sequence of stages. Finally, the sum total of variants generated is sent through an evaluative filter and the best solution is determined.

If the first strategy is commonly regarded as that of the great masters, many architectural practices today pursue strategy number 3, or even strategy number 4. Through the establishment of a clear division of labor within the design process—between those who establish the rules, and those who interpret and materialize them—rules are assigned a number of different tasks simultaneously. They provide both guidelines and evaluative filters. As derivations of given constraints on the task at hand and its developed vision, they are guidelines for deriving variants, highlighting various possibilities and directions while of course also functioning as an evaluative catalog for assessing individual variants.

If an architectural practice lacks the requisite personnel necessary for the generation of variants, then the process is restricted to that of exploratory testing. By contrast, a city has at its disposal an unimaginable number of producers of variants in proportion to its reduced number of rules.

---

9   See for example the many tower variants (working models) produced by Neutelings Riedijk Architects for their IJ–Tower Block in Amsterdam. Neutelings Riedijk Architects (1999), N. 94 —Neutelings Riedijk 1992/1999.
10 Horst W. J. Rittel and Wolf D. Reuter (1992), *Planen—Entwerfen—Design Ausgewählte Schriften zu Theorie und Methodik*. cited in Jürgen Joedicke (1976), *Angewandte Entwurfsmethodik für Architekten*, 18.

10

Synthesis—A Designed Conclusion

In 1974, Jonathan Barnett wrote in his book *Urban Design as Public Policy*: "Architects and Planners have inherited some funny ideas about themselves as the keepers of the sacred flame of culture and the guardians of society's conscience. There has been a tradition that a true professional, and certainly, a true artist, should not be too closely involved in the day-to-day process of government, or politics, or real estate development. Instead, he has sent his instructions to the policy makers as manifestos or visionary drawings, and, not surprisingly, the policy makers usually find them impossibly idealistic and irrelevant to the problem at hand."[1] Instead of delivering finished designs outside of the institutional decision-making process, Barnett recommended that architects and urban designers themselves should write and design the basic underlying rules for the envisioned space of action.

[1] Jonathan Barnett (1974), *Urban Design as Public Policy: Practical Methods for Improving Cities*, 6.

With the insight that urban design involves mediating between public and private interests, the very institutional framework becomes an element-to-be-designed, or: the rule-set itself turns into a design task and the rules into design-instruments. Whether such a method makes sense can only be judged when we show how rules function within a clearly defined design task and which operational and qualitative consequences the integration of administrative and conceptual regulations have for the resulting ensemble.

In this sense, the material discussed in the previous chapters, with its description of more than 100 rules, should be seen as an exploratory collection—an annotated sourcebook.

In the following, some case-studies and design projects, which are clearly inspired by the insights from the mechanisms and rules described in the previous chapters, will be examined and evaluated.

Thereby, the following questions are important: which urban conditions rather ask for a design framework with a certain freedom than a fixed design? Which structural parameters are necessary to produce a rule-based design framework? How are degrees of freedom defined, how is the expected result anticipated and how can this result be evaluated and modified?

In addition, it is important to show how these insights are visualized and communicated in an accessible way. The fact that a design is not fixed any more, but consists of "control and laissez-faire," confronts us inevitably with a paradox: what form should a design assume when drawing is not an option, and the simple delivery of rules does not provide understandable information?

The research project Kaisersrot[2] at the ETH in Zürich, which explores the development of dynamic rule-sets with the help of computer programmes, tries to give an answer to this question in the form of concrete design solutions in real situations. Projects are not drawn, but programmed, then simulated and finally visualized in multiple variants. This simulation and visualization process provides an important added value. The possibility to change parameters quickly and visualize the modified result turns Kaisersrot into an effective interactive tool between several stakeholders. The resulting built environment is not any more explicitly designed, but the result of a mediated process, while at the same time still enabling a powerful and visionary urban and architectural quality to emerge.

Checks and Balances—The City of Kaisersrot

[A]
Team Kaisersrot, KCAP

[L]
Schuytgraaf

The city of Kaisersrot exists as software. With regard to distribution, form, and programme, the city consistently attempts to coordinate discrete and individual requirements. The infrastructure necessary for this results from the individual desires of the participants, and is not their foundation. What is life like in the city of Kaisersrot?

People appear to lead happy lives in this city. The reason for this seems obvious, almost banal: they get what they want without enduring excessive controls over their behavior. But this place is far from a paradise!

[2] See www.kaisersrot.ch

Especially in the city's early days, we observed an above-average number of neighborhood disputes. People argued constantly, defending their individual interests and debating questions of how the public environment and territory should be constituted. Residents seemed to spend more time talking to their neighbors across their hedges than sitting on their terraces. Those were turbulent days. Inhabitants tended to occupy a piece of land only to discover it was not at all what they had envisioned, that it was too far from the forest, from the lake, from sports facilities or friendly neighbors. They looked around constantly, pegging out various plots, locations, and landscapes. Moving was difficult as well, because no infrastructure had been securely laid out, and the connecting roads changed hourly. In those times, living with constant change was tough! But after a while, people became increasingly aware of interests going beyond their individual desires. They began a productive process of negotiations that took their neighbors' wishes into account as well. The balancing of mutual interests had begun. As a result, a set of behavioral patterns or rules evolved that became one of the few, implicit principles guiding the development of the city. People realized that not all of their desires could be maximally fulfilled without risking tedious negotiations with neighbors. They had to make decisions for themselves, restrictions had to be accepted. But all of this happened quite naturally and with surprisingly little opposition. Rules were accepted, and were regarded as relationships rather than externally imposed controls.

Today, the inhabitants of Kaisersrot still stand at their hedges, not necessarily to discuss territories or mutual dependencies, but just to have a chat with their friendly, self-chosen neighbors.

In the city of Kaisersrot, the manifestation of a common will to form a settlement emerges only after the private interests of individual property owners have been formulated. This priority is clearly evident in the sequence in which the settlement's urban elements are shaped. The basic infrastructure in the form of the street layout results from the combined interplay of individual decisions, and hence emerges only at the very end. How large should my property be? Who (or what) should be the neighbors located on the other side of its boundaries? And of course, how will my property be linked to the common street network? These are the initial and highly discrete criteria. Only after these three questions have been answered for each future property owner are the layouts of the individual parcels determined, and only thereafter is the interconnected street network configured. As a public domain, the infrastructure is subordinated to private interests, and is modified accordingly.

The optimization, that is to say, the fulfillment of all individual desires is a protracted, iterative process. The building lots are placed on the territory of the settlement, after which comes an evaluation dealing with the following questions: do all of the lots conform in their reasonable forms and proportions to the territory of the settlement? Does each property owner have the desired neighbor? In short: is everyone happy? If not, everything will be rearranged.

The retrospective redefinition of the public street space through a multiplicity of private interests resembles the 19th-century redevelopment of the town of Circleville.

120 Everyone gets the neighbor he or she wants.

In the town of Circleville (p.75), the privately motivated collective reshaping of the town from circle to orthogonal grid functioned as a transition. Unavailable here in *Kaisersrot* is a grid to serve as an anticipated (infra)structure capable of fulfilling all desiderata, and differently from Circleville, where the rationale was the profit optimization of individual parcels, the range of desiderata in this instance is highly differentiated. Required here is a diversity of testing and evaluation procedures aimed at arriving at an optimal settlement layout, one in which all residents will feel at home. Countless variants must be produced and compared with one another. These test–production cycles are performed by the computer.

The rules applied are:

— minimum plot size: determined individually by each building lot owner [LS]
— vicinity: proximity of certain programmes [UG]
— infrastructural networking: each parcel is linked to a street. The total length of a given street should be as short as possible [ROB] [PSL]
— proximity elevates coercion [PC]

Lot Size Requirements
[LS] §6.02
Use Groups
[UG] §3.08
Robustness
[ROB] §4.15
Population to Overall Street Length
[PSL] §2.05
Proximity Coercion
[PC] §1.07

[A]
Team Kaisersrot

[L]
Globus-Provisorium, Zürich

Roundtableware

The *Globusprovisorium* stands directly at the center of Zürich—directly on the banks of the River Limmat, and in direct proximity to the main train station. The building's name—a direct reference to its provisional status—already indicates its fate: ever since its construction in the 1950s by the department store chain *Globus*, Zürich has debated its demolition. It stands on the former terrain of the *Papierwerdinsel*, one of the city's most prominent and hence sensitive locations. From this point, views of a number of celebrated Zürich trademarks are interrupted: from the main

Crystallization process.

train station to the *Grossmünster* church, the mountains, and the lake. An alternative, that is to say, a more harmonious replacement for the present building, is regarded by many citizens as a worthy goal. The city has proposed the continued presence of a department store in combination with a new hotel. But where on the Limmat should the new building stand? Inevitably, it will continue to block important view axes. Here, it would interrupt views of Zürich's churches, there, it would interrupt access to the river. Each potential siting has as many disadvantages as advantages. The city will have to decide! To draw up a single plan to fulfill the task seems futile. The interior of the building, however, its desired relationships within a special programme, is fixed. The hotel's main entrance is to be oriented in the direction of the train station; adjacent to it will be the lobby and a restaurant. The form and positioning of the hotel rooms would be oriented toward views of the water and other local sights, and in such a way that the integrated shopping center has no neg-

ermöglichte Blickbeziehung von Bahnhof zum Grossmünster bei Episode O

122a The restaurant crouches down to allow views from the main station to the Grossmünster.

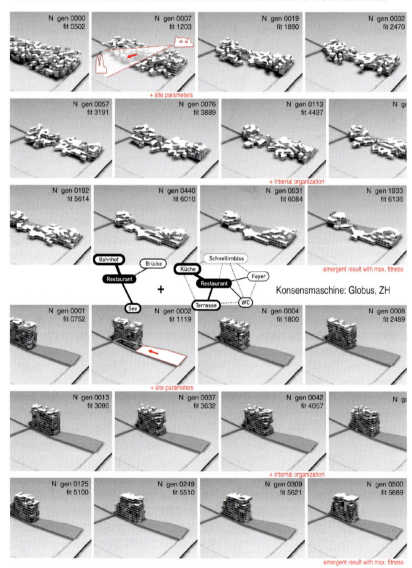

Konsensmaschine: Globus, ZH

122b Sequence of the volumetric evolution.

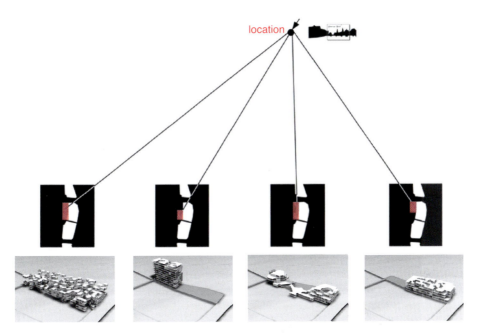

ative impact on the functioning of the hotel. The restaurant is to serve both hotel guests as well as passers-by and shoppers. These rules again can be described as relationships within a computer software programme. The building's envelope and its position along the Limmat remain flexible. The software is sent to the city, and the municipality's civil servants can decide themselves which urban criteria, which views, and which relationships are less important, and hence where the building can be placed and in which form. In each instance, they are provided with a building that functions in compliance with the internally formulated rules. They receive an overview of variants, that is to say, an instrument which supports but does not replace the decision-making process for determining appropriate alternatives to the Globusprovisorium.

The applicable rules are:
— view management (both onto and from the building) [LVM] [BP]
— programmatic proximity and relationships [UG] [PC]
— defined building envelope [UE]

Innumerable Immaterial Towers
Wijnhaven Island is located between the center of Rotterdam and the River Maas. Already standing on the terrain, entirely surrounded by water, is a blocky development of up to seven stories—one that does not use the site to its maximum allowable utilization. What is feasible is an additional densification with slender towers à la New York's Greenwich Village. But where should they stand? Such towers would also have to be constructed cautiously and in a temporal sequence to avoid burdening the area, which is already in use, with excessive construction activity. For this reason, no plan has ever been drawn up. The relevant qualities were

London View Management [LVM] §2.10
Backdrop Preservation [BP] §2.08
Use Groups [UG] §3.08
Proximity Coercion [PC] §1.07
Urban Envelope [UE] §2.12

[A] KCAP

[L] Wijnhaven Island, Rotterdam

123a See the towers grow...

123b ...from their mutual base—Wijnhaven Island with its already 7-story-tall buildings.

defined on the basis of the few rules contained in the applicable regulations. No tower may overshadow another, nor a neighboring building, in an excessive way. In general, each tower is required to provide views onto the nearby River Maas through a maximum number of windows. The towers need street addresses, and their forms should manifest a certain slenderness. High-rise slabs are not desirable.

The absence of an explicit plan and the lack of a division into stages has brought about a situation in which the first developer to erect a tower on the terrain will automatically enjoy the greatest degree of design freedom. The first to build has the greatest choice of sites, and need not orient himself to existing towers. Alongside rule-based planning, this involves an additional motivation, namely to invest in the area's future as quickly as possible.

Standing there today on the terrain in close proximity to one another are five of slender, towers. A rare surprise in a European city—and perhaps possible only due to the renunciation from the very beginning of any precise, plan-like representation of the ultimate result.

The applicable rules are:
— shadowing [2H] [DEC]
— slenderness of towers [BBK]
— address formation [TPS]
— view management [LVM] [BP]
— no skyline wall [SWS]
— phasing [PC] [TOE]

Aviary

"Big housing projects tend to look like big housing projects."[3] This characteristic, discovered by William H. Whyte, applies to many large urban projects, whether purely residential or not. The simple fact that entire ensembles of buildings are planned and built by a single hand at the same time tends to cause the constituent members to fuse together visually into megastructures. By virtue of their common characteristics and consequent internal homogeneity, such special entities are automatically delimited from their surroundings. They become hermetic. What can be done to prevent Whyte's prophecy from becoming reality?

The scene is the train station in Zürich, Switzerland, 2003. During the coming 15 years, many portions of the station, both to the left and right of the tracks, will become obsolete. The city will thereby acquire a new urban district around the station. Surrounding streets leading toward the terrain will continue, forming new blocks of buildings. Some sections can commence development already in the coming three years, others will be freed of all rail-related infrastructure only after 15 years. No plan can survive such an interval of time. As a consequence, the area will automatically be deprived of its projective consistency. It is unlikely that the total building volume, arising over a period of 15 years, will become a hermetic visual unity within the larger texture of the city. But what are the implications of such "planless planning" for the achievement of a district character? The layout of the blocks is determined by individual construction phases. Different architects are responsible for individual building blocks. As it is implemented, then, it becomes progressively less likely that the project will resemble a unified whole. For the urban designer, however, this approach entails the danger of a loss of control over the results.

A couple of additional rules can be applied; these can function as a frame, reference, or quality control for ongoing development. The building

[A]
Team Kaisersrot, KCAP

[L]
Stadtraum HB, Zürich

---

[3] Whyte (1968), 245.

blocks receive three-dimensional envelopes which set maximum heights, safeguard view axes, and, finally, counteract the urge toward a monotonous, vertical extrusion of the parcel's surface above a certain height. Within these three-dimensional building lines, the future buildings and programmes can develop more-or-less freely. A second rule also applies: a fixed percentage of the boundary of the outer envelope must come into contact with future development. This applies in particular to a building's lower portions. This endows the street zone with definition, and limits are set on the recession of architectural volume. Still applicable is the *2-Hour Shadow* rule. This does not necessarily hinder the construction of high-rises, but it does promote mixed use: not residences, but instead offices will be found where portions of buildings receive shadow for more than two hours. The minimum allowable proportion of residences will be steered indirectly by the number of towers and their forms, ensuring an adequate mix of uses. Planning is transformed gradually into a set of inter-related and interdependent regulations, one containing sufficient leeway to accommodate future modifications. If need be, the rules are subject to revision. At no point in time is such a plan endangered.

The opportunism, with its performative capacity, and the openness of the plan were manifested quite distinctly in a subsequent referendum, which asked Zürich's citizenry about their attitudes toward the project. With projects surpassing a certain size threshold, the city's inhabitants must be directly involved in the decision-making process. In the tradition of San Francisco's *Opposition Drawings*, opponents drew up a dystopian image of the area's future development, one that was excessively densified and anti-urban, and one conforming simply to private and profit–oriented economic interests. Supporters sought to cast the project in as positive a light as possible on the basis of its public qualities. The interplay between these two exaggerated, oppositional representations spanned the entire spectrum of potential development. A worst-case scenario was confronted with an idealized image. The project will develop somewhere between these two highly stylized envelopes. Success will be determined by the capacity of regulatory mechanisms to undergo subsequent adjustments.

The applicable rules are:
— 2–h shadow [2H]
— worst–best–case envelopes [UE]
— Neighborhood compatibility [NC]
— setbacks [SB] [DTE]
— light into the street [SEP] [DEC]
— mixed uses (ratio of residential to work) [UG]
— opposition drawings [OD]
— quality of street views [QSV]
— height range [HR]
— no skyline wall [SWS]
— special district [SD]
— building bulk, slenderness [BBK]

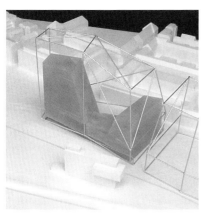

124a An aviary for future development. The urban envelope and its potential infill.

124b The opponents' poster with their opposition drawing.

124c An aviary for future development. The urban envelope.

124d The testing of the urban envelope within Zürich's city model.

125 The crude clay of London's Goodsyard Bishopsgate ...

No Design—Just Rules?

[A]
Team Kaisersrot, KCAP

[L]
Goodsyard Bishopsgate,
London, GBR

The former terrain of London's Goodsyard Bishopsgate is traversed by a viaduct, along with a series of subterranean train tunnels, and the future East London Line elevated rail. A few meters above, the area is crossed by two view corridors leading to St. Paul's Cathedral. To the west, there is pressure to allow the high-rise business district around Liverpool Street / Broadgate to encroach onto the district. Located to the east is the small-scale, multicultural neighborhood of East London's Brick Lane. The mayor of London wants to see 50% of the district dedicated to affordable housing. The pressure to develop in relation to actual buildable surface is enormous. The district is divided between the administrative districts of Hackney and Tower Hamlets.

Finally, any construction enterprise in the district is subject to "rights to light" and other limitations with regard to dimensions and distances between buildings.

Even before a new urban design confronts further determinations, the district is already saturated by rules and constraining relationships. Accordingly, the planning process involves coordinating and relating the individual constraints and rules to one another as a coherent whole.

For special criteria, a restricted number of character envelopes supply a visionary image, but without permitting the total vision to become explicit. The overall results will emerge from their superimposition.

Pedestrian Streets
[PS] §4.07
**London View
Management**
[LVM] §2.10
Urban Envelope
[UE] §2.12
Set Back
[SB] §7.02–1
Setback Street Ratio
[SSR] §4.13
Backdrop Preservation
[BP] §2.08
**Towers at Primary
Streets**
[TPS] § 2.11
Height Difference Max
[HDM] §5.07
Difference Max
[DIM] §4.03
2h Shadow
[2H] § 5.08
**Ancient Lights
Doctrine**
[ALD] § 5.11
**Skyline Wall
Syndrome**
[SWS] § 3.04
Landmarks and Icons
[LMI] §5.04
**Neighborhood
Compatibility**
[NC] §5.09
**Quality of Street
Views**
[QSV] § 4.05

The applicable rules are:
— comprehensive public space layout [PS]
— view corridors to St. Paul's [LVM]
— urban envelopes [UE]
— setbacks [SB]
— setback street ratio [SSR]
— view management on and off site [LVM] [BP]
— accessibility [TPS]
— stepping towers [HDM] [DIM]
— rights of light / 2–h shadow [2H] [ALD]
— no skyline wall [SWS]
— landmarks and icons [LMI]
— neighborhood compatibility [NC]
— quality of street views [QSF]

126a Transparency.

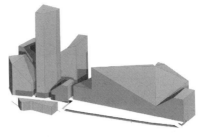

126b Landmark.

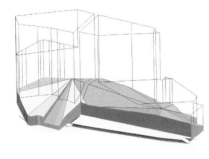

126c Daylight (off site).

126d Shadow casting (off site).

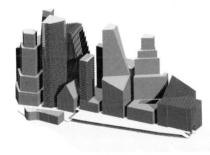

126e Diverse architecture.

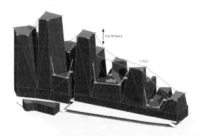

126f Stepping towers.

126 ... as a synthesis of different character–envelopes ...

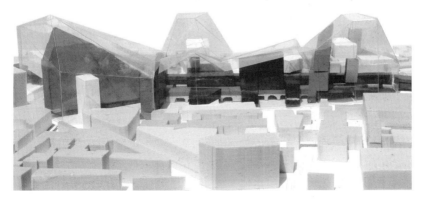

127 ... with its internal specification ...

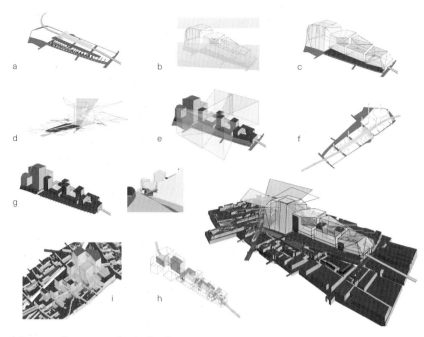

128 ... according to a set of 9 simple rules:
(a) public space layout, (b) London's view corridors, (c) envelopes with setbacks, (d) desired views on site, (e) desired views off site, (f) accessibility and address, (g) stepping height of towers, (h) programme according to shadow casting, (i) limitations for shadow casting onto adjacent buildings.

Common Ground

Common to all of the projects described is the attempt to engage in design using rule-based instruments, which is to say: to formulate statements about the form, arrangement, type, and quantity of urban material, but also to allow a degree of freedom in this respect. Methodical work with rules can be applied to a very broad spectrum of (urban) design tasks, albeit in ways involving divergent objectives and degrees of difficulty.

The availability of a heterogeneous built environment capable of accommodating programmes of various types and sizes in maximum proximity to one another, constitutes a fundamental precondition of urban complexity and liveliness, but provides no guarantee. To determine and to quantify such programmes beforehand and to materialize them in built mass involves forms of speculation concerning future user demands that are associated with tremendous uncertainty. To avoid inaccurate forecasting requires planning that is oriented directly toward demand. Such planning is achievable only when actual users have the freedom to influence a given design directly. The achievement of such freedom is a core motivation driving the methodical application of rules in the design process, and is common on divergent levels to all of the five projects described here.

Initially, the Kaisersrot Project for Schuytgraaf was regarded as an experiment, one designed to determine the degree to which end users—which is to say future residents—could be integrated into the planning process. This experiment was conceived very much in the tradition of models popular in the 1960s, which shifted the designer into the background in favor of users. In order to accommodate this desire (or dream) for participatory planning, Kaisersrot wanted to do more than distribute questionnaires, with the design process then proceeding conventionally on the basis of such wish lists. Instead, the idea was to design an algorithm capable of automatically synthesizing a functioning parcel plan on the basis of additional inputs by potential residents regarding desired lot sizes, locations, and building typologies. As applied in the Schuytgraaf project, it quickly became clear that for project developers, end users existed only as abstract magnitudes. A mix of building typologies in various quantities was substituted for the real number of future residents. In the end, the genuine freedom of residents to actively shape the plan became the freedom to choose suitable options from a broad spectrum of residential typologies and qualities. In light of the original objectives, this retrenchment allowed the experiment to "fail successfully" in the form of a real construction project. Nonetheless, the project opened up additional procedural qualities: on the one hand, the software permitted extended experimentation with mixing uses and their immediate visualization via the unrestricted entry of individual user profiles. In the best cases, such tests permit utilization distribution models to be generated that can be created by conventional planning only with great difficulty. For a new plan, the settlement as built displays an unconventional mixture of residential typologies in close proximity: single-family houses stand directly alongside townhouses, multi-unit structures and apartment buildings. Even within the limited context of a housing estate, this generates the qualities of an open structure. During the planning process itself (which can stretch out into years depending on the dimensions of a given project), moreover, changes generated by altered demand are allowed to influence such a flexible master plan without destroying it. Finally, this software constitutes an important experiment in reassessing established procedures regarding built mass: it is a question of attempting to create an instrumentarium which reverses the planning process in order to derive overarching public structures from the properties of individual elements. This pertains to the sequence and hierarchy through which the individual elements are coordinated with one another: a conventional planning approach fixes the public street network by which the parcels—and hence the buildings—are to be oriented. The Kaisersrot software functions exactly the other way around: not unlike a natural process of residential development, the point of departure for the individual buildings and parcel are now individual, private interests, while public space and public infrastructure grow out of such individual object orientations. As a consequence, public space derives its justification and its definition from the critical mass of private interests, and is not projected or superimposed onto these in a ready-made or a priori fashion. The result is a robust and desirable connection between public and private.

The revitalization project of the Wijnhaven in Rotterdam serves to illustrate an additional trait and practical goal of rule-based design, namely the possibility of phasing and stepwise development without predetermined zoning and its attendant temporal sequencing. Such an almost "natural" form of development is capable of further reinforcing the area's heterogeneous character and of densifying it sustainably: in the absence of any basic restrictions with regard to temporal development, the first tower project enjoys the greatest choice of potential building sites. The rules specifying the interrelationship of the various towers are already available, but are not yet in force, since only one tower has been planned. This means maximum leeway for the first project, and serves as an incentive for rapid project development, thereby behaving as an impetus for a heterogeneous mix of high-rises: the larger towers are separated by larger gaps, while smaller, more slender towers can be positioned subsequently in between. In contradistinction to a conventional phasing in zones and temporal segments, incidentally, this approach almost automatically offers the potential for creating architectural and programmatic diversity.

The project for the new urban district around Zürich's Hauptbahnhof exploits the maximum freedom enabled by the application of rules for the sake of increased private and individual demand orientation in planning, thereby ensuring acceptance from the economic point of view, but also in order to generate a heterogeneous area with increased mixed use. These two desiderata, however, are not necessarily complementary. The rules that are to be designed must do justice to both objectives while mediating between them.

Since this is a downtown area, the regularities of the immediate architectural context are exploited to arrive at an initial set of structural determinations. Access roads are assigned to the area together with block sizes. The *Urban Envelope* [UE] adopts the average heights with setbacks, is additionally differentiated via staggered development in height, and serves as the project's structural frame. Also shaping maximal volumes are desired vistas and view axes. Within this envelope, rules determining illumination and *Maximum Building Bulk* [BBK] serve to reduce the potential built volume and to enforce mutual deference between neighboring buildings. As mentioned above, the *2–Hour Shadow Rule* [2H] serves to encourage mixed residential and work uses without the necessity of defining a fixed percentage of either category. However, vital here is an initial appraisal of which use is successful and which merits protection. At that point, it was clear that without minimum specifications, residential uses in this location would be threatened. Accordingly, the idea was to designate everything for residential use except for ground floor zones and those volumes that would be exposed to shadow for more than two hours daily. Additional tests designed to determine the types of development made possible by these rules showed an average of 50% residential use with great variation with regard to possible uses and densities. This last approach enjoyed one advantage as well as one practical disadvantage. The advantage was strategic in nature: all of the city's interest groups were able to perceive in this arrangement whatever they wished to perceive. All of the protagonists felt as though they were in a position to contribute to shaping potential development within the envelope. To some extent, they even formulated and proposed new rules in the course of discussions. Finally, this palpable freedom within the planning process led to productive discussions between the representatives of various interest groups. A significant disadvantage of

Urban Envelope
[UE] §2.12

Building Bulk
[BBK] § 7.02–13

2h Shadow
[2H] § 5.08

such under-specification, nonetheless, was identified by project developers. Not unlike the towers at Wijnhaven, there was to be no predetermined temporal phasing or utilization figure per parcel. First come, first serve, with maximum leeway. But the necessity to take into consideration an as-yet-nonexistent future neighboring development at the very start of a project necessarily entails a certain level of insecurity, one having a bearing on the ultimate respective utilizations of each building lot. This makes calculations based on planning ahead difficult. In the worst cases, the respective developer does not know when purchasing a parcel which rates of return are possible, since these are dependent upon the potential construction dimensions, and these in turn are dependent on building measures taking place on neighboring parcels. A dynamic development with the desired side-effect of a formally and temporally differentiated architectural ensemble cannot be reconciled with the fixed determination of a maximally allowable utilization ratio per parcel.

This does not mean, however, that such a threshold makes it impossible to continue with a rule-based design. A quantitative limit still allows considerable leeway with regard to the distribution and form of potential constructive dimensions. However, in the event that such a threshold is complemented by additional limits (e.g. the formal determination of a threshold in the form of an envelope), then the leeway for future development is determined in ways comparable to that of conventional planning.

Based on experiences with such practical, rule-based projects, we can arrive at an additional rule of thumb: in order to ensure a given project sufficient leeway and an adequate degree of freedom, no more than three to four rules designed to shape relationships, plus a structural framework, should be applied simultaneously. In the context of projects constrained by preexisting and strongly determining contexts, this number can be reduced even further. In the case of London's Goodsyard Bishopsgate, it was ultimately by no means a question of the need for new or additional rules; instead, the essential task consisted in the need to analyze and reinterpret existing ones.

Finally, we come to the visualization of such rule-based projects. Essentially, there are three types of visual presentation of a given project which dispense with an explicitly determined configuration in favor of variational possibilities. A plausible, rule-based project can be represented in all three ways. To begin with, the rules themselves can be visualized—either as abstract diagrams or as framing structures within the design (e.g. as wireframe or volumetric models of the envelopes). In addition, the process is represented on the basis of temporal development or the formation of variants. This functions as a sequence of images with a fixed perspective. Finally, possible results are visualized as variations in their final architectural appearances. In this context, minimum, medium-sized, and maximum variants are chosen in relationship to a specific criterion (for example density, FAR, open space, use, ...). But not too many variants—that could be overwhelming and might create an impression of arbitrariness.

79 Density Regulators—The City of Averuni Revisited

A summary of all the rules relevant to the cases discussed above results in a list of at least 115 rules: the universal-general code of the city of Averuni. The spheres of application of these rules cannot always be distinguished clearly from one another, but the rules can be classified roughly with reference to their primary objectives: 79 of them guide or shape urban density. 77 rules influence urban form and the forms of individual buildings. 36 rules specify programmes; 52 rules allow the heights of buildings to be administered directly, and 51 pertain exclusively to aesthetic considerations. Given the tendency of rules toward inclusivity, there emerges a certain fuzziness within this classification and in the underlying web of relationships that is made up of form, density, and programme. A rule that specifies a building's form is also a potential regulator of density, and so is a rule which, for example, fixes a minimum distance between two buildings. Some rules are genuinely versatile, in fact they have an impact on form, utilization, and density in equal degrees. Zürich's 2-Hour Shadow Rule [2H] has an explicit impact on the building's form (height, volumetry), its programme (residences only in unshadowed areas), and of course, it also has an impact on the distribution of architectural masses (proximity of buildings in relation to one another), and finally on the utilization of land—this as an ancillary result of the determination of building height/ volumetry.

2h Shadow
[2H] § 5.08

As a consequence of the capacity of rules for multiple applications, the first version of the Code of Averuni and its collection of rules exhibits a degree of redundancy. Assuming the city is interested in guiding density, then all 79 applicable rules will certainly not come into play. Adequate for this purpose will be a small selection of rules with diverse territorial definitions. The criteria for the selection, accordingly, is once again the sphere of influence of the respective rule. It makes an enormous difference for the form of a city whether its density is determined by height maximums, rules governing distances between buildings, those regulating shadows, or those determining the utilization coefficient furnished with some sort of bonus rules.

And this means simply that the deliberate selection of a rule already amounts to a design choice, one that determines which abstract quantities will be linked with which qualities with regard to form, appearance, economic performance, and utilization.

We can also conclude that while the focus of most the rules is the steering of urban characteristics or urban density and its distribution, only a small number of rules actually work on this urban scale. Ninety percent of the rules discussed here operate in relation to objects, on the scale of the individual buildings or parcels. Here, the total urban expression is determined on its diametrically opposed scale. This paradox becomes palpable when we read the first version of the Code of Averuni: the city is a fiction—not because it does not really exist, a mere invention, but instead because it is based on artificial average values. This urban fantasy rests on the everyday character of the description, on the way in which objects behave toward one another.[4] These relationships form the con-

---

[4]   In this sense, this Code can be distinct from Michael Sorkin's *Local Code* (1993). If the Code of Averuni is to begin with a collection of really existing rules, then Sorkin's regulatory structure, as he himself points out, generates a utopia (127)—an ideal code for an ideal city.

text and the urban image—even there, where no real context in fact exists. To render this achievement experienceable requires the history of a "real" nonexistent city somewhere in the middle of nowhere—one that is elucidated and established through actually existing rules. The important feature of the city is precisely the fact that it did not exist prior to the reading of the codes, and most importantly, that the reader has no prior image of it. This image of Averuni, to be drawn from the imagination, is to rest solely on the clauses of the 115 rules. Each rule serves here not to analyze an existing urban situation, but instead becomes tangible as an originating and form-giving tool: emerging in the imagination through the reading process is a city—although no real image of Averuni actually exists, and none ever will. The rules become active when the reader interprets them in the form of a potential expression or form—but only piecemeal, since all 115 rules can probably not be synthesized in the imagination into a totalizing image of the city. Instead, they become active in the imagination across a wide spectrum of Averuni's urban scale and urban characteristics. Despite the many rules involved, moreover, we can assume that such images will be different for each reader, which again underscores the leeway contained in the rules.

In the first chapter, ideally, Averuni will implicitly evoke the experience of interacting with rules—an experience upon which the remainder of the book elaborates as a methodical quality and as the achievement of these rules.

Remote Control

Today, there exists a general consensus about the fact that the city does not let itself be designed but merely steered in a limited way. At the same time, the production of built environment takes place according to precise rules, consisting of *natural processes* and man-made *conventions and regulations*. In addition, several examples of big interventions, so-called "*grand projets*", can be found in the history of urbanism, showing that the conscious exertion of influence by man on his built environment can reach considerable proportions.

As an impressive example of conscious intervention, there are the Dutch reclamation projects, whereby enormous surfaces of water were turned into land and developed, with as an extreme result the city of Almere, a New-Town of meanwhile almost 200.000 inhabitants.[1]

Closer consideration of these three factors of influence on the built environment—the *natural process* of settlement, man-made *regulations* and the "*grand projets*"—provide us with some insight about the mechanisms of urban production.

The *natural process* of settlement follows fixed natural principles. One of them is the almost completely two-dimensional character of urban design: a plot or a building can generally only be *next* to another plot or building. A plot or building is generally always accessed *via* a public road. Most elements of the built environment lay *next to* and not *on top of* each other. Another natural principle is the essentially economic character of urban production. In a liberal society construction takes place according to the mechanism of the free market: demand and supply, attractive location, available land, land-price or quality of access.

The man-made *regulations* are generally the result of the need to control the natural process of settlement and protect the environment against excessive developments. They are essentially *negative*, limiting measurements, conceived to facilitate *positive*, equal chances of development. They create a condition of "freedom in bondage" in planning, the true precipitation of the democratic principle in physical space. Examples are zoning regulations, the right of land-ownership, the obligation for buildings to stay at least 5m from the property-line, the obligation to maintain a private hedge of 1.2m high on the property-line or rules to prevent noise-nuisance between apartments.

Thus, the apparent "chaos" of the urbanized landscape, as it is perceived by many people, in fact is an extremely ordered condition, a "hyperorder", the result of the influence of natural processes of settlement and man-made regulations.

The construction of the network of high-speed train tracks in Europe shows that "*grand projets*" today are still possible. On the one side, they are the result of a conscious and focused intention of a limited group of people—in other words: a design. On the other hand however this design is modified in its eventual form by a great many factors—political interests, objections, geological conditions, financial deficits, ecological motives. Thus, the eventual outcome as a result of this balancing

[1] Michelle Provoost et al. (1999), *Dutchtown: A City Centre Design by OMA/Rem Koolhaas*.

act does not often have one specific author (the designer is the collective), depends on chance until the last minute, generally shows a lack of sharpness in detail and does not produce a coherent and consistent character.[2]

In the light of the above, it is remarkable that there are still people who think that one can create a functioning piece of city by means of a fixed, "beaux-arts" urban design. The described mechanisms suggest a much more self-evident design and implementation method: if we want to create an urban design, we first formulate in a rough sketch a *"grand projet"*, a global vision for an area. Consequently, we take care that this vision is filled in according to *"natural processes"* of urban production, whereby development initiatives meet our own home-made *rules*. In my experience this is one of the few working-methods that can function in large-scale, complex urban conditions and lead to reasonably and precisely predictable results. However, in an urban design produced according to this method, something peculiar is at hand with the *rules* that are deployed. I divide them here roughly in three categories. A first category consists of dry, administrative rules that regulate certain rights and plights from a juridical perspective, for example the right to daylight access. A second category consists of rules, formulated from a more subjective (design) vision, like the above-mentioned private hedge. A third category comprises strategic steering instruments that focus on the control of dynamic variables, like for instance the balancing of the relation between plot-form and size, building typology, public space network and traffic capacity.

Somewhere in the history of urbanism, probably very early, rules differentiated themselves according to these categories and by doing so crossed an important ideological borderline: some rules developed from purely juridical instruments into creative design tools. The creative deployment of rules as design tools is what this book "Grand Urban Rules", that Alex Lehnerer wrote as a result of the research at our Institute of Urban Design at the ETH in Zürich, is setting the context for, and this also constitutes the great significance of this publication. It does not only give a comprehensive overview of the history of urban rules in the United States and other countries, but also explores how rules can be deployed in a pro-active, creative way and what potential this embodies.

In *The Metropolis of Tomorrow*,[3] Hugh Ferriss sketches architectonical interpretations, splendid visions drawn in charcoal, of the New York Zoning Resolution of 1916 and so makes a clear step into the direction of a reciprocal relationship, in which rule and design will mutually influence each other. The course of this reciprocal relationship has crystallized in innumerable forms, whereby the extreme context of Manhattan served as a laboratory for the whole of the United States. This was also possible because the grid, the rectangular pattern of streets, forms the constituting base of the city—and even a large part of the countryside—almost everywhere in America. The grid can also be seen as a simple translation of the freedom principle into a city-plan: every street and every block is

---

[2] Nicola Schueller, Petra Wollenberg and Kees Christiaanse (2009), *Urban Reports*.
[3] Hugh Ferriss (1929), *The Metropolis of Tomorrow*.

essentially equal. By applying equal rules a "generic city"—in the words of Rem Koolhaas[4]—, "a city without properties," a city with equal chances, an "Open City" emerges. However, Koolhaas, as ghostwriter for Manhattan, has shown us earlier in *Delirious New York*[5] that a "generic city" does not enjoy a long life. Through local centralization, Central Park, Broadway and other changes in form, concentration and mix, neighbourhoods of radically different character have emerged in Manhattan, reinforced by local adaptations of rules under the influence of disparities in investment pressure. This differentiation in characters of diverse mix, age, density and typology on a uniform base of the grid, in which communities of different background coexist, embodies the quintessence of the American city. The insight that very complex, well-functioning and attractive urban structures can emerge from a simple base, with a simple, steering rule-set found its climax in 1983 in OMA's design for the Parc de la Villette in Paris.[6] In this project the vision of an animated Dutch polder landscape represents the "*grand projet*", and the simple base with its organizing principles, such as the polder strips, the *rules* and the invasion of the site with variable programmes, represents the *natural process* of settlement. This concept builds a bridge between America's "Grand Urban Rules" and "rule-based design" but particularly today's strategic urbanism and exerted an irresistible attraction on the young generation of designers like Alex Lehnerer.

"..*urban design as the organizer of the common, should maintain a certain modesty towards architecture, which may flourish in a thousand flowers, in other words, urban design is about creating conditions for freedom..*"[7]

A second bridge in the development of "*rule based urban design*" is KCAP's urban design for the Wijnhaven in Rotterdam (p.249).[8] Despite the fact that no computer software at all was deployed for this project, it constitutes irrevocably a prototype for recent parametric software experiments. On the basis of a subjective design vision and with the help of precise *rules*, a *grand projèt*, a *natural process* of building initiatives in the form of slender high-rise towers, was unleashed on the existing base of blocks and streets. This project belongs to the few experiments that were actually realized and function in a successful way.[9] In the ETH research project *Kaisersrot*[10], in which Alex plays a leading role, these principles are modeled by computer simulations. In this work the testing of the *rules* may not be evaluated with splendid charcoal drawings by Hugh Ferriss, but be researched in a much wider spectrum of variables and perspectives. In this way, we have recently carried out high-rise studies for the railway station areas of Zürich Central Station (p.251) and London Bishopsgate (p.254), in which the relation between the desired city-image, building typology, orientation, view-lines, daylight and sunlight

4   Rem Koolhaas et al. (1995), *Small, Medium, Large, Extra-Large: Office for Metropolitan Architecture, Rem Koolhaas and Bruce Mau.*
5   Rem Koolhaas (1978), *Delirious New York: A Retroactive Manifesto for Manhattan.*
6   Rem Koolhaas et al. (1995), *Small, Medium, Large, Extra-Large: Office for Metropolitan Architecture, Rem Koolhaas and Bruce Mau.*
7   Kees Christiaanse (1989), *Creating Conditions of Freedom.*
8   Paul Groenendijk (2009), *The Red Apple & Wijnhaven Island.*
9   Ibid.
10 Kaisersrot. Available from: www.kaisersrot.ch.

exposure can be explored. In addition studies have been carried out for efficient lay outs and street patterns for suburban developments (p.244)and programmatic relations in buildings (p.246).

We should very much welcome the fact that Alex has taken the effort to study the roots of the deployment of *rules* in urban design in the United States extensively and particularly to look after the motive forces and effects that they produced. This book is in the first place an invitation to think about operating rules in urban design and also clearly shows that rules and software cannot design themselves. They can, when properly formulated, provide excellent tools for the development of qualitative spatial structures. Secondly, the book is a reference manual for the urban designer, where he can find certain principles, types and systems of rules from which he can start in-depth studies. Last but not least the book is an inspiration for the urban designer in his search for more effective methods to steer the contemporary city.

Kees Christiaanse
Zürich 2009

The Climatic Aspect of Architecture

We are architects and information scientists in equal measure—a rare species in a singular situation. We are able to design regulatory systems capable of colonizing our planet in seconds. We can also design regulatory systems which imitate familiar architecture to the point of confusion. Architects smell a rat, and fall back on their individual creativity, or on the nature or origin of things, thereby gaining certainty for their occupation and holding their own in the face of the onslaught of technological rationality: back to nature. The technicians disregard such resistance, blindly expanding their capacities, becoming faster and more differentiated in expectation of getting there the next time around: everything is possible.

The apple falls from the tree. A simple rule. 17th century. Many such rules were subsequently established, while the objects under consideration became smaller and more numerous. In the 19th century, the result was simple: in the absence of energy inputs, every rational system arrives at a state of equilibrium, and hence at a "cold death"—or as a negative foil, a "heat death." This is unsettling. For apparently, our existence and our living environment depend upon a very different vector. For us, a state of equilibrium would be arbitrary and improbable. Evidently, our vector succeeds on a local and temporary level in preventing systems from succumbing to equilibrium. But only locally and temporarily. Large and all-encompassing systems of rational order, then, represent threats rather than the hope for certainty.

But we have nothing other than our rationality and our machines. Except that we are uncertain in our dealings with them. Our existence is a search, a project through which we might prolong our improbable existence. There is no clear perspective, no certainty. Just a process of feeling one's way. With everything we have, including precisely our thinking and our machines. Certainty no longer lies in one book, nor even in many books/many machines/materials/the earth. It lies in code/the indeterminate/the projective/the climatic. Assuming there still is any certainty at all. From this point of view, Alex's work is a source of joy! Inquisitive. Interesting. Open.

Ludger Hovestadt
Zürich 2009

Bibliography

Alexander, Christopher 'A City Is Not a Tree', *Architectural Forum*, London, /1 (April 1965).

Alexander, Christopher *Notes on the Synthesis of Form* (Eighth printing edn.; Cambridge, MA: Harvard University Press, 1974).

Appleyard, Donald and Fishman, Lois 'High Rise Buildings Versus San Francisco', in Donald Conway, et al. (eds.), *Human Response to Tall Buildings* (Stroudsburg, PA: Dowden Hutchinson & Ross, 1977).

Banham, Reyner *Los Angeles; the Architecture of Four Ecologies* (1st U. S. edn.; New York, NY: Harper & Row, 1971).

Banham, Reyner et al. 'Non-Plan: An Experiment in Freedom', in Jonathan Hughes (ed.), *Non-Plan Essays on Freedom Participation and Change in Modern Architecture and Urbanism* (Oxford, UK: Oxford Architectural Press, 2000).

Baiter, Richard Abbott and New York Office of Lower Manhattan Development. *Lower Manhattan Waterfront: The Special Battery Park City District, the Special Manhattan Landing Development District, the Special South Street Seaport District* (New York, NY: Office of Lower Manhattan Development, 1975).

Barnett, Jonathan 'Introduction to Part III: Case Studies in Creative Urban Zoning', in Norman Marcus and Marilyn W. Groves (eds.), *The New Zoning: Legal, Administrative, and Economic Concepts and Techniques* (New York, NY: Praeger Publishers, 1970).

Barnett, Jonathan *Urban Design as Public Policy: Practical Methods for Improving Cities* (New York, NY: Architectural Record Books, 1974).

Bassett, Edward Murray *Autobiography of Edward M. Bassett* (New York: Harbor Press, 1939).

Bernard, Richard M. and Rice, Bradley R. *Sunbelt Cities: Politics and Growth since World War II* (1st edn.; Austin, TX: University of Texas Press, 1983).

Blake, Peter *God's Own Junkyard; The Planned Deterioration of America's Landscape* (1st edn.; New York, NY: Holt Rinehart and Winston, 1964).

Borges, Jorge Luis 'Die Analytische Sprache John Wilkins', in Jorge Luis Borges (ed.), *Das Eine Und Die Vielen. Essays Zur Literatur* (Munich, 1966).

Bryce, James *The American Commonwealth* (2nd edn.; London, UK and New York, NY: Macmillan and co., 1889).

Brooks, Benjamin; C. M. Gidney, Edwin M. Sheridan *History of Santa Barbara, San Luis Obispo and Ventura Counties, California*, 2 vols. (Chicago, IL: The Lewis Publishing Company, 1917).

California Department of Transportation 'The Adopt-a-Highway Programme', http://www.dot.ca.gov/hq/maint/adopt/, (2008).

Caro, Robert A. *The Power Broker: Robert Moses and the Fall of New York* (1st edn.; New York, NY: Knopf, 1974).

Chapman, Park 'Built with a Merger Here, a Bonus There—Trump Plaza', *Real Estate Weekly*, December 6, 2000.

Charle, Suzanne 'New Laws Protect Rights to Unblocked Sunshine', *New York Times*, July 20 1980.

Christiaanse, Kees 'Creating Conditions of Freedom', *World Architecture*, 6 (1989).

Clark, William Clifford and Kingston, John Lyndhurst *The Skyscraper; a Study in the Economic Height of Modern Office Buildings* (New York, NY, Cleveland, OH: American Institute of Steel Construction Inc., 1930).

Comey, Arthur C. *Transition Zoning* (Harvard City Planning Studies V; Cambridge, MA: Harvard University Press, 1933).

Le Corbusier *When the Cathedrals Were White* (New York: McGraw-Hill, 1964).

Costonis, John J. *Icons and Aliens: Law, Aesthetics, and Environmental Change* (Urbana, IL: University of Illinois Press, 1989).

Dunlap, David W. 'Owners of Too-Tall Tower Offer to Renovate 102d St. Tenements', *New York Times*, August 4, 1988.

Dunlap, David W. 'Grand Central Owner Seeks Broader Use of Air Rights', *New York Times*, May 3, 1992.

Ferriss, Hugh *The Metropolis of Tomorrow* (New York, NY: Ives Washburn, 1929).

Fédération Internationale de Football Association *Laws of the Game* (Zürich, CH: FIFA, 2008).

Fitzgerald, F. Scott 'My Lost City', in Edmund Wilson (ed.), *The Crack-Up : With Other Uncollected Pieces, Note-Books and Unpublished Letters ; Together with Letters to Fitzgerald from Gertrude Stein ... [Et Al.] ; and Essays and Poems by Paul Rosenfeld ... [Et Al.]* (New York, NY: New Directions, 1956).

Fonorof, Allan 'Special Districts: A Departure from the Concept of Uniform Control', in Norman Marcus and Marilyn W. Groves (eds.), *The New Zoning: Legal, Administrative, and Economic Concepts and Techniques* (New York, NY: Praeger Publishers, 1970).

Ford, Larry R. *Cities and Buildings, Skyscrapers, Skid Rows, and Suburbs* (Baltimore, MD: The Johns Hopkins University Press, 1994).

Fortune Magazine 'Skyscrapers: Pyramids in Steel and Stock', *Fortune* 2, (August, 1930).

Foucault, Michel *Die Ordnung Der Dinge —Eine Archäologie Der Humanwissenschaften* (Frankfurt a.M.: Suhrkamp, 1971).

Freund, Ernst 'Discussion', *The Third National Conference on City Planning* (1911).

Garvin, Alexander *The American City : What Works, What Doesn't* (New York, NY: McGraw-Hill, 1996).

General Outdoor Advertising Co. Vs. Department of Public Works, 289 MA 149, 193 NE 799 (1936).

Goldberger, Paul 'When Planning Can Be Too Much of a Good Thing', *The New York Times*, December 6, 1987.

Goldberger, Paul 'When Developers Change the Rules During the Game', *New York Times*, March 19, 1989.

Goldberger, Paul 'The Skyline, Now Arriving', *The New Yorker*, (1998).

Groenendijk, Paul *The Red Apple & Wijnhaven Island* (Rotterdam, NL: 010 Publishers, 2009)

Haar, Charles Monroe; Kayden, Jerold S. and The American Planning Association *Zoning and the American Dream: Promises Still to Keep* (Chicago, IL: Planners Press American Planning Association in association with the Lincoln Institute of Land Policy, 1989).

Harden, Blaine 'A Bankroll to Fight a Behemoth; Rich Neighbors Open Wallets to Battle Trump's Project for Residential Skyscraper' *New York Times*, September 8, 1999.

Hardin, Garrett 'The Tragedy of the Commons', *Science*, /162 (December 13, 1968).

Hartman, Chester W. *The Transformation of San Francisco* (Totowa, NJ: Rowman & Allanheld, 1984).

Hayek, Friedrich August von *Individualismu. Und Wirtschaftliche Ordnung* (Erlenbach-Zürich, CH: Eugen Rentsch Verlag, 1952).

Hayek, Friedrich August von *The Constitution of Liberty* (Chicago, IL: Regnery, 1972).

Hegemann, Werner *Das Steinerne Berlin 1930 —Geschichte Der Grössten Mietskasernenstadt Der Welt* ((Aufl.3, unveränd.) edn.; Braunschweig, Wiesbaden: Vieweg, 1979).

Hersey, George L. and Freedman, Richard *Possible Palladian Villas (Plus a Few Instructive Impossible Ones)* (Cambridge, MA: MIT Press 1992).

Holl, Steven *The Alphabetical City* (New York Pamphlet Architecture, 1980).

The City of Hong Kong 'Guidelines on Specific Major Urban Design Issues—Heritage and View Corridors', *Chapter 11: Urban Design Guidelines for Hong Kong (6.2.6 – 6.2.7)* (Hong Kong, CN: HK Planning Department, 2005)

The City of Hong Kong *Urban Design Guidelines for Hong Kong—Preservation of View to Ridgelines/Peaks—Executive Summary* (Hong Kong, November 2002).

Horsley, Carter B. 'In the Air over Midtown: Builders' New Arena', *New York Times*, February 11, 1979.

Horsley, Carter B. 'Is It One Building or Two? New Project Halted by Dispute', *New York Times*, January 14, 1979.

Howard, Ebenezer and Osborn, Frederic James *Garden Cities of To-Morrow* (Cambridge MA: MIT Press, 1965).

Huxtable, Ada Louise 'Towering Question: The Skyscraper', *New York Times*, June 12, 1960

acobs, Jane *The Death and Life of Great American Cities* (New York, NY: Random House, 1961).

oedicke, Jürgen *Angewandte Entwurfsmethodik für Architekten* (Stuttgart, DE: Krämer, 1976).

Kanton Zürich 'Anleitung Zur Bestimmung Des Schattenverlaufes Von Hohen Gebäuden, Die 2-Stunden-Schattenkurve', in Amt für Regionalplanung (ed.), *Grundlagen zur Orts- und Regionalplanung im Kt. Zürich* (Zürich, 1967).

Kayden, Jerold S. The New York Dept. of City Planning and The Municipal Art Society of New York, *Privately Owned Public Space: The New York City Experience* (New York, NY: John Wiley, 2000).

Kelly, Kevin *Out of Control: The New Biology of Machines, Social Systems and the Economic World* New York, NY: Basic Books, 1994).

Koolhaas, Rem *Delirious New York: A Retroactive Manifesto for Manhattan* (New York, NY: Oxford University Press, 1978)

Koolhaas, Rem et al. *Small, Medium, Large, Extra-Large: Office for Metropolitan Architecture, Rem Koolhaas and Bruce Mau* (Rotterdam, NL: 010 Publishers, 1995).

LaGrasse, Carol W. 'The Wall of Cars', *New York Property Rights Clearinghouse*, Vol.6 No.1 (May 2002).

Lehnerer, Alexander 'Tit for Tat and Urban Rules', in Walz Borries, Böttger (ed.), *Space, Time, Play* (Basel, Boston, Berlin: Birkhäuser, 2007).

Lewyn, Michael 'Zoning without Zoning' *Planetizen—The Planning & Development Network* (2003); http://www.planetizen.com/node/109.

The City of Los Angeles 'City of Los Angeles Municipal Code', in The City of Los Angeles (ed.), (Sixth Edition edn., Ordinance No. 7,000: American Legal Publishing Corp., 2007).

The City of Los Angeles 'Mulholland Scenic Parkway—Specific Plan', in City of Los Angeles—A Part of the General Plan (ed.), Ordinance No. 167, 943, 1992).

The City of Los Angeles 'Mulholland Scenic Parkway Specific Plan—Design and Preservation Guidelines', in A part of the General Plan—Community Plans/Specific Plans City of Los Angeles (ed.), (pursuant to Ordinance No. 167,943; City of Los Angeles, 2003).

The City of Los Angeles 'Wilshire—Westwood Scenic Corridor—Specific Plan', in City of Los Angeles—A Part of the General Plan (ed.), (Ordinance No. 155,044; City of Los Angeles, 1981).

oyer, François *Paris Nineteenth Century : Architecture and Urbanism* (1st American edn.; New York, NY: Abbeville Press, 1988).

ynch, Kevin *The Image of the City* (Cambridge, MA: Technology Press, 1960).

Lynch, Kevin *Site Planning* (2nd edn.; Cambridge, MA: MIT Press, 1971).

Lyons, Richard D. 'Beheading a Tower to Make It Legal', *New York Times*, February 28, 1988.

Mandelker, Daniel R. 'The Basic Philosophy of Zoning', in Norman Marcus and Marilyn W. Groves (eds.), *The New Zoning* (New York: Praeger Publishers, 1970).

Manville, Michael and Shoup, Donald 'People, Parking, and Cities', *Access*, No. 25 (2004).

Martin, Leslie 'The Grid as Generator', *Urban Space and Structures* (London, UK: Cambridge University Press, 1972).

Martin, Leslie and March, Lionel *Urban Space and Structures* (London, UK: Cambridge University Press, 1972).

Mayor of London, Housing—the London Plan Supplementary Planning Guidance (Spg) (London, UK: Greater London Authority, November 2005).

Mayor's Task Force on Urban Design *The Threatened City* (New York, NY, 1967).

Neutelings Riedijk Architects *N.94 —Neutelings Riedijk 1992/1999* (Madrid, ES: ElCroquis, 1999).

The City of New York '81–272 Alternative Height and Setback Regulations—Daylight Evaluation—Features of the Daylight Evaluation Chart', *Zoning Resolution. Article VIII: Special Purpose Districts* (The Department of City Planning, 2007).

The City of New York '81–274 Alternative Height and Setback Regulations—Daylight Evaluation—Rules for Determining the Daylight Evaluation Score', *Zoning Resolution. Article VIII: Special Purpose Districts* (The Department of City Planning, 2007).

The City of New York *Development and Present Status of City Planning in New York City* (New York, NY: Board of Estimate and Apportionment, Committee on the City Plan, 1914).

The City of New York 'Zoning Resolution. Article VIII: Special Purpose Districts', (The Department of City Planning, 2007).

The City of New York *Zoning Handbook* (January 2006 edn.; New York, NY: Department of City Planning, 2006).

The New York Times Editorial 'First Detailed Official Plans of the New York Central's Improvements', *New York Times*, March 27. 1910.

The New York Times Editorial 'Mayor Criticizes Moses on Zoning—Makes Light of Attack on Floor Area Ratio Plan to Prevent Overbuilding', *NY Times*, June 8, 1960, Wednesday 1960.

The New York Times Editorial 'The Design of the City', *New York Times*, February 13, 1967.

The New York Times Editorial 'A Little Zoning Is a Good Thing', *NY Times*, March 2, 1977, Wednesday 1977.

The New York Times Metropolitan Desk 'Man to Defend His Unmown Lawn in Court', *New York Times*, September 16, 1984, Sunday 1984.

City of Passic Vs. Patterson Bill Posting 72 NJL 285, 62 A 267 (1905).

People Vs. Stover 12 NY 2d 462, 191 NE 2d 272 and 240 NYS 2d 734 (1963).

Platt, Rutherford H. and Lincoln Institute of Land Policy *The Humane Metropolis: People and Nature in the 21st-Century City* (Amherst, MA: University of Massachusetts Press in association with Lincoln Institute of Land Policy Cambridge, 2006).

Pommer, Richard and Otto, Christian F. *Weissenhof 1927 and the Modern Movement in Architecture* (Chicago, IL: The University of Chicago Press, 1991).

Provoost, Michelle and et al. *Dutchtown: A City Centre Design by OMA/Rem Koolhaas* (Rotterdam, NL: NAi Publishers, 1999).

Reps, John W. *The Making of Urban America— a History of City Planning in the United States* (Princeton, NJ: Princeton University Press, 1965).

Rittel, Horst W. J. and Reuter, Wolf D. *Planen—Entwerfen—Design Ausgewählte Schriften Zu Theorie Und Methodik* (Stuttgart, DE: Kohlhammer, 1992).

Rossi, Aldo *The Architecture of the City* (Cambridge, MA & London, UK: MIT Press, 1982).

Rowe, Colin and Koetter, Fred *Collage City* (Cambridge, MA: MIT Press, 1978).

The City of San Francisco *The Downtown Plan—Proposal for Citizen Review* (San Francisco, CA: Department of City Planning, 1983).

The City of Santa Barbara 'Attractions Guide—the Courthouse', www.santabarbara.com, (2008).

The City of Santa Monica 'Planning and Zoning—Fence, Wall, Hedge, Flagpole', in The City of Santa Monica (ed.), *City of Santa Monica Municipal Code* (9.04.10.02.080; Seattle, WA: Quality Code Publishing, 2007).

Scenic America 'Background on Billboards', http://www.scenic.org/billboards, (2008).

Schueller, Nicola; Wollenberg, Petra and Christiaanse, Kees *Urban Reports* (Zürich, CH: GTA Publishers, 2009).

Schuman, Wendy 'Soho a 'Victim of Its Own Success'', *New York Times*, November 24, 1974.

Scott, Mel *The San Francisco Bay Area : A Metropolis in Perspective* (2nd edn.; Berkeley, CA: University of California Press, 1985).

The City of Seattle *Downtown Seattle Height and Density Changes—Numbers of Projected New Buildings by Height Range* (Strategic Planning Office, 2002).

The City of Seattle The Downtown Urban Center Neighborhood Plan (Seattle: Downtown Urban Center Planning Group, 1999).
Shultz, Earle and Simmons, Walter *Offices in the Sky* (1st edn.; Indianapolis, IN: Bobbs-Merrill, 1959).
Smith, Adam *The Wealth of Nations* (London, UK, New York, NY, 1966).
Sorkin, Michael *Local Code: The Constitution of a City at 42°N Latitude* (New York, NY: Princeton Architectural Press, 1993).
St. Louis Gunning Advertising Co. Vs. City of St. Louis 235 MO 99, 137 SW 929 (1911).
Stern, Robert A. M.; Gilmartin, Gregory and Mellins, Thomas *New York 1930: Architecture and Urbanism between the Two World Wars* (New York, NY: Rizzoli, 1987).
Stern, Robert A. M.; Mellin, Thomas and Fishman, David *New York 1960: Architecture and Urbanism between the Second World War and the Bicentennial* (New York, NY: Monacelli Press, 1995).
Sullivan, Louis H. and Bragdon, Claude Fayette *Kindergarten Chats on Architecture, Education and Democracy* (1st edn.; Washington, DC: Scarab Fraternity Press, 1934).

Toll, Seymour I. *Zoned American* (New York, NY: Grossman Publishers, 1969).

United Kingdom Legislation *Town and Country Planning Act 1990, Chapter 8: Section 106* (London: Office of the Deputy Prime Minister, 1990).
Unwin, Raymond *Nothing Gained by Overcrowding! Or How the Garden City Type of Development May Benefit Both Owner and Occupier* (third edn.; London, UK: Garden Cities and Town Planning Association, 1912).
U.S. Department of Transportation (Deputy Executive Director Vincent F. Schimmoller) Memorandum: Adopt-a-Highway Signs —Interpretation (Ii-477(I) —"Advertising on Adopt-a-Highway Signs"), (April 27, 2001).

Venturi, Robert; Brown, Denise Scott and Izenour, Steven *Learning from Las Vegas* (Cambridge, MA: MIT Press, 1972).
Village of Euclid Vs. Ambler Realty Co 272 US 365, (1926).

Walker Smith, Voorhees & Smith *Zoning New York City; a Proposal for a Zoning Resolution for the City of New York* (New York, NY, 1958).
Waldram, Percy J. 'The Measurement of Illumination; Daylight and Artificial: With Special Reference to Ancient Light Disputes', *The Journal of the Society of Architects* Vol. 3 (1909).
Waldram, P. J. and Waldram, J. M. 'Window Design and the Measurement and Predetermination of Daylight Illumination', *The Illuminating Engineer*, Vol. XVI (1923).

Weaver, Clifford L. and Babcock, Richard F. *City Zoning—the Once and Future Frontier* (Chicago, IL: Planners Press: Order from American Planning Association, 1979).
Weinstein, Richard How New York's Zoning Was Changed to Induce the Construction of Legitimate Theaters', in Norman Marcus and Marilyn W. Groves (eds.), *The New Zoning: Legal, Administrative, and Economic Concepts and Techniques* (New York, NY: Praeger Publishers, 1970).
Wheaton, William C. 'Zoning and Land Use Planning: An Economic Perspective', in Charles Monroe Haar, Jerold S. Kayden and American Planning Association (eds.), *Zoning and the American Dream : Promises Still to Keep* (Chicago, IL: Planners Press American Planning Association in association with the Lincoln Institute of Land Policy, 1989).
Whyte, William Hollingsworth *The Last Landscape* (1st edn.; Garden City, NY: Doubleday, 1968).
Willis, Carol *Form Follows Finance: Skyscrapers and Skylines in New York and Chicago* (1st edn.; New York, NY: Princeton Architectural Press, 1995).
Wolfe, Tom 'Electrographic Architecture', *Architectural Design*, (July, 1969).

Yick Wo Vs. Hopkins 118 US 356, (1886).

Zoll, Stephen *Superville: New York—Aspects of Very High Bulk* (Massachusetts Review 14, 1973).

Image Credits

Hersey and Freedman (1992), Possible Palladian Villas (Plus a Few Instructively Impossible Ones). MIT Press.
Plan of the City of New Babylon, Kansas ... er. The City of New Babylon on Paper, drawn by A. C. Warren, from Albert Richardson, *Beyond the Mississippi*. Hartford, ... 867. A. Printed in Reps (1965), The Making of Urban America—a History of City Planning in the United States, 369.
The City of New Babylon in Fact. View of New Babylon, drawn by George W. White, from Albert Richardson, *Beyond the Mississippi*. Hartford, 1867. Printed in Reps (1965), The Making of Urban America—a History of City Planning in the United States, 370.
Triborough Bridge and Tunnel Authority, New York.
From a painting by G. W. Wittich in 1870, ... Williams Brothers, *The History of Franklin Pickaway Counties*. Ohio, Cleveland, 1880. Printed in Reps (1965), The Making of Urban America—a History of City Planning ... the United States, 489. (Olin Library, Cornell University, Ithaca, New York)
Illustration based on Manuscript plans of Circleville, Ohio, drawn by John W. Reps in ... 955. Printed in: Reps (1965), The Making of Urban America —History of City Planning ... the United States, 490.
Garvin (1996), The American City: What Works, What Doesn't, 433.
Voorhees (1958), Zoning New York City; ... Proposal for a Zoning Resolution for the City of New York, 40.
Cartographer J. T. Palmatary, published by Braunhold & Sons (Chicago). Chicago Historical Society, ICHI–05656.
The City of Chicago, showing the Burnt District. Published in Harpers Weekly, August 1, 1874. From a colored print published by Currier & Ives.
Lithograph by Arno B. Reincke, 1916.
Shultz and Simmons (1959), Offices in the Sky, 285.
Map by Richard Hurd in Hurd (1924), Principles of City Land Values., reprinted ... Willis (1995), Form Follows Finance: Skyscrapers and Skylines in New York and Chicago, p.171.
Plate 132 from The Plan of Chicago, 1909. Burnham et al. By Jules Guerin, Delineator. On permanent loan to The Art Institute of Chicago from the City of Chicago, 28.148.1966.
A panorama of Santa Barbara from the Mesa, by Alfred Robert Edmondson, 1914.
Hegemann (1930), Das Steinerne Berlin 1930—Geschichte Der Grössten Mietskasernenstadt Der Welt, 213, 230. Basel: Birkhäuser, 2000 (4th edition, 978-3-7643-6355-0).
Edwards (1924), Good and Bad Manners ... Architecture.

30 Panoramic view of 1893 World's Columbian Exposition in Chicago. Library of Congress, LC–USZ62–128873.
31 LaGrasse (2002), The Wall of Cars. Photograph by Kenneth Walter.
33 Robert Venturi, courtesy of Venturi, Scott Brown and Associates, Inc.
34 City of Las Vegas, Planning & Development Department (2007), Chapter 19.06, Special Purpose and Overlay Districts.
35–37 City of Las Vegas, Planning & Development Department (2007), Chapter 19.14, Sign Standards.
40 The picture was taken in 1974 at the time of a public referendum to curb high rise development in San Francisco. Courtesy of Berkeley Simulation Laboratory, Peter Bosselmann.
42a–c Illustrations based on the San Francisco General Plan—Building Bulk. The City of San Francisco (2000–2008).
43 Illustration according to the San Francisco General Plan—Quality of Street Views. The City of San Francisco (2000–2008).
45 Courtesy of Adam Hardy
46a Illustration based on the View Protection Guidelines of the City of Vancouver (December 1990).
46b Illustration based on information of the False Creek Official Development Plan by the City of Vancouver (April 1998).
48a–b Illustration based on the Urban Design Guidelines for Hong Kong
—Preservation of Views to
Ridgelines/Peaks
—Executive Summary.
The City of Hong Kong (2002).
50–51 Illustrations based on the London View Management Framework Draft SPG. Mayor of London (April 2005).
52a Mayor of London (April 2005), London View Management Framework Draft SPG.
56 Ferriss (1929), The Metropolis of Tomorrow.
58b Illustration based on Anleitung Zur Bestimmung Des Schattenverlaufes von Hohen Gebäuden, Die 2–Stunden Schattenkurve. Kanton Zürich (1967).
59 Anstey and Harris (2006), Anstey's Rights of Light—and How to Deal with Them, 60. RICS, Michael Cromar (illustrator).
61 Illustration based on Anstey and Harris (2006), Anstey's Rights of Light—and How to Deal with Them, 96.
62a–g Courtesy of the Department of City Planning, City of New York.
64 New York City Department of City Planning.
69 Ford et al. (1931), Building Height, Bulk, and Form; How Zoning Can Be Used as a Protection against Uneconomic Types of Buildings on High-Cost Land.
72 Stern et al. (1995), New York 1960:

Architecture and Urbanism between the Second World War and the Bicentennial, 342., rights: Joseph E. Seagram & Sons, Inc. New York.
80 Voorhees (1958), Zoning New York City; a Proposal for a Zoning Resolution for the City of New York,129–30.
81–83 Clark and Kingston (1930), The Skyscraper; a Study in the Economic Height of Modern Office Buildings.
84 (Urban Design Group, New York, ca. 1970).
90a Jacobs (1961), The Death and Life of Great American Cities, 179.
94 Illustration based on information by the Seattle Strategic Planning Office, 2002.
105 The City of New York (2007), Zoning Resolution. Article II: Residence District Regulations. Chapter 4—Bulk Regulations for Community Facility Buildings in Residence Districts. Amendment from 10/17/07.
113 Courtesy of Civitas, New York City.
115 Based on Unwin (1912), Nothing Gained by Overcrowding! Or How the Garden City Type of Development May Benefit Both Owner and Occupier, 4.
116 Martin and March (1972), Speculations, 52. Cambridge University Press.
117 Martin (1972), The Grid as Generator.
118 Holl (1980), The Alphabetical City, 60.
119 Hisao Suzuki.
120, 122a–c Kaisersrot.
121 Aerial photo by Aerodata International Surveys, 2008. Schuytgraaf, NL, project by KCAP, Rotterdam.
124a,c Courtesy of KCAP.
125, 127 Models executed by students of the 2005 ETH London Bishopsgate Studio.
126af, 128 Renderings executed for KCAP.

The author has made every effort to secure the permissions necessary to reproduce the visual material in this book. Any omissions will be corrected in subsequent editions.

Acknowledgements

Special thanks to: Kees Christiaanse, my doctoral advisor and discussion partner, together with whom I have been able to test out my ideas over the past few years in the context of actual urban design projects, which ultimately provided the impulse for this undertaking. And to Ludger Hovestadt, the second reader of my doctoral dissertation, for his input, for work on many joint projects, and for his unwavering belief in my work. Thanks also to Peter de Winter, 010 Publishers. To Kaisersrot: Markus Braach, Benjamin Dillenburger, and Oliver Fritz. To Sandra and Bruno Oppermann for their far-reaching support. To Mark Michaeli, Sandra Oppermann, and Christian Salewski as critical readers. To Joost Grootens and Annemarie van den Berg for the graphic design of this volume. To Ian Pepper for the English translation. To Niels Lehmann for graphic assistance. To Florian Meuser, Thomas von Pufendorf, Stephan Renner, Christoph Stark, and Jonas von Studnitz for making available illustrative materials. To the ETH chairs of Kees Christiaanse and Ludger Hovestadt for making pursuit of my research possible, for financial support for the present publication, and for our time together at the ETH in Zürich; to the students in my seminars at this same institute. And finally, to the Netherlands Architecture Fund for generous financial assistance without which the present publication would not have been possible.

A. L., Chicago, Sept. 2009

Book Credits

This publication has been made possible by the generous support of the Netherlands Architecture Fund, the Chair of Prof. Kees Christiaanse and the Chair of Prof. Dr. Ludger Hovestadt at the ETH Zürich.

Illustrations: Alex Lehnerer
Book design: Studio Joost Grootens
(Joost Grootens, Annemarie van den Berg)
Printed by: Lecturis, Eindhoven

© 2009
The author and 010 Publishers, Rotterdam

ISBN 978–90–6450–666–6
www.010.nl